Next Steps to Ministry

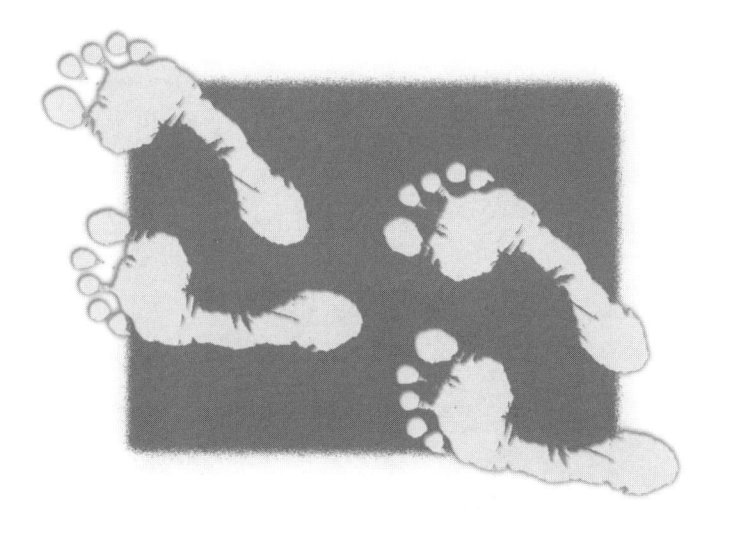

NEXT STEPS TO MINISTRY

ENTERING A LIFE IN CHRISTIAN MINISTRY

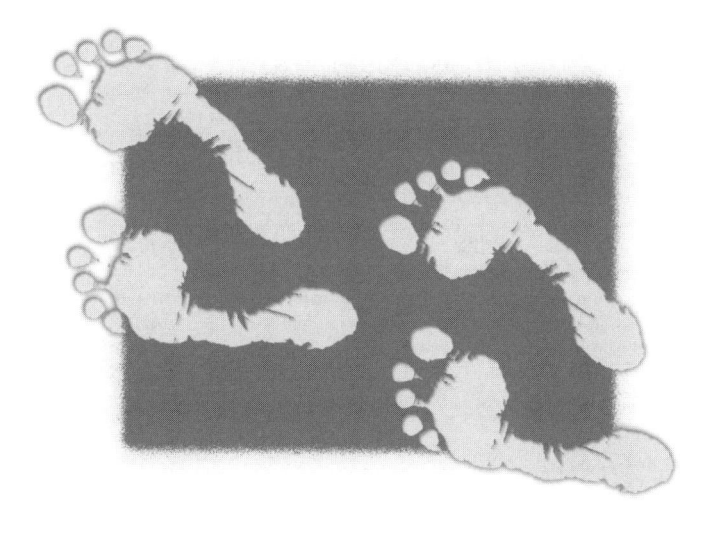

DAVID MARKLE
GENERAL EDITOR

Warner Press
Anderson, Indiana

ANDERSON UNIVERSITY PRESS

copublished by Warner Press, Inc., and Anderson University Press

Copyright © 2007 by David E. Markle. All rights reserved. No part of this publication may be reproduced, stored in a retrieval system, or transmitted in any form or by any means—electronic, mechanical, photocopy, recording or any other—except for brief quotations in printed reviews, without prior written permission of the publisher. For this and all other editorial matters, please contact:

Coordinator of Communications and Publishing
Church of God Ministries, Inc.
PO Box 2420, Anderson, IN 46018-2420
800-848-2464 • www.chog.org

To purchase additional copies of this book, to inquire about distribution and for all other sales-related matters, please contact:

Warner Press, Inc.
PO Box 2499, Anderson, IN 46018-9988
877-346-3974 (toll free) / 765-644-7721
www.warnerpress.com

Scripture quotations, unless otherwise indicated, are from *New Revised Standard Version Bible*, copyrighted 1989 by the Division of Christian Education of the National Council of the Churches of Christ in the United States of America; and are used by permission. All rights reserved. Scripture quotations marked CEV are from the *Contemporary English Version* © 1991, 1992, 1995 by American Bible Society. Used by permission. Scripture quotations marked MSG are from the *THE MESSAGE*. Copyright © by Eugene H. Peterson 1996, 1994, 1995, 1996, 2000, 2001, 2002. Used by permission of NavPress Publishing Group. Scripture quotations marked NIV are from the *Holy Bible, New International Version*®. NIV®. Copyright © 1973, 1978, 1984 by International Bible Society. Used by permission of Zondervan. All rights reserved. Scripture quotations marked NKJV are from the New King James Version. Copyright © 1982 by Thomas Nelson, Inc. Used by permission. All rights reserved. Scripture quotations marked NLT are from the *Holy Bible, New Living Translation*, copyright © 1996. Used by permission of Tyndale House Publishers, Inc., Wheaton, IL 60189 USA. All rights reserved. Scripture quotations marked RSV are from the *Revised Standard Version of the Bible*, copyright 1946, 1952, 1071 by the Division of Christian Education of the National Council of Churches of Christ in the USA. Used by permission.

Cover design by Mary Jaracz
Layout design by Carolyn Frost
Editing by Joseph D. Allison and Stephen R. Lewis
ISBN-13: 978-1-59317-175-9

Library of Congress Cataloging-in-Publication Data

Next steps to ministry : entering a life in Christian ministry / David Markle, general editor.
   p.   cm.
  Includes bibliographical references.
  ISBN 978-1-59317-175-9 (pbk.)
  1. Pastoral theology. 2. Church work. 3. Christian leadership. I. Markle, David.
BV4011.3.N49 2007
253'.2--dc22   2007004974

Printed in the United States of America.

07 08 09 10 11 / EP / 10 9 8 7 6 5 4 3 2 1

In Memoriam

Richard W. Shockey
1948–2005

Friend, Christian educator, pastor to pastors,
Kingdom of God strategist, mentor to many,
poised to give himself to a new generation,

Our Lord called you to himself far too early for our liking.
Nevertheless, we know:

"Blessed are the dead who die in the Lord…they will rest from their labors, for their deeds follow them" (Rev 14:13 NIV).

Dear brother, with this volume, we join our labors with yours for the sake of those who come after us!

CONTENTS

Foreword ix
Preface xi

Being—Maturing Who We Are as Followers of Jesus the Lord 1

Knowing Yourself
    by Gregory A. Wiens 3

Faith Development in a Postmodern World
    by Gilbert W. Stafford 27

Being a Person of Integrity
    by Edward L. Foggs 43

Growing a Teachable Spirit
    by Arlo F. Newell & Andy L. Stephenson 59

Becoming—Following Christ into a Life in Christian Ministry 79

Discovering and Affirming Your Approach to Ministry
    by Martin D. Grubbs 81

Finding a Placement That Fits
    by Cynthia Rembert James 97

Working with People: A Case Study in Effective Communication
    by Rand & Phyllis Michael 113

Living into the Call
    by Christina T. Accornero 123

Continuing Education in Ministry
    by Fredrick H. Shively 135

Doing—Basic Responsibilities of a Life in Christian Ministry 147

Care for Souls
    by David E. Markle 149

Equip for Ministry
    by Steven L. Rennick 171

Contextualizing the Gospel
  by Steven Lewis 185
The Art of Influence: Learning to Be a Leader
  by Douglas L. Talley 203
Effective Meetings and Anointed Budgets
  by Ronald V. Duncan 223

Afterword: The First Five Years 241
Biographies 249

Foreword

As a pastor and theological educator, it is my esteemed privilege to introduce this collection of readings in ministry and leadership formation authored by some highly gifted leaders. As I reflect on the rich tapestry of perspectives presented here, I am reminded of how the apostle Paul was a mentor to Timothy, his son in the ministry (2 Tim 4:1–5). Paul exhorted Timothy to "fulfill your ministry" as he charged him to aspire to the achievement of a lofty standard of excellence as a pastor, teacher and leader. The essays in this book demonstrate how Paul's exhortation to excellence in Christian character and commitment remains urgent and relevant for ministry in our own time.

Where does one find a roadmap for this journey called ministry? These readings provide some key pathways, signposts, and milestones for followers of Jesus Christ who are discerning the call to lead God's people in the twenty-first century. Whether novice, seminarian, or seasoned pastor, all will find inspiration in these words from reliable witnesses who have thoroughly tested the terrain leading from call to fulfillment in ministry. Indeed, this book is a virtual roadmap for ministry, charting connections between various locations and destinations, a practical guide for one's journey in service to the Lord and his church.

These chapters are organized to explore three dimensions of formation for ministry and leadership in today's world: being, becoming and doing. In the section on Being, Greg Wiens, Gil Stafford, Ed Foggs, Arlo Newell, and Andy Stephenson bring attention to maturity in knowing who we are as followers of Jesus, inviting the reader to engage critical questions,

Next Steps to Ministry

cultural themes, the concept of integrity, and the call to mentoring relationships. Next, in Becoming, Marty Grubbs, Rand and Phyllis Michael, Christine Accornero, and Fred Shively demonstrate approaches to following Christ into a life in Christian ministry in their reflections on modern megachurch ministry, case studies in communications, pursuing the call to ministry, and the value of continuing education in fostering lifelong learning. In the third and final section on Doing, David Markle, Steve Rennick, Steven Lewis, Doug Talley, and Ron Duncan address basic responsibilities of a life in Christian ministry: care for souls, equipping via mentoring, the task of contextualization, leadership as the art of influence, and the practical administration of meetings and budgets.

We are blessed to have such capable men and women of God whose keen insights are represented in this stimulating collection of essays, stories and reflections. With full awareness of the crises and challenges we face in a culture that so easily and readily diverts our attention from the things of God, I present these readings as a rich resource for the preparation and equipping of leaders who can guide the church to a future with hope.

Cheryl J. Sanders
Washington, DC
September 2006

Preface

In 2001, Warner Press published *First Steps to Ministry,* for which I was editorial coordinator. The purpose of *First Steps* was to be a "practical guide for persons who believe God has called them" to Christian ministry. Even at the time of publication, we felt the need for a follow-up volume that we always referred to as *Next Steps*.

First Steps is for persons considering and exploring a call to Christian ministry; *Next Steps* is for those who have made the commitment and now seek to grow deeper in their calling. The call for these two books emerged from the Leadership Development Task Force of the Church of God (Anderson, Indiana) under the leadership of Jim Davey. The task force felt a widespread need for a tool that would assist the church in clarifying the call to ministry and a deep sense of need for leaders formed in the image of Christ.

While there continues to be a great deal of talk about leader*ship* development, many are beginning to turn their focus to *leader* development.

Ironically, the process of developing godly leaders—one of the central challenges for the church in the twenty-first century—is nearly never mentioned in the Bible. The Bible is full of leaders of every stripe: from Moses to Paul, from Ahab to Darius, from Saul and David to Herod, from Deborah to Priscilla and Aquila—the good, the bad, and the ugly. The judgment of God and Scripture is that leaders who adhere strongly to God's call, connecting most strongly to that relationship, are the great leaders. Those who do not, regardless of their skills as politician, diplomat, or general, are not great leaders.

Next Steps to Ministry

God describes David, arguably one of the greatest leaders in our history, as a "man after God's own heart." The development of leaders is more about the formation of godly persons than it is about building skill. If we can focus our attention more on the emergence of Christlike leaders and their spiritual and moral formation, then the development of skills comes easily. A skilled leader unformed as a Christian leader is both dangerous and at risk. A leader who has been formed as a Christian leader is simply a learner.

This book is organized according to the same divisions as *First Steps*—being, doing, becoming—and is born out of the conviction that the priorities of Christian ministry are seen most clearly in the physical position that Mary took in relationship to Jesus, sitting at his feet. It is born out of the conviction that the life of Christian ministry is seen most clearly in the call of Jesus on his disciples to be perfect. It is born out of the conviction that the heart of Christian ministry is seen most clearly in the physical position that Jesus took in relationship to his disciples—the one who washes the feet of others.

The book begins with fundamental matter—to whom do I belong and who am I? (being)—and discovers that the answer to those questions comes by sitting at the feet of Jesus.

"But the Lord answered her, 'Martha, Martha, you are worried and distracted by many things; there is need of only one thing. Mary has chosen the better part, which will not be taken away from her'" (Luke 10:41–42).

We continue from that "lowly place" to matters related to life and ministry. We discover insight into these matters in our journey toward holiness (becoming).

"You call me Teacher and Lord—and you are right, for that is what I am. So if I, your Lord and Teacher, have washed your feet, you also ought to wash one another's feet. For I have set you an example, that you also should do as I have done to you." (John 13:13–15).

We continue our work with others, growing into work as washing the feet of those we serve in Jesus' name (doing).

PREFACE

"As God's chosen ones, holy and beloved, clothe yourselves with compassion, kindness, humility, meekness, and patience. Bear with one another and, if anyone has a complaint against another, forgive each other; just as the Lord has forgiven you, so you also must forgive. Above all, clothe yourselves with love, which binds everything together in perfect harmony" (Col 3:12–14).

This book is offered to the church and its leaders in order to help those who, answering God's call, find themselves in leadership of a local congregation. It is offered with a prayer that they might continue to learn, discover, and grow as Christian ministers—fully developed disciples of Jesus Christ.

Arthur M. Kelly
Anderson, Indiana
November 2006

I.
BEING

maturing who we are as
followers of Jesus the Lord

In his work *Catch Your Breath: God's Invitation to Sabbath Rest*, Don Postema suggests a helpful exercise in quieting our self before God.[1] We are invited to read the text of Psalm 37:7:

"Be still before the Lord, and wait patiently for him."

Then shorten the text at each reading, savoring each line:

>*Be still before the Lord, and wait patiently for him.*
>*Be still before the Lord and wait patiently...*
>*Be still before the Lord and wait...*
>*Be still before the Lord...*
>*Be still...*
>*Be...*

Or, similarly, Psalm 46:10:

>*"Be still, and know that I am God!"*
>*"Be still, and know that I am..."*
>*"Be still, and know..."*
>*"Be still..."*
>*"Be..."*

This section presents a call to be who you are in Christ Jesus. There is little more important that you will discover than a solid sense of self grounded in the person of our Lord Jesus Christ. It is prerequisite to all that is good in our life together in Jesus Christ.

Larry Hein, Brennan Manning's spiritual director, said to him, "Be who you is, because if you is who you ain't, you ain't who you is."[2]

---

[1] Don Postema, *Catch Your Breath: God's Invitation to Sabbath Rest* (Grand Rapids, MI: CRC Publications, 1997:19).

[2] Brennan Manning, *Lion and Lamb* (Old Tappan, NJ: F. H. Revell, 1986:24).

CHAPTER ONE:
Gregory A. Wiens: *Knowing Yourself*

No matter how you measure living in these turbulent decades, change is rampant all around us. In times of instability, we need pastors with keen insight, pastors who see themselves clearly and know themselves intimately. They must be able to look at themselves and, without flinching, know what they can do, what they can't do, and what they can learn to do. This is essential, because as the world changes around them, they must be able to adapt in how they lead the church to impact the world.

The best athlete can adapt to any opponent. Great teams study game films of their opponents. As individuals and teams, they look for ways to do what they do well in a way that will overcome the adversary. They don't try to be a different team with different strengths, but they focus on what they do well and they prepare to make adjustments in the midst of the game to compensate for changes they note in their rival's offense or defense.

Pastors must use these same tactics. In order to lead a church in mission, pastors must know what they can do well, know what they should not do, and know what they can learn or change to overcome the world. Pastors must develop the discipline of knowing themselves through an intentional and ongoing discovery process.

The landscape of churches is littered with men and women who have dropped out of pastoral ministry because they weren't able to answer these three questions about themselves: What do I do well? What do I not do well? What can I learn to do well?

Next Steps to Ministry

Many of the friends who entered ministry with me twenty-five to thirty years ago are now casualties along the ministry roadway. They accepted positions or roles and, very simply, tried to be people they weren't created to be. From the outside, these casualties look different from each other, but if you look deeply you will see that these pastors burned out because they were operating outside their strengths or they refused to set boundaries on their time, energy, or resources. Their marriages may have ended due to a number of reasons, but often underlying this relational failure is a lack of insight into how they needed to change their way of relating to their spouse, their church, or others. Had many of these individuals developed a keen insight into the answers to these three questions, they would still be on the ball field today. It would be game day for them and they would be competing for the prize (1 Cor 9:24).

Too many students of Christ's ministry are not running intentionally to win the race; they are just trying to finish the race. Either they don't expect to win or they don't know how to help themselves run to compete for the prize. Runners study themselves. They videotape their form to identify their strike and stride. I have run five marathons; I know that if you want to finish well, you must study running—your own and that of others. All runners have a natural form of strike and stride which should be trained, tweaked, and changed. My observation is that good runners study themselves more closely than most pastors do. Too many pastors simply accept who they are without intentionally studying themselves from a variety of perspectives to know what they are good at, what they are bad at, and what they can change to be better.

In the not-too-distant past, pastoral preparation models didn't attempt to answer these three questions. Educational institutions and seminaries assumed that everyone could learn to do everything, at least moderately well. There seemed to be a prevailing mentality that all pastoral students should be trained to be proficient in the same areas equally. If you weren't a good speaker, you were taught and taught such until the preaching was at least good enough to pastor a small church. If you weren't inclined toward nurturing, you were given enough coursework and assignments until you could at least offer decent bedside manners for those suffering in the hospital.

In the past, most pastoral preparation coursework was designed around a one-size-fits-all model. Students were educated in the minimum competencies of all of the essential roles and expectations of pastoral ministry. In times of stability, this approach was fine, but the playing field has changed today. Pastors who were educated in this model of ministry found themselves wonderfully equipped to deal with a church and world that no longer existed. They tried to do everything moderately well with little self-awareness of their own natural and gifted ways. They found themselves expending enormous amounts of energy trying to do that which they were not good at and with little time or energy left to develop what they were good at.

Too much of their time was spent in activities that consumed them rather than invigorated them, and the kingdom of God profited little from their efforts. Many of these pastors left the ministry tired, burned out, and defeated. They gave it all they had, yet it simply wasn't good enough.

Ironically, the problem wasn't with their commitment. It wasn't with their faith. It wasn't with the energy they poured into the ministry. It was that they never clearly understood that they were created uniquely. They were not created to do it all. They were created much differently than other leaders or pastors. They were created to do some things that no one else would be able to do like they do. On the flip side, they were created *not to do* some things that others would excel at. Their role in the church would look much different from those of their friends and colleagues. Their role would probably even differ from their predecessor at the church to which they were called.

Before we move on, let us also acknowledge that churches also expected a one-size-fits-all kind of pastors. They wouldn't allow their pastors to have different strengths than preceding pastors. Or they wanted their pastor to possess the strengths that the growing church down the road had. Obviously, this problem is pervasive within the church today, but it is not the focus of this study. Let us start with helping pastors and ministry students answer these three questions about themselves, and hopefully, with time, we will educate our churches.

You Are One of a Kind

King David tells us in Psalm 139:14 that he was fearfully and wonderfully made. He continues to remind us that all of his days were ordained before one of them took place. David obviously had great confidence in who God had created him to be. He saw himself as unique, one specifically chosen by God to fulfill a divine call. He recognized that God had worked throughout his life to form him to function in God's kingdom uniquely.

Too many of us think, of course David would believe that. After all he was the king of Israel, the one whose heart sought after God. But let us remember that he was raised as the runt of the family. He had seven older brothers (1 Sam 16) who were chosen and valued by their father to become king. In fact, David's father had to be reminded that he had another son out in the fields. Obviously, David was not one of the favored sons growing up. Even after his kingly anointing, David was assigned to fast-food delivery when the real action was in fighting the enemy (1 Sam 17). His brothers also did not respect him or believe in him.

Yet, as David later wrote Psalm 139, he knew God had uniquely equipped him through all of those experiences to serve him. David was not nearly as gifted a warrior as some of those who fought with him; however, he was the best at being David: a poet-warrior-king. There were things that David wanted to do, but, because of who God had created him to be, David would never be able to do them. Because King David fulfilled his God-given calling, David would not be able to fulfill his own dream. He expanded the borders of Israel and established peace with her neighbors. That was his calling. God assured him of victory in these pursuits as he fulfilled his unique contribution to the kingdom (1 Sam 7). But, precisely because of David's obedience to his unique calling, he was kept from fulfilling his lifelong dream of building the temple of God (1 Chron 22:8). He had shed too much blood to be allowed to build the temple, yet he had to do that to be who God made him.

As you begin to answer these three questions for yourself, you will find out precisely what God has uniquely gifted and called you to do for the kingdom. But don't be surprised if you find out (like King David) that because of your unique calling, you may never accomplish *your* dream—even though your dream may glorify God just as David's did.

Often through answering these three questions, pastors and leaders are freed up to be who God created them to be, sometimes for the first time in their lives. But in the same way, they may find that they will never see what they wanted become a reality. God's calling is more fulfilling than our dreaming.

Assessment Practiced

To answer the three questions, you will need to assess yourself in a variety of ways. Assessment isn't something new; in fact, it can be seen throughout the Bible.

When God called the reluctant Gideon to recruit an army to free Israel from their oppressors in Judges 6 and 7, we see assessment in action. Gideon was surely not confident in his own abilities. First, God had to convince Gideon that he had called him to lead; then he had to teach him how to select his team for the fight. God told Gideon to release those who were afraid to fight and most of Gideon's recruits left. Then God told Gideon to do one more assessment. He instructed Gideon to lead his men to the water and watch how they drink it. God used this seemingly unrelated assessment to identify the three hundred men who made the final cut. God used a behavioral assessment of drinking water to indicate a fighter's ability to persevere under the pressures of battle.

Moses seemed to have been out of touch with his strengths and corresponding weaknesses. Though at the burning bush he stated that he stuttered and wasn't a good speaker, it seems that his self-insight was limited to that physical limitation. Moses needed someone who knew him well yet was unafraid to speak the truth to him. To Jethro, Moses' father-in-law, it was obvious that Moses was trying to do it all. You see, Moses had been adopted and had lived as a foreigner in his own land most of his life. This life experience uniquely equipped him for leading the exile, but it also set him up for wanting to do everything by himself and not trusting others. It also inevitably caused him to miss the promised land. His temper and need for control appears to have been a blind spot for Moses.

Next Steps to Ministry

In Mark 4:33, Jesus shared "as much as they could understand." Jesus knew how much the people could understand because he assessed their ability and context. Surely Jesus had divine discernment, which allowed him to know exactly where his listeners were (better than the rest of us will ever be able to do), but he chose to use his assessment skills to lead and teach others. Also, Jesus purposely chose disciples whose strengths varied greatly. There was the impetuous Peter, the inviting James, the reflective John, the precise Matthew, and the cautious Thomas. Each apostle made unique contributions to the kingdom, both before and after Jesus' departure from earth.

Paul was clearly a man on a mission. After his calling on the road to Damascus until his death in Jerusalem, we see an apostle with a clear vision of what his calling looked like. Paul seems to have been aware of his strengths and corresponding limitations. Though he clearly states he tried to be all things to all people so that some would come to Christ (1 Cor 9:24), he limited his time to areas of his strength. When Barnabas assessed that the culture in Antioch required someone with a background and passions different from his own (Acts 11:25), he went to Tarsus and found Paul. Raised as a Jew in a Gentile land, Paul's background, culture, gifts, and passions clearly matched the leadership needed in Antioch and the church flourished.

Paul's drivenness is clear in Acts 15 when he and Barnabas get into a sharp dispute over the handling of John Mark. Here we see a difference of calling, gifts, and passions leading to conflict. Both of these men responded in gracious ways, which led to a multiplication of ministry for the kingdom of God. Barnabas redeemed John Mark so that later Mark would be very useful to Paul (2 Tim 4:11), while Paul continued with Silas (and others) to plant many more churches around the Mediterranean Sea.

Assessment Taught

Throughout the New Testament, we find that God's people are never held accountable for what they don't have, only for what has been given. In Matthew 25:14–30, Jesus used the parable of the talents to describe our heavenly Father's response to our use of what he has given us in life. The question is never why one servant doesn't produce as much as another.

The question ringing in the ears of the servant given the least amount of money is, What did you do with what I gave you? God is ultimately concerned with what we do with what he has given us for the expansion of his kingdom. He will not hold us accountable for what we cannot do! God wants to know, What did you do with what I gave you? To answer this question of our Lord, we must be able to answer our three questions: What do I do well? What do I not do well? What can I learn to do well?

Calling

A great deal of confusion arises over a person's calling today. Obviously, your calling clearly is related to answering these three questions. Unfortunately, you must answer these questions in the midst of active ministry not before ministry. So how do we define our call (at least initially) if we are not yet clear on what we do well?

My answer to that question is that you must at least start. You must make some initial attempts at this process, knowing that the feedback and self-exploration process will continue for the rest of your active ministry years. Some things can only be learned as you do them. Defining and clarifying your call is one of these issues. That is why this chapter talks about *knowing* yourself rather than *know* yourself. *Knowing* implies an ongoing process, one without end. This side of eternity, you will never know yourself completely (1 Cor 13:12b). You will obviously go through stages in life where you learn more about yourself than in other phases. However, the process of learning and refining should never end.

There are at least three times in your ministry when it is critical for you to assess your answers to the three questions and determine how they relate to your calling. One is when you start ministry. As you evaluate your initial ministry position, ask yourself these questions and use the feedback methods described below. A second time for intentional evaluation is whenever you change ministry roles or positions. During times of change, it is critical that you evaluate your life in light of what you have learned about yourself from previous ministry assignments. A third time of assessment is required when you transition from one stage of ministry to the next.

Next Steps to Ministry

As you evaluate your calling, consider these two aspects of your calling: the push and the pull.

Push

The call of God on your life involves an internal sense, a push—God works inside you to push you toward his desire for your life. This aspect of your call always begins deep in the soul fed on the Word and Spirit of God. God's call is exactly that: God's call. It is Spirit calling to spirit. God begins to push you toward his desire as you spend time in the study of his Word. He continues to push you toward his call on your life as his Spirit leads you into the wilderness. These times are focused periods of quietness alone with God, times of prayer and meditation. They are times of reflection and fasting, searching the heart of God for direction.

The call is pushed by a deep awareness of the three questions. God gives you insight into how he has uniquely equipped you to labor in his kingdom. This push is just as clear as you become aware of what he has *not* gifted you to do. You are able to say no to opportunities that are plainly outside of your giftedness. As you continue to explore the areas you can grow in, God's call will become clearer. Often times, his call involves preparing you for future ministry that you are completely unaware of today.

Pull

As God is working to push you from the inside, he also works in the Body to confirm his call, to pull you into open opportunities for you to fulfill his desire for your life. Too often, I hear young ministers tell me of the great push in their life and yet they are frustrated because there is no pull, no opportunity to pursue their push. In such times, I affirm these ministers to go and seek outside input into their push. Find individuals who know you and will be honest with you and ask them these three questions. Usually if there is no pull, there is more work on the push. Often God is pulling you in a direction that you simply do not want to go. Like King David, you have a dream that is not part of God's call on your life; unlike David, you may not have followed God away from that initial dream yet.

Every person who dreams of being a pastor is not called. This is where the pull comes in; the body of Christ must confirm the pull of the call. God will bring opportunities or individuals to give feedback in sharpening the answers of these three questions. This process should be a vital part of each pastor's ministry preparation.

Knowing Yourself from the Inside

Now let us turn to look specifically at how we are to go about answering these three questions. We first must look inside ourselves.

One of the primary ways to answer these questions is for you to journal. This kind of journaling is not the kind you do for forty days, but a discipline which becomes a lifelong habit. A journal is not a chronicle of the events of your life. But rather, this kind of journal is about your reactions to success or failure in life. It is a record of your thoughts, your fears, and your pain. These reflective insights are gained over years of learning to write for self-assessment, not for posterity. I have kept this kind of journal for twenty-four years. I keep the journals in a very safe place, and they will probably be burned when I die. I have written for God to speak to me, not for me to speak to anyone else. I have written many things I am ashamed of; however the journal is a record of my real emotions and reactions. They always haven't been Spirit led.

But I have twenty-four years of accumulated insight into myself. No one on the earth knows me better than those pages reflect. Even those who know my outside behaviors well don't always know what is going on inside my heart and head. My wife and I have an understanding at this point that she can read the journals if she so desires, but usually she doesn't and I don't write them with the understanding that she will. You must work out an appropriate understanding with your spouse. Whatever agreement you make, do it in a way that allows you to be totally candid in your journal.

Ask God specifically to give you insight into yourself through the journaling. Learn to develop an attitude of openness to input. When others challenge you and you want to react, intentionally don't react, but journal about the event later. Or when you sense your emotional reaction has been out of line with the situation, spend time reflecting on why; ask God to guide you insight.

When you are frustrated, ask yourself why. Identify your own expectations, determine where they may have come from and who receives the glory when they are fulfilled. Be honest with these two factors; the answers do not disqualify the expectations from being God's as well as yours. After a major setback, look inside and ask yourself why you feel as you do. In the same way, when you feel fulfilled, stop and identify why.

It will probably take you a couple of years to cultivate an attitude through journaling that allows you to learn from yourself.

For me, it is always essential to follow up my reflective journaling with Scripture reading. During this time, I resist the urge to study the Scriptures for teaching it to someone else, and simply ask, "Father, what does your word say to me this morning?" For this reason, I read out of a different paraphrase or translation (currently *The Message*) than I am used to. I am not worried about the exegetical considerations, but the personal application. God continually shows me tremendous insight into myself through his word.

No other process has produced the personal insight into these three questions that journaling has for over two decades of my life. Through this continual reflection on life, reading of God's Word, and openness to the Spirit, God has totally reoriented my life through the answers to these questions. About twelve years ago, through my personal journaling process, I began to identify the answers to the first question about what do I do well. I clearly saw five key strengths that express my uniqueness. Since that time I have added one more. I call them, simply, my six Cs:

- Create Chaos (or Challenge the Status Quo)
- Communicate Truth
- Coach Leaders
- Cast Vision
- Critically Think (or Creatively Think)
- Closely Relate to a Few

These strengths are what I do well, and the Lord will hold me accountable for how I have invested my life in these areas (and not others). These are the traits that distinguish me from others. You must work through the process for yourself to discover your own list of characteristics that distinguish you from others around you.

In order for journaling to produce insight into what you are good at, you must continue to ask yourself these three questions as you journal. For example, How do my feelings about the confrontation I had yesterday with the elder give me insight into what I am good at, what I am not good at, or what can I learn? Your reactions, emotions, thoughts, successes and failures must all be seen through this three-part grid over a long period of time to gain insights into yourself.

Many people simply choose to drift through life with little depth of insight into themselves or others, thereby settling for much less than God's design for their call; they simply are not willing to discipline themselves for a lifelong journey of seeking God's input. One of the observations that God used to convince me to begin this journey of journaling twenty-four years ago was that most of the men and women of God that I truly desired to emulate in life were people who kept journals.

In the 1981 movie *Chariots of Fire*, Eric Liddell is quoted as saying, "I believe God made me for a purpose, but he also made me fast. And when I run I feel his pleasure." This is the kind of insight that comes from journaling. We don't know if he actually wrote those words, but we do know he gained similar insights because he kept a journal. As the movie aptly illustrates, Eric Liddell was confident he knew the answers to these questions.

When I was struggling eighteen years ago with the concept of calling and strengths and weaknesses as they relate to my calling, my mentor told me, "Do what you have an unfair advantage over others doing." One of the critical ways I have of knowing this is through journaling. It has been through this discipline that I have come to see that there are some things that only I can do the way I do, and that is what God is holding me accountable for. I don't have to do everything others want me to do, but only that which God wants me to do and what he helps me do very well. When I do these things, I feel his pleasure.

Knowing Yourself from the Outside

Your ability to gain insight from the inside is related to your ability to solicit input from the outside. In his book, *Revolution in Leadership: Training Apostolic Leaders for Tomorrow's Church*, Reggie McNeal asserts that leaders will only be able to lead in the twenty-first century to the extent that they are in peer-mentoring relationships in learning clusters with other leaders. We must cultivate relationships with a few that give us input and insight into our lives.

If you want to pastor for effectiveness in the twenty-first century, then you need to build healthy, transparent, and vulnerable relationships with other pastors who not only see into your life but speak into it as well. Paul was not afraid to acknowledge his painful past. He writes, "But for that very reason I was shown mercy so that in me, the worst of sinners, Christ Jesus might display his unlimited patience as an example for those who would believe on him and receive eternal life" (1 Tim 1:16 NIV). Paul is listed with at least forty-seven individuals throughout the New Testament. Obviously, he was with people and openly shared his life with them. So resist the temptation to isolate or insulate yourself.

Assessment Tools

There are many assessment tools available today to help you better understand how you operate in ministry and relationships. Included in this section are a number of tools that you may find helpful. However, since there are at least seven factors or domains that influence everyone's behavior, it is unrealistic to expect one or even two instruments to perfectly describe your behavior in any given environment. Seven possible domains influence your behavior: (1) your personality or temperament, (2) your thinking, (3) your values (spiritual transformation), (4) your emotional needs (healthy and unhealthy), (5) your physiological needs, (6) your perspective, and (7) your environment.

Certain assessment instruments assess specific domains very well, but at any point in time, other factors may be influencing your behavior. Therefore, it is very beneficial to be assessed from a variety of perspectives. The following instruments will assess one or two of the mentioned domains. The assessment instruments may be purchased, found on the Web, or obtained from a qualified assessment professional.

DiSC

The DiSC instrument is used to assess temperament or personality. DiSC was originally developed to identify how someone approaches a task in the context of a team. The instrument is simple, yet it allows for a variety of profiles to be generated. DiSC assessments measure your need for control (D), your need for influence with others (I), your need for stability (S), and your need to conform to exacting standards (C). Your scoring may be high, medium, or low on any combination of these scales. This allows for over a hundred possibilities, yet it is very simple to understand and use. The advantage of this instrument is that everyone in a team context can take this assessment and learn a great a deal about what the team members value as they work together.

You can find many derivations of this instrument using animals (lions, dogs, and otters), colors (red, blue, green) or other terms. They are all basically the same and may be found on the Web from a variety of vendors for relatively inexpensive fees (usually under $20).

16 PF

The 16 PF instrument is the abbreviated name for 16 Personality Factors. This is an instrument that not only looks at your personality but also at some of the emotional or thinking domains. The sixteen factors it measures are

- Warmth
- Reasoning
- Emotional Stability
- Dominance
- Liveliness
- Rule-Consciousness
- Social Boldness
- Sensitivity
- Vigilance
- Abstractedness
- Privateness
- Apprehension
- Openness to Change
- Self-Reliance
- Perfectionism
- Tension

15

As one can see from these factors, the 16 PF is a much more complex instrument. Unlike other such instruments that are based on what is wrong with you (pathological), the 16 PF is based upon health. For this reason, this instrument is useful in exploring how you relate to your spouse, your leadership style, and other such complex relationships. While the DiSC instrument can be taken almost any time, the 16 PF would be appropriate during transition times of ministry. Because of its complexity, the 16 PF is difficult to use in a large-team context and it is expensive yet insightful.

Spiritual Gifts

The New Testament teaches the concept of spiritual gifts (Rom 12, 1 Cor 12, Eph 4, 1 Pet 4) as a basis for our contribution to the building up of the church. God selected certain spiritual gifts for individuals specifically (1 Cor 12). All believers are to develop these gifts as Paul advised Timothy in 1 Timothy 4:14 and 2 Timothy 1:6. However, gifts by their very nature identify something you are especially good at while other people aren't. Each gift brings a divine ability to contribute to the kingdom in a unique way.

The lists of gifts found in Scripture vary somewhat based on translation and theological perspective. The churches in Rome, Ephesus, and Corinth all received a different list from Paul in the letters he wrote to them. These variations in the lists seem to indicate that Paul did not have a master list from which he was working. Here is one listing of gifts with their scriptural references:

- Helps/Service (1 Cor 12:28, Rom 12:7)
- Giving (Rom 12:8)
- Mercy (Rom 12:8)
- Encouragement (Rom 12:8)
- Faith (1 Cor 12:9)
- Wisdom (1 Cor 12:8)
- Knowledge (1 Cor 12:8)
- Discernment of Spirits (1 Cor 12:10)
- Evangelism (Eph 4:11)
- Leadership (Ruling, Rom 12:8)
- Administration (1 Cor 12:28)
- Teaching (Rom 12:7, 1 Cor 12:28)

- Prophecy (Rom 2:6; 1 Cor 12:10, 28–29; Eph 4:11)
- Hospitality (1 Pet 4:9)
- Pastor-Shepherd (1 Pet 5:1–4; Eph 4:11)
- Apostleship (Eph 4:11)
- Pastor-Teacher (Eph 4:11)
- Miracles (1 Cor 12:10, 29, 39)
- Healing (1 Cor 12:9, 28, 30)
- Tongues (1 Cor 12:10, 28, 30)
- Interpretation (1 Cor 12:10, 30)

There are no perfect gifts for a pastor to possess. The gift mix of a pastor will, in many ways, determine the best style or type of ministry. A pastor with the gift of encouragement or mercy will have a totally different style of preaching than a pastor with the gift of prophecy. Also the gift mix of the pastor will determine the kinds of activities they choose to fill their days. Since spiritual gifts are given for the building up of the body and pastors are part of the body, when pastors use their spiritual gifts, they should be also built up. If pastors finds themselves loathing certain roles of the pastorate, it is a probably because that role is not in their gift mix.

Because spiritual gifts are essential to the pastor and the church, there is probably no more important assessment to begin with than spiritual gifts. However, gifts are always confirmed in the context of the Body through practice. An assessment doesn't prove you have a gift any more than a thermometer proves you are healthy. It is simply an indicator that gives you a place to begin using your gifts in the Body. If others in the Body do not affirm that you have the gift through seeing the fruit of your labor in action, it is time to again seek outside input. Some assessments (such as the Web site listed below) include ways to ask others for feedback, which is then incorporated into the assessment. This is always helpful. Most of us have seen pastors who are convinced they have a gift of teaching when those listening would beg to differ.

There are many good spiritual gift assessments. A good (and free) assessment of spiritual gifts using the above list can be taken online at www.gregwiens.com. The scoring is immediate and automatic. The full definitions of each gift, probable characteristics of those who demonstrate the gift, and examples of biblical persons with these gifts is available in a fifty-page booklet that can also be downloaded free from the site.

Strengths Finder

The Clifton Strengths Finder is based upon the research of Marcus Buckingham and Donald O. Clifton of the Gallup organization. In their book titled *NOW, Discover Your Strengths*, they have identified thirty-four strengths. Their assessment identifies your top five strengths. The appeal of the strengths finder is that these thirty-four strengths in many ways complement the two preceding assessments. They give insight into how your gifts may be utilized in the church. They also identify places where your temperaments (DiSC) may be used. They group the strengths into themes of how you relate to others, how you influence others, the way you work, and the way you think. Below is a listing of these themes and strengths within each theme:

Relating Themes (Working with people)
Communication	Includer (formerly Inclusiveness)
Empathy	Individualization
Responsibility	Relator
Harmony	

Impacting Themes (Influencing people)
Command	Maximizer
Competition	Positivity
Developer	Woo

Striving Themes (Working hard)
Achiever	Belief
Restorative	Discipline
Activator	Focus
Self-Assurance	Significance
Adaptability	

Thinking Themes (Working smarter)

Analytical	Deliberative
Input	Futuristic
Arranger	Consistency (formerly Fairness)
Connectedness	Ideation
Intellection	Learner
Context	Strategic

You may purchase this assessment online at www.strengthsfinder.com. Better yet, for the same price as taking the assessment only, you can buy the book *NOW, Discover Your Strengths*; on the inside of the dust jacket is a code for taking the test on this Web site. The book usually costs around $25.

Time Line

A helpful assessment tool in identifying issues is an instrument called a time line. A time line is a linear depiction of your life. You start out with a long sheet of paper. On the left end, about half-way up the paper, write the date you were born. On the right end of the paper, write today's date. Now create a time line by drawing a horizontal line connecting the two dates. Next, identify each of the major defining moments of your life along that line. Write down events of trauma and excitement, success and failure, joy and sorrow—any and all events that have had an impact in making you who you are. Only do this after you have spent some time in reflection and prayer asking God to give you such insight necessary to complete this.

Next, draw a line angling up or down depending on the impact of the event. If the first major event of your life was negative, you would start angling down from birth until this event. You would continue this process until you have completed connecting all of the events of your lifetime. With this instrument, it is especially helpful to ask a coach or group for feedback as you explain it to them. Often times, others will see influences of your behavior long before you see them.

Another instrument used in a similar manner is a social family history, or a genogram. If you feel you are struggling with issues that can be traced back to preceding generations, then this is a good exercise to practice in order to gain insight and overcome such behaviors. You will benefit most from having a professionally trained coach or counselor unpack the results of this instrument.

The 360° Assessment

A useful assessment tool for pastors of all ages is to intentionally solicit input from those who know you well. Consider people who know you from a variety of perspectives and who will be honest enough to give you truthful feedback. Ask twenty to forty individuals to spend some time reflecting on your life and behavior. Have them answer these four questions and respond to you in writing by a certain date:

- What do I not do well?
- What do I do well?
- What have I learned to do well?
- What is it that only I can do, that I have an unfair advantage over others in doing? In other words, what can I do that others cannot or that if I don't do it, others won't be able to do it?

Take all of the responses you receive and sit down in a quiet place to read them all together. Write out the themes or consistent messages that come through many of the responses. If any of the responses are totally different from the others, try to understand why. Think it through. Next, give the set of responses to someone you respect and who is objective, mature, and has the gift of discernment. Ask the reviewer to read the responses and tell you what he or she sees in them. Listen very carefully, ask questions, and be willing to accept the insights.

Keep Long-term Perspective

Most pastors spend the first half of their ministry trying to prove who they are and the second half trying to defend it. They should spend the first half learning about themselves and the second half fully ministering out of who they are.

Too many pastors drop out of ministry because they judge their effectiveness over too short of a time frame. As you continue to learn more about yourself throughout your lifetime, you will continue to sharpen your focus on your strengths, weaknesses, and areas of growth. Early in your life, don't become so consumed with a vision of how you think God will use you, such that if it doesn't come to reality you will give up and leave the ministry.

Don't allow your expectations to rob you of the privilege of ministering out of who God created you to be. There is no unredeemable ministry failure, as illustrated by John Mark leaving Paul in Acts 13:13. Later in Acts 15:37, Paul implies that John Mark is of no use to him on the second missionary journey and that causes a major argument between Paul and Barnabas. Yet, in 2 Timothy 4:11, Paul tells Timothy to bring John Mark with him because "he is of great use to me" (NIV). God sees everything that happens and is able to redeem every failure if we let him.

There are no wasted courses in God's training room. Every event can be used if we assess its impact in our lives and the potential asset it can become if we allow God to use it to sharpen our understanding of who we are.

In addition to reading the journals of great men and women of the faith, it is essential to read biographies of individuals who have been dead at least thirty years. This time span allows for most of the sentimentalism to have worn off. After this period of time, their biographers and you can begin to understand them for who they really were and for what they did.

Ask yourself the question, How long did this individual take before he or she began to have a clear understanding of the answers to the three questions? Most of the time, you will find that their clarity didn't come until the second half of their life, so be patient. The goal again is not to know yourself, but to continue knowing yourself. You will become a lifelong traveler who ever more clearly understands the uniqueness that your heavenly Father created in you, through you, and for you.

Not So Fast

Before we close, I need to affirm the practice of working on your weaknesses. Consider two specific instances when you must identify and work on weaknesses in your life: (1) when you find yourself in roles which

Next Steps to Ministry

require a strength you don't have and (2) when your past continues to present itself in a destructive way in the present.

Everything I have said thus far is predicated upon knowing yourself and developing the uniqueness that God had endowed in you. But that is not a reason to refuse to work on areas that are tripping you up. All good athletes have had to learn to compensate for weak areas in their game. Certainly, they develop and work on their strengths, but if there is some area of extreme weakness, they learn to deal with it in such a way that it doesn't knock them out of the competition. At times in our lives, all of us will find ourselves in roles that require us to work outside of our strengths, gifts, or passions and we must learn to deal with these areas in ways that won't knock us out of ministry.

Every role I have filled in the ministry from growing layperson, to leading layperson, to intern, to associate staff, to senior staff, to state pastor has required me to do something I was not exceptionally good at and most of the time simply didn't enjoy. But all of us have to do some of those things. So what do you do? I would suggest that you first try to change the expectation of that role. However, if you are not free to rewrite the ministry description for the role you are in, let me suggest three options that can be part of adjusting those expectations: (1) staff it, (2) structure it, and (3) train it.

Staff It

If you find yourself in a role where the expectations cannot be changed and the performance that is needed is not one of your strengths, there are several possibilities for survival. The first is to staff to your weakness. One of the joys of a church with multiple staff members is that the pastoral staff can align responsibilities along gifting lines. If you are hiring someone to join your team, be sure to consider the kinds of assessments we have discussed in this chapter. Ask yourself, what kind of person do I need on staff to complement my weaknesses? Look for someone who not only can cover the assigned responsibilities but who brings strengths and passions that are different from yours. Always staff to your weaknesses!

Knowing that I wasn't a very nurturing person, when I pastored a church of three hundred, I broadened the job description of the youth pastor into a pastoral care position. He was exceptionally gifted in this area and it freed me up from doing hospital visitation. (Well, it didn't completely free me: That was a major shift in expectations on the congregation's part; however, through great pain I eventually convinced them that the minister of pastoral care had gifts that would actually help them feel better in the hospital, unlike me!)

Structure It

If you can't staff for a required strength that you don't possess, then try to structure or systematize it. Often you can develop systems that will operate in a way to compensate for your not having a required strength in a role. Find some way to develop a structure that will function in a way to alleviate you from having to practice the area of weakness.

When I planted a church, we averaged fewer than two hundred people in attendance for years, and I didn't have the luxury of having a leadership team of multiple staff members, so I structured the church around small groups. This structure allowed congregational care to take place from within the context of small groups. If someone needed care, the small group ministered to them appropriately. By structuring the church accordingly, I only visited the hospital once in fourteen years of pastoring that church!

Train It

The last (or possibly first) resort of dealing with a nonstrength is to train it. Seek help from outside experts who can help you deal with this expectation in a way that does not cause you major trauma. The goal of this training is not to make you proficient in this area, but just to help you perform well enough that this weakness doesn't negatively impede your ministry.

Let me give you another example from my own ministry. I am not an overly structured person by nature, but when I learned that I had to be more structured in ministry than I was, I took a number of time management courses. I learned to prioritize and make lists. I read a great deal about the need to plan your work and work your plan. All of this helped me considerably. I began to set annual goals, which changed my life and improved my ministry. However, I have never become a fully organized person.

I spent time disciplining myself to use a Daytimer, which I did for years. Then when PDAs came out, I allowed the system of a PDA to tell me when I had to leave for an appointment or when I didn't have enough time to squeeze one more thing in. I have used PDAs for almost a decade now and they serve me well. I used training and systems to compensate for this area where I could be tripped up continually.

So if your role requires you to possess a strength which you lack, you can either staff it, structure it, or train it.

It's Your Baggage, So Deal with It!

As you begin the process of knowing yourself, you may find areas in your life that derive from some pathology or dysfunctional part of yourself that needs to be addressed. It's not enough to simply identify one or more areas of inappropriate behavior as simply a weakness and move on. When you find yourself face to face with some issue that arises from a past experience, you have a choice: you can either enter the dark tunnel of chaos and deal with this issue (which in the long-term will free you to be a person fulfilling the call of God on your life) or you can settle for significantly less than God's intent because you were unwilling to face issues that will impede your ministry effectiveness.

Again, past models of pastoral preparation fail us here. Seldom were individuals helped to see how their relational or emotional hang-ups continued to undermine healthy ministry. Most institutions simply did not ask the faculty to deal with these non-academic issues, which often could be seen in the classroom. As you complete the self-discovery steps in this chapter, I pray that someone you encounter during the process will care enough to give you some insights into these relational or emotional impediments to ministry. Listen carefully and thoughtfully, and then seek help from someone trained to coach you through it. Don't give in to the enemy or yourself when the progress is slow; the kingdom of God is worth your becoming the best at who you are!

One More Thought on Fruitfulness

So who did God create you to be? How will God assess your ministry? God's ultimate assessment comes when we meet him face to face. Don't judge the efficacy of your calling or the effectiveness of your assessment by the fruit you see in the short term. Often God uses a different scorecard to measure our success than we do. At times, he will use brokenness to clarify your understanding of yourself. At other times, God will teach you how to use your strengths by ordaining the long dark night of the soul that's been written about by so many of the church fathers.

Moses spent forty years in the wilderness, David spent years running from Saul, and Paul spent years in Tarsus while the church in Jerusalem did very well without him (Acts 9:31). Every biblical and historical Christian leader has gone through a time of breaking that helped refine their character, identify their strengths, and define their call.

As I've been writing the closing words to this chapter, I've received an e-mail from a pastor whom I have coached through the most difficult time of his ministry life. He left a contentious board situation and spent over a year out of ministry dealing with physical illness, emotional pain, financial struggles, and marital stress. Previously, he had pastored for several decades in one of the larger churches in his denomination, but he had come to feel that he was washed up. However, as he has sought assessment from and listened to those who loved him and as he has worked on the issues that were tripping him up, he has grown significantly. He has just accepted a call to another pastorate in a church that now appreciates his polished, or seasoned, perspective. He is free to be who God has called him to be now. He has a much greater understanding of himself and appreciates what God has created him to be. He will no longer try to be who he is not. He knows what he can do, what he can't do, and what he is learning to do. For that reason, he is now entering one of the most freeing, fulfilling, and fruitful seasons for his ministry and for the kingdom.

And that is God's desire for you: that you know who he created you to be, that you know who he created you not to be, and that you know the places you can still learn and grow. Even more than you want to be effective in ministry, God wants you to be fully prepared and empowered as the unique and gifted warrior he has created you to be.

Reference List

Benner, David G. 2004. *The Gift of Being Yourself*. Downer's Grove, IL: InterVarsity Press.

Buckingham, Marcus, and Donald Clifton. 2001. *Now, Discover Your Strengths*. New York: The Free Press.

Clinton, Robert. 1988. *The Making of a Leader*. Colorado Springs, CO: NavPress.

Crabb, Larry. 2001. *Shattered Dreams*. Colorado Springs, CO: Waterbook Press.

Dotlich, David, and Peter Cairo. 2003. *Why CEOs Fail*. San Francisco: Jossey-Bass.

Hagberg, Janet, and Robert Guelich. 1995. *The Critical Journey of Faith*. Salem, WI: Sheffield Publishing.

Kinnaman, Gary, and Alfred Ells. 2003. *Leaders That Last*. Grand Rapids, MI: Baker Books.

MacDonald, Gorden. 1984. *Ordering Your Private World*. Nashville, TN: Thomas Nelson.

McNeal, Reggie. 1998. *Revolution in Leadership*. Nashville, TN: Abingdon Press.

McNeal, Reggie. 2000. *A Work of Heart*. San Francisco: Jossey-Bass.

Quinn, Robert. 2004. *Building the Bridge as You Walk on It*. San Francisco: Jossey-Bass.

Willard, Dallas. 2002. *Renovation of the Heart*. Colorado Springs, CO: NavPress.

Other Resources
www.gregwiens.com (Free spiritual gift and personality tests)
www.talentsmart.com/products/surveys.php (Excellent assessments for a fee)

Chapter Two:
Gilbert W. Stafford: *Faith Development in a Postmodern World*

Premodern, Modern, Postmodern

To begin with, we need to define some terms. What is a postmodern world? In order to understand that, we have to understand what a modern world is, and in order to understand that, we have to understand what a premodern world is.

In **premodernism,** the assumption is made that the way one's own group views things is the only right way, and therefore, everybody else's way needs to be changed to "our" way. This leads to cultural and religious wars. Since our culture is the best and all others are deficient, we need to change all other cultures to be like ours. Since our religion is the true religion and all others wrong, we need to convert all who are not in our religion to ours.

Modernism changed that way of looking at things. According to modernism, a universal religious spirit is expressed in a variety of ways depending on the cultural settings in which one finds oneself. The important thing, therefore, is to identify the universal principles of religious life and then discover how those are developed in different ways throughout the world. The assumption is that humankind the world over has a common way of reasoning and that as we enter into dialogue with people around the world, we are able to communicate with them about these universal principles and come to a common understanding as to how those principles are the same whether in their cultural and religious life or in our own.

In premodern thought, the emphasis is on conflict and conversion. In modern thought, the emphasis is on dialogue and common understandings. In premodern thought, the focus is on "our" way over against all other ways. In modern thought, the focus is on "our" way as one of many expressions of universal understandings. In premodern thought, it is a matter of multiple disconnections; in modern thought, it is a matter of universal connections. In premodern thought, the focus is on distancing ourselves from others; in modern thought it is a matter of discovering that which is common to us all.

That brings us to **postmodernism**. In postmodernism, the idea of universal reason and of a universal religious experience is denied. No longer is an attempt made to identify the underlying religious experience that makes each religion simply a cultural expression of the one universal religious spirit. Instead, each religion has to stand on its own and is to be understood within the context of its own historical and cultural setting apart from any supposed universal religious principles. The idea of universal truth is denied. It is a matter, then, of a multiplicity of religious truths, each of which makes sense only within its own historical and cultural context. This postmodern approach can be applied, not only to religious traditions, cultures, and societies, but also to individuals, in which case the emphasis is strictly on what is true for "me," what works for me, what makes sense to me.

It is within this postmodern context that we find the word *deconstruction* in use. To deconstruct an idea, an assumption, a concept is to take it apart so that we can take another look at the issues involved without being encumbered by a widely held way of looking at it. One can do this with anything in any sphere of life and thought. Let me illustrate it in relation to marriage and family life. A deconstructive attitude asks whether it is really the case, as is widely assumed, that marriage is to be only between one male adult and one female adult. Why not between two adults of the same gender? Furthermore, why not between one man and more than one woman, or between one woman and more than one man? Why not between a person of one gender and two or more persons of both genders? To go further, why must marriage have to be between persons of legal age? Is not such an age merely arbitrary? In fact, why does a sexual relationship have to be legalized? Why not allow for free expression of sexual urges in the same way that we allow for the free expression of eating urges? A related issue is whether children really need both male and female influences in their home life. Questions such as these flourish within the framework of a postmodern world that no longer makes the assumption that there are universal truths applicable to every one in every culture.

But the issue may arise as to whether questions such as these differ all that much from those raised in the course of good education. Does not good education encourage the questioning of general assumptions?

Three Types of Educational Approaches

In fact, it *is* true that in the course of good education, assumptions about God and the world are put under the searchlight of probing questions, broader studies, and intellectual analysis. In the midst of this kind of educational process, one often breaks apart assumptions that for a long time have been held to be obviously true and therefore nonnegotiable. Often one hears this process referred to as deconstruction. And, to be sure, this kind of deconstruction has always been part and parcel of what we call *liberal arts education*. Liberal arts education is designed to introduce students to a broad spectrum of thought in science, history, literature, religion, philosophy, and the arts. Its aim is to help students think critically about the world, cultural life, and religious faith. In other words, the goal of liberal arts education is to move students from merely accepting the traditions that have been handed down, on the one hand, to examining them in the broader context of human exploration, experience, knowledge, and multiple traditions, on the other. The emphasis in liberal arts education is not so much on how one feels about a matter but on intellectually and historically analyzing it.

This liberal arts approach to education is to be distinguished from two other very different approaches. One is *the informational approach* with its emphasis on conveying a body of information, viewpoints, and conclusions, the knowledge and acceptance of which is the goal of the educational endeavor. The other is *the skills approach* with its emphasis on learning how to do what needs to be done in a particular field. One sees all three of these approaches in relation to Christian ministry: The liberal arts emphasis is primarily on breadth of thought and on learning how to think critically about Christian faith within that broader framework. The informational emphasis is primarily on communicating a particular interpretation of the Christian tradition and its superior value to all other interpretations. The skills emphasis is primarily on how one does ministry in particular contexts and how to do it well.

A risk in the liberal arts approach is that it may be unduly hesitant to introduce students to the richness and values of the Christian faith and of a particular interpretation of the faith, and hesitant to help them to develop skills of effective ministry. A risk in the informational approach is the absence of both the broader context of thought and critical considerations. A risk in the skills approach is that one may end up knowing how to do ministry without knowing much about the Christian tradition and without critical skills for evaluating the theological basis for doing what one does.

Regardless of the kind of education one has, however, the fact remains that as a participant in the larger culture, one inevitably finds oneself functioning in a postmodern world where universal truth is questioned and deconstruction is encouraged. But what is the difference between the deconstructive thought that takes place in liberal arts education and that which is part of the culture in general?

Perhaps this distinction will be helpful: Those involved in liberal arts education are encouraged by *pedagogical design* to move beyond simply accepting that which has been given to them, and therefore, in that sense, they are going through an academic process of supervised deconstruction. This is not to be confused with deconstruction in the postmodern sense of disavowing on the basis of *philosophical orientation* that there are any universals that are common to the whole human family, common to all religions, and common to Christian faith. Liberal arts education at its best does not assume, as extreme postmodernism does, that when all is said and done, it boils down to one's own personal view of things, that and nothing more. That is not the tradition of liberal arts education. The tradition of liberal arts education is that there is a broad human expression of knowledge and that in order to understand any one part of it adequately one must be informed by that broader human experience. It is only within this broader context that one asks critical questions about one's own tradition, culture, experience, and explorations. Christian liberal arts education holds that faith examined is faith strengthened. Faith that is unexamined does not stand up well in the give-and-take of life in general.[1]

Questions to Be Answered in the Contemporary Context

In regards to faith development within a postmodern world, it needs to be said that just because we live in a postmodern world does not mean that we must function as postmoderns. Just as premoderns continued to function in the modern world, even so premoderns and moderns continue functioning in a postmodern world. Just as Americans can continue being Americans in a European context without becoming European and Muslims can continue being Muslims in a Christian context without becoming Christian, even so premoderns and moderns can continue being such in a postmodern world without actually becoming postmoderns. The first basic question that each of us is called upon to answer in the postmodern world is this: *Is truth universal or is it simply truth for me?* For example, when I say that God is love, do I mean that regardless of what anyone else thinks, the reality is that God is love, or do I mean simply that I personally am convinced that God is love but this is simply my way of looking at things?

The second question is, *What will I do with the conclusion that I come to regarding the first question?* If there is no universal truth—if, for instance, the claim that God is love is simply my perception of things and not the way things really are—is there any criterion by which to argue against the idea that God is loveless? Am I willing to live with the conclusion that God is not actually love even for those who are convinced otherwise? Am I willing to live with the conclusion that the claim that God is love is nothing more than the conviction that I, along with others, hold but that such is not the case universally? If, on the other hand, truth *is* universal reality, and not just my personal perception, then how do I relate to those who reject this truth or who have a contrary perception of truth?

The third question grows out of the conviction that truth is universal: *How will I relate to those who do not accept the truth?* Will I relate to them in a coercive way or in an evangelical way? The coercive way tries to make others cave in, whereas the evangelical way shares, lives, proclaims, and demonstrates the truth as good news for the whole world.

We have important lessons to learn from all three—premodern, modern, and postmodern ways of thinking. From premodernism, we can learn the power of proclaiming the truth as "good news of great joy for all the people."[2] From modernism, we can learn that there is a universality of the human experience to which we can all relate. From postmodernism, we can learn to show respect for those who have different understandings, commitments, traditions, and outlooks on life.

Christians and the Bible in a Postmodern Context

As Christians, the beginning point for understanding God and the world is the Bible. It is the spiritual autobiography of the ancient people of God who are our ancestors in the life of faith.[3] The Bible is a collection of writings from across many centuries of experience. It did not drop down out of heaven. It is not the product of a single human author. It does not consist of pieces of literature all of which are of the same type. Instead, it is a collection of many different literary styles. In fact, one finds within this body of writings itself much evidence of both critical reflection on the tradition as well as new understandings that emerge as a result of ongoing experience and reflection.[4] And yet, as these very diverse writings are brought together for the benefit of the people of faith, a story line emerges that includes common themes about God, the world, and salvation. Over the centuries people who have been engaged by the message of this book have discovered new life, transformative purpose, and divine mission.

No other book in the history of the world has been so minutely studied, analyzed, and critiqued as the Bible. One finds in it the questioning of tradition and of assumptions widely held—there is a deconstructive process in Scripture itself. This, in fact, was very much part of the tension between Jesus and the religious leaders of his day. So, to be engaged in depth with the Bible is inevitably to be engaged in critical thinking about God and the world. This critical thinking, however, has a spiritual and religious track record; it has an historical context that includes the life experiences of common everyday people as well as prophets, priests, and rulers.

As we, the postbiblical people of faith, reflect on the whole story in the Bible—something that only we can do (those within Scripture could not by the nature of things reflect on the *whole* story of the Bible)—certain features of the biblical God emerge, such as the following: God is eternal. God is the creator of life, the sustainer of life, the redeemer of life, and the perfecter of life. God is the eternal thrice personal unity of the mysterious One who is beyond the adequacy of human understanding, the revealed One who comes to dwell with us, and the connecting One who is related to everything and every body in every time and place. God is the triune Father, Son, and Holy Spirit. God is holy. God is love. God is just. This is only a sample of what we can say, on the basis of Scripture, about God.

The church is called to be the ongoing people of biblical faith. For some two thousand years, the church has been reflecting on its faith in the biblical God. The result of that reflective work finds expression in creeds, confessions, hymns, songs, theologies, sermons, books, and personal testimonies. We shortchange ourselves whenever we fail to avail ourselves of this rich and enriching heritage. Here again, the importance of critical reflection is crucial to the right use of these just mentioned resources. To be sure, one can point to instances in church history when the absence of critical reflection led to disastrous consequences. Without critical reflection the church tends to become oppressive, heavy-handed, and repressive. Creative life is squeezed out of it, and traditionalism and authoritarianism displace the ongoing ministry of the Spirit and Word. In order for the church to function as intended, voices from the margins of church life need to be heard.[5] That does not mean that those voices are always right and that the voices at the center are always wrong. What it means is that the voices at the center always need to be engaged with the voices from the margins, listening to their questions, grappling with their issues, and asking whether they as persons at the center have, indeed, overlooked something important. But this conversation between the voices at the center and the voices on the margins goes two ways. In may be that the voices from the margins simply do not understand the issues with which the voices at the center are dealing; perhaps they do not adequately understand the Christian tradition for which those at the center claim to have a special stewardship.

What is needed is for the voices at the center to be at the same time voices from the margins, that is to say, those in positions of official power in the life of the church need always to be asking critical questions about matters of faith; and for voices on the margins to be at the same time voices from the center, that is to say, those who are not in positions of official power in the life of the church need always to be well-informed by the history of the faith.

Faith Itself as the Basis for Faith Development

In order for both those at the center and on the margins to grow in Christian faith requires first and foremost, of course, the experience of the gift of faith. Faith is the result of the work of God upon and in our lives. Faith is not something we conjure up. It is not something we set out to build. Rather, faith is God's gift to us. It is God's internal working within the soul so that when we indeed come to faith, we have the overwhelming awareness that we had nothing to do with it; it was all of God. The apostle Paul expresses this in Ephesians 2:8–10:

> For by grace you have been saved through faith, and this is not your own doing; it is the gift of God—not the result of works, so that no one may boast. For we are what he has made us, created in Christ Jesus for good works, which God prepared beforehand to be our way of life.

God provides the church to serve as a community that nurtures us toward faith, sends forth evangels of the gospel to introduce us to faith, and blesses many of us with families who provide an intimate environment for coming to faith; but in the last analysis, only God can bring us to faith.

Many important things could and ought to be said about the nature of Christian faith[6]; however, the most important thing is that genuine faith takes place when a person has a new self-understanding in relationship to God, to others, to the world, and to themselves. Consider Paul's words in 2 Corinthians 5: 16–18:

> From now on, therefore, we regard no one from a human point of view; even though we once knew Christ from a

human point of view, we know him no longer in that way. So if anyone is in Christ, there is a new creation: everything has become new! All this is from God, who reconciled us to himself through Christ, and has given us the ministry of reconciliation.

Those who are in Christian faith understand themselves as the reconciled children of God; they understand themselves as divine emissaries to others regarding the offer of this new identity; they understand themselves to be good stewards of the world that God created, sustains, and redeems; and they understand themselves to be forgiven and set apart for divine purposes.

Faith development is about spiritual growth that is informed by this new self-understanding, whose development takes place in the context of the church at the center of which is the biblical message. As my pastor once put it in a sermon, we simply will not make it as Christians unless we are informed by the inspired Word of God and are deeply committed to participation in an inspired community of Christian faith.[7] I agree.

The Church as the Community for Faith Development

I call attention to eight components of church life that are crucial for faith development:

1. Preaching and Teaching

First and foremost is the preaching and teaching of the message of the Bible. Preaching is the *proclamation* of God's Word; teaching is *instruction* in it. Preaching is a *declaration to us*; teaching is *discussion with us*. Preaching *addresses us with answers*; teaching *listens to our questions*. It is this ongoing engagement with the message of the Bible that provides us with the context for faith development. While a sermon in worship may be both preaching and teaching, it is preaching that should be uppermost. And while a lesson in class may be both, it is teaching that should be uppermost. We need both preaching in worship and teaching in classes. We need to hear the Word declared to us, calling us to transformation, and we need to study the Word so that our transformation is well-informed.[8]

2. The Lord's Supper

The second dimension of church life is the Lord's Supper. This is the Lord's way of keeping the main thing the main thing in the life of the church. At the center of the church's life is the saving life, death, resurrection, and lordship of Jesus Christ. The holy meal designed by our Lord keeps before us the centrality of his redemptive work. How easy it is for us to forget what the center of church life is! It is about Jesus the Christ, who lived in first-century Palestine, was crucified under Pontius Pilate, was raised from the dead on the third day, and is even now the reigning Lord at the right hand of the Father. When Jesus broke the loaf and gave it to his disciples, he told them, "This is my body" (Mark 14:22). When he gave them the cup, he told them that it was the "blood of the new covenant" (Mark 14:24). That the loaf is his body means that in this way our Lord makes his ongoing life present among us. That the fruit of the vine is the blood of the new covenant means that because of his life and death we are in a new relationship with God. Apart from the sacrificial life of Jesus Christ, there is no Christian gospel. The Lord's Supper[9] is often referred to as the Eucharist[10], which means a time of thanksgiving—thanksgiving for God's sustaining grace for bodily nourishment and for God's redeeming grace through Christ. It is also referred to as Holy Communion[11], which refers to the fact that at the holy meal, we commune not with a deceased Lord but with the risen, living, and reigning Lord. It is at the table that the church holds conversation with her Lord. As the Lord's Supper, it is hosted by none other than our Lord himself for our spiritual nourishment.

3. The Experience of the Kingdom

The third feature of life in the church is the experience of the church as the community of the kingdom of God. The kingdom is the inbreaking into human history of the reign and rule of God. The Old Testament promises of the kingdom came to fulfillment in the person of Jesus Christ. The kingdom revealed in its fullness is none other than Jesus Christ. The only way to enter into the kingdom is to enter into his life by faith. When by faith we are "in Christ, there is a new creation: everything old has passed away; see, everything has become new!" (2 Cor 5:17). We enter into the kingdom by being incorporated into Christ, and the kingdom thereby reigns within us, blessing and directing us. Just as Paul refers to both our being in Christ (2 Cor 5:17) and Christ's being in us (Gal 2:20), even so through him we are both in the kingdom and the kingdom is in us. It is in the life of the church that we learn kingdom values of justice, love, grace, and peace. It is in the church that we witness signs of the kingdom such as miraculous healings, miraculous grace in suffering, miraculous dedication to the cause of Christ, miraculous stewardship of life's resources, and miraculous transformations of lives and relationships. It is here that we experience reconciliation, victory, and hope—reconciliation between ourselves and God, between ourselves and others, and within ourselves; victory over sin and death; and hope in the God of the resurrection, who always stands on the horizon of new possibilities.

4. Corporate Worship

The fourth component is the corporate worship of the church. Of course, all of the above relate to corporate worship, but here I have in mind the whole service of worship, which includes the singing of "psalms, hymns and spiritual songs among yourselves, singing and making melody to the Lord in your hearts, giving thanks to God the Father at all times and for everything in the name of our Lord Jesus Christ" (Eph 5:19–20).

Psalms have to do with the recital of God's faithfulness to the people of God; hymns have to do with the theological adoration of God; spiritual songs have to do with the personal experience of God. We are stunted in our faith development if any one of these musical expressions is missing. In terms of our spiritual development, we need to sing recitations of the faithfulness of God to his people (e.g., Miriam's song in Exodus 15:21 after the crossing through the Red Sea: "Sing to the Lord, for he has triumphed gloriously; horse and rider he has thrown into the sea."). We need to sing our theological adoration of God (e.g., the song of the twenty-four elders in heavenly glory in Revelation 4:11: "You are worthy, our Lord and God, to receive glory and honor and power, for you created all things, and by your will they existed and were created."). We need to sing personal testimonies of the experience of God in the soul (e.g., Mary's song during her pregnancy with our Lord as recorded in Luke 1:46–48a: "My soul magnifies the Lord, and my spirit rejoices in God my Savior, for he has looked with favor on the lowliness of his servant."). Just as the Bible has all three, even so church singing should include all three; we should embrace all three not on the basis of our personal preference but because of our spiritual need for wholesome faith development.

Singing, however, is only one component of corporate worship. Others are prayers, testimonies, confessions of faith, the preaching of the Word, the Lord's Supper, and the offering of ourselves and of our resources to the Lord. Other components are repentance, the empowerment of the Spirit, exhortation to conform our lives to the will of God, and celebrations of conversions through baptism. In addition, corporate worship often includes other celebrations, such as of births, marriages, educational and vocational accomplishments, and deaths in Christ. Corporate worship provides opportunities for church revival, for personal renewal (as in services of foot washing), and for refocusing on personal vocation and the divine mission.

5. Service and Mission

The fifth dimension of church life is that of service and mission. Faith development requires involvement both in compassionate ministries and in evangelical outreach beyond the boundaries of corporate worship. We are called, not only to "give a cup of cold water" (Matt 10:42), but also to go to the whole world with the gospel. Matthew includes both emphases: Not only does our Lord tell us that "this good news of the kingdom will be proclaimed throughout the world, as a testimony to all the nations; and then the end will come" (Matt 24:14) and commission us to "make disciples of all nations" (Matt 28:19), but he also clearly declares that the final judgment will be based on kingdom values as to whether we feed the hungry, give drink to the thirsty, welcome the stranger, clothe the naked, care for the sick, and visit the imprisoned (Matt 25:31–46). It is by doing kingdom deeds and going with the kingdom message that our faith is developed. It is by involvement in the divine mission that we grow in our understanding of the faith.

6. Small Groups

The sixth feature of church life is that of smaller, intimate fellowships that pray and eat together, play and work together, share and care together, and hold each other accountable. I have in mind that which is called by several different names: class meetings, cell groups, small groups, house churches, home groups.[12] It is here that individuals can share their inner lives more readily, develop strong relationships that sustain one through the difficulties and challenges of life, and find a place to process doubts, ideas, and questions. It is in such close, intimate groups that accountability can be experienced, decisions processed, issues grappled with, and perspectives developed. It is in this kind of setting that one can learn new skills of communicating about matters of faith and put into practice the understandings of the faith. In such settings, our peers are in a position to observe us up close and engage us about matters that those who are in a more formal relation with us perhaps would not be free to do.

7. Prayer

The seventh component is the prayer life that is nurtured by close association with those who gather specifically for the purpose of praying. I have in mind prayer that is other than the corporate prayers in worship services and other than the praying that is part of a smaller, intimate group. The kind of experience referred to here is the gathering that has only one purpose, that of prayer. It is in such prayer meetings that we hear the heart throbs of people to whom we may not be close otherwise. It is here that we discover the passions of fellow believers, unite in concerted intercessions, and rejoice in the power of united prayer. Certainly, the church spoken of in the book of Acts was a church that gathered for the purpose of earnest prayer. Acts 4:31 describes such a prayer meeting: "When they had prayed, the place in which they were gathered together was shaken." Acts 12:5 reports that "while Peter was kept in prison, the church prayed fervently to God for him" and that, in fact, he was delivered. A young maid named Rhoda was so overjoyed at his appearance at the prayer meeting that instead of opening the gate for him, she ran to tell the others about the answer to their prayers. Young Rhoda, no doubt, experienced faith development that night as she participated in the church at prayer.

8. Educational Settings

The eighth and last dimension to be discussed here is the educational work of the church: classes, instructional sessions, seminars. It is through the teaching ministry of the church that faith development takes place not only as one is in the student role but also in the teaching role. I often hear those who teach say that it is the very best way to learn. When one prepares to teach, one tends to study in greater depth in order to be prepared to contribute well to students and to anticipate issues that might come up in the course of the study sessions. Often teachers report that they have overly prepared. But that is good because it provides additional opportunity for one's own faith development.

The questions raised by students provide teachers with issues and perspectives that perhaps are new; they provide new paradigms for consideration. As a longtime teacher in church, college, and seminary, I learned a long time ago that questions are gifts to me in that they provide me with new opportunities to think through issues.

Faith development in a postmodern world requires the gift of faith itself, a basic understanding of the nature of the postmodern world, and deep involvement in the life of the church.

Endnotes

[1] While liberal arts education is intentional about the examination of faith, I realize that such examination is not limited to the liberal arts experience. Indeed, persons in an informational school experience or in a technical skills experience or for that matter in none of the above can nevertheless be in the mode of examining the faith. Also, I realize that a liberal arts education does not guarantee that one actually will be very serious about examining the faith even within that setting. Having recognized that the forms of educational experience do not necessarily dictate the reality, the main point here is that the pedagogical deconstruction that takes place as part of liberal arts education is not the same as the philosophical deconstruction that grows out of postmodernism.

[2] The words used by the angel of the Lord to the shepherds at the time of our Lord's birth, in Luke 2:10.

[3] For a fuller treatment of the nature of Scripture, see chapter 3, "The Church's Book of Faith," in Stafford (1996).

[4] For examples, see Amos 5:21–24; Matt 5: 21–48; James 2:14–17.

[5] Examples of voices from the margins are the young, the old, minorities of all sorts, those who have special causes, any who are not in official places of church responsibility. The reference in this section to voices at the center refers to those who have official church responsibility or who have attained the status of authority, either by experience or by academic attainment.

[6] See my treatment in chapter 17, "Discipleship Faith," and chapter 18, "The Gift of a New Identity," in Stafford (1996).

[7] David Markle, Park Place Church of God (Anderson, Indiana), June 5, 2005.

[8] I will say more about worship as such in section 4 and more about classes in section 8.

[9] 1 Cor 11:20.

[10] See Matt 26:27; Mark 14:23; Luke 22: 17, 19; 1 Cor 11:24.

[11] See 1 Cor 10:16 in the King James Version.

[12] This last phrase is used by Randy Frazee (2001, 164). The value of Frazee's book is that he shows the necessity of participating in intimate authentic community for faith development.

Reference List

Bloesch, Donald G. 2002. *The Church: Sacraments, Worship, Ministry, Mission.* Downers Grove, IL: InterVarsity Press. (An overview of the doctrine of the church informed by Scripture and history)

Callen, Barry L. 2001. *Authentic Spirituality: Moving Beyond Mere Religion.* Grand Rapids, MI: Baker Books. (A resource for understanding the nature of the Christian life)

———. 1999. *Radical Christianity: The Believers Church Tradition in Christianity's History and Future.* Nappanee, IN: Evangel Publishing House. (An historical survey of that tradition of Christian faith which emphasizes the church as a "disciple community" [Hall 1996, 22, 259, 264])

Finger, Thomas N. 2004. *A Contemporary Anabaptist Theology: Biblical, Historical, Constructive.* Downers Grove, IL: InterVarsity. (A comprehensive theology that grows out of the conviction that the church is a "disciple community")

Foster, Richard J. 1998. *Streams of Living Water: Celebrating the Great Traditions of Christian Faith.* San Francisco: HarperSanFrancisco.

(An introduction to major streams of Christian thought and practice and how they enrich each other)

Frazee, Randy. 2001. *The Connecting Church: Beyond Small Groups to Authentic Community.* Grand Rapids, MI: Zondervan. (A plea for churches to structure themselves so that people discover genuine oneness with each other)

Hall, Douglas John. 1996. *Confessing the Faith: Christian Theology in a North American Context.* Minneapolis, MN: Fortress Press.

Larson, Lloyd, and Frank Ponce, eds. 1989. *Worship the Lord: Hymnal of the Church of God.* Anderson, IN: Warner Press. (A statement of Christian faith in song)

Lundin, Roger. 1993. *The Culture of Interpretation: Christian Faith and the Postmodern World.* Grand Rapids, MI: Eerdmans. (A Christian critique of postmodern culture)

Melander, Rochelle, and Harold Eppley. 2002. *The Spiritual Leader's Guide to Self-Care.* Bethesda: Alban Institute. (A fifty-two-week plan for nurturing one's soul to health)

Schweitzer, Friedrich L. 2004. *The Postmodern Life Cycle: Challenges for Church and Theology.* St. Louis: Chalice. (A discussion of how postmodernism affects our understanding of the stages of life)

Stafford, Gilbert W. 1996. *Theology for Disciples: Systematic Considerations about the Life of Christian Faith.* Anderson, IN: Warner Press. (A theology that is designed to help the church as a "disciple community" to reflect on its faith)

———. 2000. *Church of God at the Crossroads.* Anderson, IN: Warner Press. (A critique of the Church of God at the turn of the millennium)

———. 2002. *As Christians, Here We Stand.* Anderson: Church of God Ministries. (A Church of God confession of Christian faith in primarily biblical language)

———. 2002. *Vision for the Church of God at the Crossroads.* Anderson, IN: Warner Press. (A practical approach to meeting the challenges faced by the Church of God)

Withrow, Oral. 1998. *Thinking about Our Faith: A Guide for Growing and Learning.* Anderson, IN: Warner Press. (A series of lessons designed for both church leaders and new Christians, using Stafford [1996] as a resource)

CHAPTER THREE:
Edward L. Foggs: *Being a Person of Integrity*

Introduction

"If I speak in the tongues of men and of angels, but have not integrity, I am only a resounding gong or a clanging cymbal. If I have the gift of prophecy and can fathom all mysteries and all knowledge, and if I have a faith that can move mountains, but have not integrity, I am nothing. If I give all I possess to the poor and surrender my body to the flames, but have not integrity, I gain nothing" (1 Cor 13:1–3, paraphrased from NIV).

The apostle Paul, of course, was writing about love. The clear inference, however, is that one may have the ability to do good and wonderful things without the love of God, thus negating the worth of what they do. By the same reasoning, one who lacks integrity can do outwardly splendorous things, but the absence of integrity negates the value of such service in the eyes of God.

I checked several definitions of integrity and they all include these elements: soundness, completeness, wholeness, entirety, and honesty, without duplicity or pretense. Integrity is involved in every decision we make, every relationship we have, every stance we take, every influence we exert, and every endeavor we pursue. It is the inescapable governor of how we live.

History, in both ancient and recent times, is replete with ministry leaders who somewhere along their journey lost their integrity. The loss of integrity is seldom deliberate and intentional. Rather, one slides down the slippery slope of carelessness, dishonesty, indifference, and inattention. Little by little, integrity begins to erode. Often its full impact is not recognized until some major calamity occurs. Then, in retrospect, one can look back and see where and when it all began.

Richard Dortch, a former Assemblies of God minister and pastor and former president of PTL, wrote an insightful account of his involvement with PTL and Jim and Tammy Baker and the downfall of that ministry. He titled his book *Integrity: How I Lost It, and My Journey Back*. Although his humiliating fall resulted in his being sentenced to eight years in prison, he is to be commended for the candor and honesty with which he describes his fall from integrity and his recovery. The volume merits reading.

Dortch wrote that the true test of integrity comes when no one is looking, when the cameras are turned off and the audience has gone home. This insight is simple but profoundly true. As a boy I often heard adults say that reputation is what people think you are but that character is what you are. Integrity is the essence of character—what and who you are when you are alone and unaware of anyone watching.

Integrity Is a Matter of the Heart

Numerous volumes have been written about integrity, but problems of integrity, or the lack thereof, persist. There are more than twenty biblical references to integrity. In David's prayer of praise for all that God had allowed him to lead the people of Israel to do in preparation for building the temple, he utters these words: "I know, my God, that you test the heart and are pleased with integrity. All these things have I given willingly and with honest intent" (1 Chron 29:17 NIV). *Honest intent* is one of the hallmarks of integrity. We all make mistakes. All of us, in our humanness, are subject to missing the mark sometimes, but honest intent is a strong evidence of integrity. It finds credence in the oft-used expression: It was a mistake of the head, not an intent of the heart.

Honest intent has much to do with our motives. Why do we do what we do? What motivates our behavior? Are we doing the right things for the wrong reasons? When Jesus taught his disciples and said to them, "Blessed are the pure in heart," he spoke directly to the importance of right motivation. Jesus uttered some of his strongest condemnations and warnings to the Pharisees who were skilled at doing things with impure motives (see Matt 23). Ministers too can be caught in the trap of being wrongly motivated. The desire for success can overshadow the demands of integrity. The need to always be right can overshadow the demands of integrity. The need to be first can override the demands of integrity.

Do we offer insincere compliments, really fishing for a return compliment? Do we accept speaking engagements based chiefly on audience size or compensation expected rather than on an inner sense of God's guidance? Are we motivated chiefly by the desire for position, prestige, and status? Do we pretend to be something we are not? Do we seek more to please others than to please God?

Several years ago I knew a man who had been indicted for murder. During the period between the time of the indictment and the trial, he reportedly told his alleged accomplices to go to church and Bible study. Get in there and pray with the best of them because it will look good in court. How's that for honest intent and pure motivation?

I heard too of a mother who had guests for dinner. When time came to eat, she asked her little girl to offer the prayer for the meal. The girl told her mother that she did not know how to pray. The mother told her to just say what she heard her say. The girl prayed: "O Lord, why on earth did I invite these people over for dinner?"

The apostle Paul spoke passionately of his concern for integrity in ministry in his second letter to the Corinthian Christians. "Therefore, since through God's mercy we have this ministry, we do not lose heart. Rather, we have renounced secret and shameful ways; we do not use deception, nor do we distort the word of God. On the contrary, by setting forth the truth plainly we commend ourselves to every man's conscience in the sight of God" (2 Cor 4:1–2 NIV).

In our quest to be persons of integrity, we need often to pray the psalmist's prayer: "Search me, O God, and know my heart; test me and know my anxious thoughts. See if there is any offensive way in me, and lead me in the way everlasting" (139:23–24 NIV).

Two verses from Proverbs speak further about integrity. "The man of integrity walks securely, but he who takes crooked paths will be found out" (10:9 NIV). "The integrity of the upright guides them, but the unfaithful are destroyed by their duplicity" (11:3 NIV). Here, again, honest intent is earmarked as a hallmark of integrity. Dishonesty and duplicity are twin adversaries of integrity.

When Nehemiah had completed rebuilding the wall of Jerusalem, he placed his brother Hanani in charge of the city. He gave as his reason for appointing Hanani that "he was a man of integrity and feared God more than most men do" (7:2 NIV). *Fearing God* is another hallmark of integrity. People who are called upon through their leadership to be in charge must be persons who fear God. To fear God is to recognize and acknowledge our reliance on him for discernment, insight, wisdom, courage, strength, and grace. It is when people begin to feel arrogant and self-sufficient in their own ability that their integrity is at risk.

As for ministry leaders, there is hardly a higher compliment paid than to David in Psalms 78:72 (NIV): "And David shepherded them [God's people] with *integrity of heart*; with skillful hands he led them." Integrity is a matter of the heart. It is not essentially about credentials, position, prestige, status, or the like. These external attributes are not to be viewed as negative, but without integrity of heart, they are more damaging than helpful.

The citing of these biblical references is intended to emphasize that our concern for integrity is about more than current social or cultural norms. It is at the heart of God's desire for those who are ministry leaders in the church. Even the critics of Jesus, as they sought to entrap him, were compelled to acknowledge that he was a man of integrity (see Matt 22:16 and Mark 12:4 NIV). He is the master of integrity and stands ready to equip us to be persons of integrity.

Integrity Requires Accountability

We tend to think of integrity as being a personal and private matter. Ultimately, it is. Practically, however, it also is a community affair. We do not live in isolation but in relationship. When integrity falters, it typically finds expression in relationship to others. Our influence is damaged so that we have to engage in damage control. Others are hurt and wounded. The kingdom of God suffers. The reputation of the church is damaged. Our families are embarrassed. The effects of integrity failure are far reaching. We, therefore, have an obligation to each other to help one another be persons of integrity.

This is why I contend that every leader, especially ministers and pastors, need one or more knowledgeable, spiritually perceptive, and *trusted critics*. I am not thinking of critics as destructive adversaries. Unfortunately, some leaders seem to regard every critic as an adversary. Properly understood and utilized, however, a *trusted critic* can enhance our integrity.

A colleague of mine, now deceased, told me that he belonged to the Communist Party for one day. Why only one day? When he shared his action with one of his friends, his friend responded by saying to him: "You must be two people, because one person could not be that stupid." He quit the Party.

Who is there who challenges our thinking, counsels us against unwise decisions, cautions us when we overreact, tells us the truth—*even when it is the awful truth*—and stands ready to help us when we have faltered by reason of immature or premature judgments? Who is there who safeguards us against our blind spots? Who is there who raises issues and questions we may not have considered? Who is there who helps us to distinguish between caring critics and unloving critics?

There emerged a proliferation of books during the late 1980s and the 1990s when clergy scandal dominated much of the news. One of those was a volume by Richard Exley titled *Perils of Power: Immorality in the Ministry*. In writing about mutual support and discipline for the pastor, he said: "He [the pastor] will need a circle of peers, usually no more than four or five, with whom he can develop a relationship of mutual accountability. When he strays, they can correct him; when he grows weary, they can strengthen and encourage him; when he becomes confused, they can provide guidance; and when he celebrates, they can celebrate with him!" (1988, 148).

This has all in the world to do with integrity, for if we go our own way and do our own thing—feeling accountable to no one but God—we become vulnerable to pitfalls that lead to a loss of integrity. So often the loss of integrity is rooted in stubborn resistance to accountability and denial of problems or needs. The failure to discern one's own frailty, the refusal to hear wise counsel, the insidious and deceptive notion that success and achievement, power and status, prestige and influence are adequate protections against the loss of integrity—these all are a part of the pride that comes before a fall.

We have a three-year-old grandson who steadily resists being helped. He wants to put his shoes on, put on and zip up his coat, and open the car door when he's ready to get in—even though he sometimes is frustrated in his attempts. His favorite words are, "Do it myself." Now there is merit in his quest for self-reliance and independence. As he grows and matures, however, he will discover that there are some arenas in which "do it myself" will not lead to the desired results. A part of the honesty in integrity is the recognition and acknowledgement that we sometimes need help to overcome perils that endanger our integrity. Even wise persons need the counsel and encouragement of trusted critics.

In citing Jimmy Swaggart's moral failure, Exley quotes Swaggart as having written these words just before his sin was made public: "I have always taken pride in my spiritual strength. I have always believed that in my relationship with God, if he promised me something, I could have it. I can't recall, in all of my life, ever going to anybody and asking them for help…Now I realize that if I had turned to my brothers and sisters I surely would have found the help I needed…" (Exley 1988, 18–19).

Although I have used the term *critic*, I do understand that we frequently tend to distrust our critics because, in our humanness, we really don't like to be criticized. Our emotional insecurities rise to the surface in the face of criticism. Therefore, a word needs to be said about qualities and characteristics of those to whom we can turn and be accountable. I have compiled a short list of qualities I desire in a trusted critic.

- A trusted critic has at heart the best interest of the one being criticized—always wishing him or her well.
- A trusted critic does not desire to embarrass or humiliate the one being criticized.

- A trusted critic is eager for the one being criticized to benefit from the criticism.
- A trusted critic typically criticizes privately rather than publicly.
- A trusted critic aspires to allow one the benefit of the doubt in the spirit of 1 Corinthians 13:4–7.
- A trusted critic has no personal axe to grind.
- A trusted critic shares not only the negative, but the positive as well.

This is a tall order, but the payoff is well worth the investment. The reality is that we can benefit even from the criticism of an adversary; how much more then from that of trusted critics who hold us accountable.

In the preface to their book *Overcoming the Dark Side of Leadership: The Paradox of Personal Dysfunction*, McIntosh and Rima assert that because ambition is easily disguised in Christian circles and couched in spiritual language (e.g., the need to fulfill the Great Commission and expand the church), the dysfunctions that drive Christian leaders often go undetected and unchallenged until it is too late (1997, 14). They go on to say that the aspects of life that push us in a positive way toward success can also exert a negative pull, destroying our effectiveness (27).[1]

In the face of shortcomings, ineffectiveness, or failure, we are inclined to argue that it's not my fault. Facing up to the truth about ourselves is not always easy. The desire for success can overshadow the demands of integrity. The need to be first can blind us to the demands of integrity. The need to always be right can threaten our integrity. Others can help us to be persons of authentic integrity if we have established avenues of accountability.

Integrity in Congregational Life

One has only to observe a few church fights and church splits to recognize that integrity often is sacrificed in the midst of tensions and conflicts. Charges, countercharges, accusations, private agendas, self-centered desires, out-of-control tempers, bad attitudes, and a broad range of other behavior dysfunctions leave integrity sadly lacking. What is worse, this so often happens in the name of the Lord.

Next Steps to Ministry

I remember hearing about a church that was in the midst of major conflict. They invited in a counseling minister to help them resolve their situation. After listening for some time to their debate, hearing members on each side assert what the Lord had told them, and sensing their utter state of confusion, he finally with a chuckle said, "You'd be better off to listen to me." His point? If what the Lord was telling them resulted in all this confusion, they undoubtedly had misheard him.

I have seen both pastors and laypeople whose attitudes toward each other seem to be mutually destructive. Both fall far short in the exercise of integrity. My focus, however, is the role of the minister in evidencing integrity. God never intended the pulpit to be a place for the airing of our gripes, frustrations, anger, and wrath. The pulpit is God's platform for proclaiming the good news. If ever we stoop to fighting our people from the pulpit, our integrity is slipping.

The late Dr. Benjamin F. Reid, Sr., shared with me an experience he had in the earlier years of his ministry. He told me about a board meeting in which there was considerable dissent and disagreement between him and a member of the board. When Dr. Reid preached the next Sunday, he proclaimed the word with anointing and power. This board member came to him in tears and embraced him after the service. He told him that this was the first time he had ever had a disagreement with a pastor when he did not hear it preached about later in the pulpit. That's integrity! That also was the bridging of a relationship that might have resulted in accelerated conflict.

There is some distance between feeding the flock and beating and bruising the flock. There are some theories of church life that seem to suggest that you ought to banish your critics and lovingly pastor only those who are "in your corner." I understand that discipline is necessary to church life, but that discipline ought to be centered around the Word and not around private and personal grievances. Otherwise, our integrity may rightly be called into question.

While the pastor is not solely responsible for the well-being of the congregation, he or she is the primary leader. The pastor can set the tone for relationships. The pastor can model those attributes and qualities of life that enable him or her to say, "Follow me as I follow Christ." The spirit of the leader can and will be inculcated into the spirit of the people.

Integrity with Ministerial Colleagues

I have heard it said that there are two things preachers will do. They will fight each other, and they will take up for each other. In the first instance, the assertion is that they find it hard to get along with each other. They are presumed to be competitive, envious, unwilling to lend a helping hand to a struggling colleague, and at times uncharitable toward one another. In the second instance, the allegation is that they will defend each other at all costs—even when a colleague has behaved irresponsibly. Both of these could hardly be true *at the same time*. Yet these perceptions circulate widely.

Permit me to cite some areas of interest and concern in the arena of integrity among ministerial colleagues:

How often do the tensions between younger ministers and older ministers give rise to integrity concerns? I have known situations where older ministers have all but smothered the gifts and aspirations of younger ministers for fear that someone may emerge to threaten their places of prestige and influence. By the same token, I have known younger ministers who treated older ministers with virtual disdain, as if only the new has merit. In so doing, they fail to acknowledge the very foundations on which they must build. Both, in my understanding, violate principles of integrity designed to maintain the unity of the Spirit in the body of Christ.

Younger leaders need to treat older leaders with due respect. Remember that if you continue to live and serve, you eventually will be the older leaders. Younger men and women (the young Turks) may someday challenge some of your cherished ideas and will see some things differently than you see them. If you have treated older leaders with respect, you are more likely to be treated with respect when you become the older leaders. Older leaders, likewise, should treat younger leaders with respect. Remember that someday you will transition from your roles of leadership and they will become the key decision-makers. If you have treated them with respect, they are more likely to be open and responsive to your counsel. My experience has been that many of the doors of opportunity that have been open to me in my retirement years are from leaders whom I respected and for whom I opened doors of opportunity during the prime years of my leadership.

There can be cliquishness on the part of ministers befitting Paul's description and admonition in 1 Corinthians 1:12. "I am of Paul, I am of Apollos, I am of Cephas"—suggesting that I have use only for those in my camp, those who hold my position, those who think just as I think—even as all of us claim to be "of Christ." This too violates principles of integrity designed to maintain the unity of the Spirit among believers, especially among ministry leaders.

We lack adequate forums in the church to face each other brother to brother and sister to sister and deal honestly and constructively with our differences in the spirit of charity and understanding. It sometimes appears that we may even lack the desire and the will to engage in such interaction. If the latter be true, integrity concerns begin to loom.

We really have no secrets. All of God's secrets are open secrets. If God has piloted me through dark and difficult days, I owe it to my colleagues to share what God has done rather than silently watch them struggle. Am I so embarrassed about my struggles that I cannot help a colleague whose struggles are akin to mine? If so, I may be facing an integrity issue.

By the same token, am I tempted to isolate myself, rejecting help that could readily be available to me? Am I more concerned about my reputation than about my well-being? If so, I also may be facing an integrity issue.

The integrity we model among colleagues will be one of our finest contributions to the strength and vitality of the church. It will help to answer one of today's pressing questions: Can the church be trusted?

Speaking of trust, persons of integrity can be trusted—trusted with persons of the opposite sex, trusted with children, trusted with money, trusted with power, trusted with responsibility, trusted with success, trusted to be persons of integrity in life's most trying of circumstances. *Trust, however, is not an automatic grant.* Trust is gained in the crucible of life. Persons who are honest come to be trusted. Persons who are responsible come to be trusted. Persons who consistently make wise decisions come to be trusted. Persons who relate well with other people come to be trusted. Persons who are not always grousing and complaining come to be trusted. Persons who acknowledge their humanity and their mistakes come to be trusted. Persons of humble spirit come to be trusted. The American Heritage Dictionary defines trust as "firm reliance on the integrity, ability, or character of a person." There can be no lasting trust without integrity. Thus, trust soon erodes when others become aware that integrity has been violated.

Integrity in the Marketplace

In the latter stages of writing this chapter, I decided to go on the Internet and explore references to integrity. I visited the Google Web site and was impressed by the scope and range of references to integrity. Volumes totaling 826,000 pages were cited. I saw references to corporate integrity, structural integrity, personal integrity, physical integrity, semantic integrity, research integrity, academic integrity, public integrity, environmental integrity, bio integrity, and the list goes on. There were topical references to integrity and change, the price of integrity, the road to integrity, the truth about integrity, what integrity looks like, the power of integrity, leadership and the quest for integrity, selling with integrity, preaching with integrity, integrity and conscience, integrity and change, threats to integrity, and the integrity gap.

There is strong evidence that the subject of integrity is being addressed in many arenas in our society, triggered, I suspect, in part by public events of recent years. The church and clergy have been one of those triggers.

Ministers do not live in isolation. If ever there was a time when ministers lived in ivory towers, such clearly is a past tense experience. We are influenced not only by our peers but also by the society around us. Much of our society has very limited interest in the church or ministry. Many hold values that run counter to Christian values. How is integrity maintained in a society that minimizes absolute values? In a society of relativism and situational ethics? In a society where many high-profile leaders evidence no claim to high moral values? In a media-dominated culture where values often are regarded as secondary to success, fame, popularity, and power? In a society where it is not uncommon to wink at departures from integrity?

I pose these questions because temptation is ever present and the pressures of our society can be strong. Even those of us who claim biblical principles as our mantra can be led to wonder if integrity requires "all this." Must I always be truthful? Am I not occasionally justified in shading or stretching the truth? Is it not all right to leave false impressions if doing so will not hurt the other person and may benefit me? Others more highly regarded than me are doing it. Why not me? Can I really be ethical all the time? If I do not cover for (i.e., protect) myself, who will? What if I seem to be the only one who holds such a high view of integrity? What if my colleagues assert that I am too sensitive about matters of integrity?

It was in the midst of such a secular society that the apostle Paul wrote these words to the Roman Christians: "Do not conform any longer to the pattern of this world, but be transformed by the renewing of your mind. Then you will be able to test and approve what God's will is—his good, pleasing, and perfect will" (12:2–3 NIV). God has not called us to the impossible. Nor has he called us to do anything that he will not enable us to do through the strength that comes to us in Jesus Christ.

My sense is that, in growing numbers, people are seeking persons and places where they can be assured of integrity. The question surfaces in every arena: Who can I trust? Yes, it surfaces even in the church. How tragic it would be were people to come to church and find integrity lacking in ministry leaders! Of all people, ministry leaders have the call and obligation to be persons of integrity. God forbid that ministers be among that group that Jesus identified with these words: "They say, and do not do" (Matt 23:3 NKJV). In other words, they do not practice what they preach. They expect others to live by one set of values and standards while they live by another.

I have tried to formulate some clues that can alert us to when our integrity is slipping. The list is not exhaustive, but it does provide signals that can caution us. I think our integrity is slipping when:

- Convenience reigns over conscience (see Est 4:16).
- Expedience prevails over conviction.
- Our comfort rather than our calling governs our behavior.
- We seek to dominate and be served rather than to serve.
- We are more attentive to social, political, and economic constraints than we are to biblical mandates.
- Our regard for success becomes greater than our regard for truth.
- Our private life is not consistent with our public profession.
- We allow ourselves to become partners in dishonest relationships.
- We are unwilling to go where we are trying to point others.
- We treat people as expendable in order to achieve our personal goals and our private agendas.

Integrity Is a Lifetime Pursuit

Life is not static. The challenges to our integrity continue as long as life lasts. Therefore, our integrity may be at risk at any given time. We can never be smug in the false assumption that there is no way our integrity can slip.

Most ball games are lost in the last quarter. A team may play exceptionally well during the early and middle stages of a game and flounder badly in the last quarter, thereby forfeiting victory. Likewise, leaders may excel during their peak years of ministry and stumble badly in their declining years. We need to be ever mindful of the words of Jesus in John 10:10 (NIV): "The thief comes only to steal and kill and destroy." Our spiritual adversary has as his ultimate objective to defeat and destroy us. He does not quit trying because it is the last quarter of our lives. He enjoys nothing more than for a gifted and respected leader to falter badly as he or she nears the end of their journey.

In the context of history, we are but custodians of whatever office or leadership we hold. We eventually will have to pass leadership on to others. Our term may expire. Our popularity may wane. Our adversaries may drive us from office. The aging years may render us unable to function with the same vigor we once did. Will our integrity remain intact when we are no longer at the pinnacle of leadership? How will we behave when, as one of my colleagues often says, we go from being "who's who" to "who's he"? Will we fall prey to bitterness, mean spiritedness, envy, and other pollutants to integrity?

Several years ago, the late Dr. E. E. Wolfram, a popular preacher and national church leader, wrote an article titled "Coming Down Alive." I used the article in many settings while he was alive with his personal permission. I had the privilege of knowing him as a colleague in ministry, although he was several years my senior. He was gracious in making this helpful, and I think classic, article widely available to the church. I quote from it in his memory and honor.

> Mount Everest had just been conquered by two men. It was the first time any human being had ever set foot on top of this—earth's highest peak. Tensing Norkey and Edmund Hillary bowed their heads in prayer on this great occasion and prayed, asking God to help them get down alive. Tensing remarks in his book that more mountain climbers are hurt or killed on the way down than climbing up.
>
> I had not known about this risk of coming down a mountain. I thought much about it. Other mountain peaks came to my mind. Then I remembered the many casualties I had seen who never made it down 'alive' from their mountain peaks.
>
> We have many books and instructors telling us how to succeed. How to work with others in getting ahead. How to discipline oneself in making a truly worthwhile contribution in life. But, there is very little help that shows us how to come down the other side of the mountain of success. Where do we go from the peak if our health breaks, if our strength is affected by reason of age, if circumstances have changed and we must come down from our high places? Can we make it down alive? How we come down indicates what type of motive we had going up.

"I will lift up my eyes to the hills. From whence does my help come? My help comes from the Lord" (Ps 121:1–2 RSV). The hills are challenging and inspiring, but our true inner strength and drive must come from the Lord who made both the peaks and the valleys. There is a beautiful settlement of saints in the valley who can look back to the wonderful mountain peaks with fond sacred memories. They are still alive, useful, and ready for any other peaks because they can take them or leave them and live.

A television commercial advertises the Lincoln Navigator with the slogan, "There are those who travel and those who travel well." I have paraphrased that slogan for ministry purposes to say, "There are those who finish and those who finish well." The reality is that everybody finishes. It's inevitable. A part of finishing well is finishing with our integrity intact.

The more chronologically gifted I become (a euphemism for aging), the more keenly aware I am of my need to guard my integrity. Proverbs 4:23 (NIV) says it well: "Keep your heart with all diligence, for out of it springs the issues of life."

ENDNOTES

[1] I have recommended this volume in a number of settings where I have been privileged to serve as guest leader and have sold dozens of copies. It is a significant resource for any Christian leader, especially ministers and pastors, who wants to avoid dangers and pitfalls that can and often do lead to integrity failure.

Reference List

Anderson, Leith. 1992. *A Church for the 21st Century*. Minneapolis: Bethany House Publishers.
———. 1994. Winning the Values War in A Changing Culture. Minneapolis: Bethany House.
Biehl, Bob. 1993. *Why You Do What You Do*. Nashville, TN: Thomas Nelson Publishers.
Blanchard, Ken. 1999. *The Heart of a Leader*. Tulsa, OK: Honor Books.

Next Steps to Ministry

Bowling, John C. 2000. *Grace-Full Leadership*. Kansas City, MO: Beacon Hill Press.

Covey, Stephen R. 1989. *The 7 Habits of Highly Effective People*. New York: Simon and Schuster.

Dortch, Richard. 1991. *Integrity: How I Lost It, and My Journey Back*. Green Forest, AR: New Leaf Press.

Exley, Richard. 1988. *Perils of Power: Immorality in the Ministry*. Tulsa, OK: Honor Books.

Finzel, Hans. 1994. *The Top Ten Mistakes Leaders Make*. Wheaton, IL: Victor Books.

Jones, Laukrie Beth. 1995. *Jesus, CEO: Using Ancient Wisdom for Visionary Leadership*. New York: Hyperion.

MacArthur, John. 2004. *The Book on Leadership*. Nashville, TN: Nelson Books.

MacDonald, Gordon. 2004. *A Resilient Life*. Nashville, TN: Nelson Books.

Mannoia, Kevin W. 1996. *The Integrity Factor: A Journal in Leadership Formation*. Indianapolis, IN: Life and Light Communications.

Markle, David, ed. 2001. *First Steps in Ministry: A Primer on a Life in Christian Ministry*. Anderson, IN: Warner Press.

McIntosh, Gary L., and Samuel D. Rima, Sr. 1997. *Overcoming the Dark Side of Leadership: The Paradox of Personal Dysfunction*. Grand Rapids, MI: Baker Books.

Swindoll, Charles R. 1988. *Living Beyond the Daily Grind,* Book One. Dallas, TX: Word Publishing.

Tidwell, Gary. 1993. *Anatomy of a Fraud: Inside the Finances of the PTL Ministries*. New York: John Wiley & Sons, Inc.

Wiersbe, Warren W. 1988. *The Integrity Crisis*. Nashville, TN: Thomas Nelson Publishers.

CHAPTER FOUR:
Arlo F. Newell & Andy L. Stephenson:
Growing a Teachable Spirit

Life is a learning laboratory. It offers many opportunities to develop and to discover the potential that God has given to each of us. This is especially true of individuals whom God has called into the Christian ministry. Every experience in life challenges us to learn by expanding our knowledge or extending our relationships. Our daily prayer should be, "Teach us to number our days aright, that we may be given a heart of wisdom" (Ps 90:12 NIV).

Having a sound biblical faith in God and a healthy acceptance of our personal strengths and weaknesses, we have responded to God's call, religiously pursued preparation in college and seminary, and have become pastors. Now, it seems, we are on our own.

Here is a teachable moment! A time of divine discovery! Our first pastorate should bring an awareness that even in ministry we need the love, wisdom, and experience of other like-minded persons who have gone into pastoral work before us. Such persons can walk beside us, even call us to accountability. As Paul mentored ministers of the early church, he advised, "But while knowledge makes us feel important, it is love that strengthens the church. Anyone who claims to know all the answers doesn't really know very much. But the person who loves God is the one whom God recognizes." (1 Cor 8:1b–3 NLT).

We need to remember that our freedom in Christ is the freedom to learn from each person that we meet. Our sensitivity and receptivity will enable us to assimilate such knowledge for our continuing maturity in Christ. This attitude and outcome are the essence of Christian mentoring.

Mentoring is the result of observing, conversing with, and serving alongside someone whom you respect. What aspect of your ministry will have the most lasting effects? Will it be the sermons you preach, the books you write, the churches you pastor, the buildings they erect, or the professional recognitions you receive? Perhaps the most enduring aspect of your ministry will be the mentoring, the influence of your life upon persons with whom you share the incarnational ministry of friendship. Someone has said that "mentoring is a process of opening our lives to others, of sharing our lives with others; a process of living for the next generation" (Davis 1991, 16).

The Bible refers to Christian discipleship as being "conformed to the image of Christ" (Rom 8:29 NIV). His love, compassion, discipline, and desires are reproduced in us as he guides us, counsels us, and understands us even when we fail. Here one finds the magnetic appeal, the attractiveness of the Christian life; it is an example of what others desire to emulate. Paul's admonition to "imitate" his faith (1 Cor 4:16, 11 NIV) implies that every minister should live so that others will want to know about the Christ whom that minister serves. The Christlike life that you live—that is Christian mentoring in the broadest sense.

Such a life is evidence of your continuing spiritual growth in Christ, expressed in your human relationships. One's faith draws people first to the mentor and then to the Christ he or she serves. A brittle, legalistic faith may appear to be strong, but the mature Christian has discovered that God's strength is made perfect in weakness (2 Cor 12:7–10 NIV). Christian mentoring requires continual dependence upon God as we humbly serve him, even as Christ washed the disciples' feet (John 13). While the CEO model of pastoral leadership may challenge some people, it seldom allows them to walk with, listen to, and find answers for life's questions in the victories and failures which a pastor experiences.

An Expanded Ministry

Mentoring will enable you to expand your pastoral ministry, overcoming some of the obstacles that hinder other types of outreach. A one-on-one mentoring relationship can be carried out on a jogging path, in the local gym club, the public library, or other settings. It entails very little expense. Nor does mentoring depend on an organizational structure for regular meetings. Mentor and mentee are free to set regular times for meeting, which can be adjusted to their individual schedules. Scripture is basic and vital in any Christian mentoring relationship, but its meaning is discovered while seeking and finding God's will through the Word, rather than studying a prescribed doctrinal outline of biblical faith. Healthy church growth is enhanced by a pastor's mentoring ministry, in which there is mutual respect and acceptance. Such a ministry has no predetermined goals or established timeline for development. When a layperson's need for the pastor's personal support and encouragement no longer exists, the friendship will continue, but the mentoring relationship will be brought to a close. A true mentor finds great satisfaction when the mentee has developed to the point of discipling others.

Models for Mentoring

Biblical models of mentoring other ministry leaders can be found in both the Old and New Testaments. Elijah, the prophet of Mt. Carmel, became the mentor for Elisha. Walking with the older prophet, Elisha learned a life of obedience and faith. His character was shaped, not only by the traditional teaching of Elijah, but also by the opportunity to observe the lifestyle and values of the mentor. Being fully aware of the human weaknesses of Elijah (e.g., his times of discouragement and running from God), Elisha saw in his mentor those elements he desired in his own life. So strong was the influence that when Elijah was taken up in a chariot of fire, Elisha desired a double portion of his blessing (2 Kings 2:9).

In the New Testament, we find the mentoring relationship between Paul and Timothy (2 Tim 1). While we have much of Paul's instruction of Timothy recorded in the Pastoral Epistles, it was Timothy's living with, listening to, and following the apostle that shaped the faith and life of the young pastor.

While other examples could be considered, these two demonstrate that the most lasting influence of persons of faith has not been the text taught but the spirit caught. Ministry leaders' spirit of faith in God captures the attention of ministry mentees, helping to transform their lives. Emerging out of these biblical examples are some key elements for the mentoring relationship:

- Devotion to the spiritual disciplines in life
- Sensitivity and discernment of human need
- Spiritual commitment and holiness of conduct
- Maturity in personal and relational skills
- Transparency and accountability in life
- A life that inspires the best in others
- Humility and a willingness to learn

Mentoring Is Intentional, Not Accidental!

One of Arlo's colleagues, pastor of a local church, was elected as president of a small college. Having never served in the capacity of administrator, fundraiser, and spiritual guide, he found this decision was not easy to make. His hesitancy was accompanied with fear and trepidation. However, he accepted the presidency and determined to become what he believed a church-related college president should be. To that end, he sought out and attempted to meet personally with Christian leaders who met those standards. When he passed through a city where such a person served, he would call for an appointment, introducing himself and the purpose of his call. While sometimes rejected, he discovered that truly great leaders are more humble and approachable than we sometimes assume. In this manner, he had the privilege of meeting with college presidents, political leaders, and pulpit giants—all because he intentionally sought out a brief mentoring relationship.

A pastor is sometimes the mentor and at other times the mentee. In one relationship, we open the doors of our lives to others, allowing them to enter and get to know us personally. In the other, we are privileged to share the experiences of others who have already traveled the ministry road before us. Either way, we are making the journey together.

Arlo has always had a keen interest in aspiring young pastors, particularly those with a passion for preaching. However, at the age of eighty, his contact and acquaintance with high school youth is very limited. Hearing of such a young man gifted in preaching, Arlo asked his father for an introduction. Let him share in his own words how this relationship unfolded:

Patience was required to assure the young preacher that all I wanted was to learn of him rather than to manipulate or make him into my concept of what a minister should be. Having gradually won first his friendship and then his confidence, my role shifted from mentee to mentor. He had opened my eyes to the youth culture. Now he had questions for me about ministry, education, and dating relationships. I recognized the reality of Psalm 37:25 (NIV): "I was young but now am old . . ." My young friend had never traveled this way before, and he was seeking answers and information. While not having all of the answers, I could share experiences and observations for him to consider in his decision making. As mentee he did not need me to dictate decisions but to expose him to possible options for life. He was a high school senior when we were first introduced, and the mentoring relationship continued through college and into seminary. While closure has come to the mentoring process, the friendship continues with an open door to serve as a sounding board for the questions of life.

Mentoring is a ministry that is not limited by age, education, or financial success. It is willingly and unselfishly sharing yourself with another, pouring your life into one whom you have come to value and respect. Andy Stephenson is the son of a ministerial colleague of Arlo's. Remembering Andy as a precocious preacher's kid, Arlo was surprised to meet a mature, self-confident, disciplined young adult. Intellectually, Andy had successfully negotiated the academic minefields, keeping his faith intact as he earned his PhD. Physically, he had disciplined his body with healthy eating habits and exercise. Above all, Arlo was impressed by his deep spiritual commitment to Christ, the church, and God's Word. So he was caught off guard when Andy called his office, asking if they could meet together on a regular mentoring basis. Sensing the need for such a connection in his own ministry, Arlo readily accepted.

Sometimes our roles have run together. We have mentored each other as we shared experiences, asked questions, explored ideas, and called one another to accountability. Out of this relationship across several months, this chapter on mentoring has emerged. We hope that it will be useful to you and that God will give you wisdom on your journey.

Qualities of Healthy Mentoring

1. Desire

Continuing growth in Christian ministry is in direct proportion to one's personal desire and willingness to be "conformed to the image of Christ" (Rom 8:29). A desire to be like Jesus in attitude and action is essential to both parties involved in the mentoring process as learners together. The prophet Jeremiah tells us, "You will seek me and find me; when you search for me with all your heart" (29:13 RSV).

Desire Is the Motivation for the Mentor, a Desire to...
- be filled with the Holy Spirit and used of God.
- enable others to grow spiritually.
- serve as a role model, an example.
- be transparent and vulnerable.
- live a life of holiness and purity.
- be faithful, obedient to the Holy Spirit.
- be accepting and non-judgmental.
- be trustworthy, deserving of trust.

Desire Is the Motivation for the Mentee...
- to grow in spiritual understanding.
- to accept the revelation of the Holy Spirit in the study of the Word.
- to be teachable, following the example shared by the mentor.
- to be open and honest, maintaining integrity.
- to be self-disciplined and accountable.
- to develop Christian character and values.

Arlo's Perspective
"What do you want to be when you grow up?" asked my Sunday School teacher one Sunday. Calling to mind one of the older pillars in the church, I called his name and said, "Like him." Her response was never to be forgotten. "To be like him you had better begin now because it takes a long time." I knew the kind of man I desired to be, a man like Brother Loewen. Unbeknown to him, he became one of my first mentors. His friendly smile greeted me every time I came to church. His strong handshake gave me a

sense of security, and the integrity of his consistent life gave evidence of his love for Christ and the Church. Growing up with his boys, Rudy, Pete, and Chuck gave me the opportunity to observe what a Christian gentleman should be.

This desire has been a persistent reminder of my need to grow spiritually and relationally. Biographies of great leaders—scholars, athletes, missionaries, educators, ministers—all create in me the desire to be mentored, to stretch, and to grow through all of life.

2. Attraction

What captures your attention could be the open door to a mentoring relationship. A person with the characteristics or attributes that you respect—integrity, humility, sincerity, giftedness—a person with whom you would like to talk, one from whom you could learn, that person could become your mentor.

Mentoring is not a prepackaged program driven by a consumer market; it is the attraction of persons with a mutual desire to be like Jesus. Mentoring is a two-way street, allowing for both parties to share and learn together. "You use steel to sharpen steel, and one friend sharpens another" (Prov 27:17 MSG).

Many leaders may have charisma, possess incredible communication skills, and be physically attractive, but time alone will tell who that person is inside. Those things wane, but character never fades. When it comes to attraction, there are many different factors that draw us to people, but you can always rely on character rather than outward appearance. Character is what will last.

Mentor Characteristics That Attract
- Sincerity
- Authenticity
- Maturity
- Adaptability
- Availability
- Dependability

Mentee Response Indicators
- Willingness to receive guidance
- Ability to listen and learn
- Desire to share and trust
- Openness in expressing feelings
- Disciplined in keeping appointments

Andy's Perspective
One of the things that attracted me to my present mentor was the incredible track record he has as a man of integrity. In any movement or organization, there are many voices of opinion, but men and women of character are able to navigate the differences and to be respected for who they are, not necessarily agreed with, but respected.

As a boy and now as a man, I have watched my mentor at a distance as he dealt with people and listened to what others have had to say about him. In dealing with those who disagreed with him, he did so with grace, staying true to his values while at the same time respecting those who differed with him. As I watched and listened to others talk about him, I realized he was highly respected by numerous individuals, many of whom held opinions different from his. I wanted to learn and grow from a man like this.

In my ministry, I have also sought out one of the leaders in the Willow Creek Association. The attraction to him was again a consistent track record (twenty years in student ministry) and impeccable integrity.

3. Connection

Caring is sharing, the willingness to enter into another's life, a covenant exemplifying incarnational intimacy. The kind of spiritual intimacy that releases us to share our personal stories, good and bad, without fear or rejection. Such trust and intimacy enables the mentor and mentee to connect at a level wherein the Holy Spirit uses their personal stories to bind them together. No secrets, no facades, simply telling the story to one in whom we have placed our trust. "The first thing Andrew did was to find his brother Simon and tell him…" (John 1:41 NIV).

Covenant Connections Call for Commitment!

Mentor	Mentee:
Loyalty	Trust
Right intention	Respect
Discretion	Conscientious
Patience	Persistence
Humility	Submission
Harmony	Unity

Arlo's Perspective

Desiring to develop in discipleship, I was attracted to the examples of persons who had achieved personal goals in life. Returning from World War II, I was a high school dropout with little hope of going to college. At twenty years of age, discharged from the Navy, I returned home wanting to relive some of my high school experiences. The Church of God youth camp was in session, so my friend Chuck Loewen and I attended. It was here that I first connected with Dr. Carl Kardatzke of Anderson College; he was the camp conference leader. As head of the college's educational department, it was obvious that he had achieved academic goals, and his Christian spirit was evidence of his commitment to Christ. During the week, we talked about life, about becoming the person God wanted one to be, and before leaving, he encouraged me to attend college. Knowing that I had not graduated from high school, he told me about the GED test and assured me that all things were possible. That connection with Dr. Carl led me to Anderson to college and into an exciting life in ministry.

Connecting with a mentor who journeyed with me across four years—observing his humility, his ability to laugh, his patience with my struggles, and his loyalty as a friend—enabled me to trust his guidance and follow his example.

4. Goals

The primary task of spiritual mentoring is to sensitize the mentee to her or his own uniqueness as a child of God. The mentor, as a facilitator, helps the mentee to hear and respond to the inner voice of the Holy Spirit. The intent is not to give advice, nor to teach or give pastoral advice as a psychological counselor, nor even to serve as a confessional, but to discern

God's will through the Holy Spirit. "Not by might nor by power, but by my Spirit, says the LORD Almighty" (Zech 4:6).

Goal-Setting Caution!
"When mentoring becomes reduced to technique and systems, then the spirituality of mentoring is in danger. Spiritual mentoring is any of the ways we 'come alongside' to assist another to listen to God, to discover the already present action of God in that person's life" (Anderson & Reese 1999, 51).

Mentoring that makes a difference enables the mentee to discover God's will for her/his life, distinguishing between selfish personal ambition and God's purpose of servanthood. Developing a sensitivity to the Holy Spirit, one discovers that God never calls us to unrealistic goals. Someone has said, "Unrealistic expectations become the seedbed of depression." A healthy, growing mentoring relationship will release the mentee to sense God's direction and to pursue God's goal.

Healthy Mentoring Goals
(Anderson & Reese 1999, 50)
- Enhance intimacy with God
- Aid in recognition of the Holy Spirit working in the life of the mentee
- Formation of Christian character and values
- Discernment of God's will
- Counsel for making life's decisions
- Establish foundations in biblical faith
- Develop a source of encouragement/hope

Arlo's Perspective
In my first experience in ministry, I served as youth minister with D. L. Slaybaugh, a successful pastor and exceptional preacher. For twenty-five years, he had pastored a growing church in a very small rural community, most of that time as a bivocational minister. He was my mentor as I watched his life, sharing about sermon preparation, hospital visitation, and funerals. Together we laughed at mistakes, learned from them, and moved on toward the goal, the goal of my becoming a pastor and preacher. For over fifty years, I have walked in his shadow, the shadow of a spiritual mentor who helped me achieve a very special goal.

Pastoring requires not only the desire to preach; it also requires the ability to relate to people within the church and in the community served. I was fortunate to have in my first congregation (120 people) a very successful business man, Guy E. Kinney of the Silverknit Hosiery Mills. Observing his ability to relate to and work with people from all walks of life, I sought him out as a mentor. I observed his tactfulness in business meetings, listened as he talked with bankers about church business, and then had the opportunity to discuss with him how to best negotiate differences of opinions in the business of the church. I moved from that church in 1960 but the influence of his life is still evident in how I deal with people as we seek to achieve God's goals together.

Sometimes the task to which one is called is larger than the mentee can handle. At such a time, a trusted mentor becomes your best friend and confidant. Having never been an editor or journalist, serving as editor in chief of Warner Press was a daunting experience. However, in my predecessor, Dr. Harold Phillips, I found a true mentor. When I felt the task was too much for me, his words "You can do it!" enabled me to survive. He had made the journey before me; he knew how to read the constituency of the church, how to test the theological waters, and how to send up a trial balloon to see how the wind was blowing. When the water was deep and the storms of controversy raged, his short note, "This too will pass!" was just what a mentor should do, help me to trust in God to fulfill his goal in my life.

5. Free to Be!

Spiritual mentoring is directed toward freeing the mentee to become her or his unique self in Christ. Strengthened in a saving relationship with Christ, sustained by a sanctified sense of self-worth, the individual has gained the courage to become all that God expects her/him to be and do. In the words of Paul, "Christ has set us free to live a free life. So take your stand! Never again let anyone put a harness of slavery on you" (Gal 5:1 MSG).

Guided by the character and conduct of the mentor, the mentee is enabled to recognize their potential as a child of God, one who is loved for who they are, equipped to serve responsibly, and released to become.

Next Steps to Ministry

Path to Freedom
1. Personal recognition, encouragement, and support.
2. Realistic perspective of the Christian life of holiness, discipline, and continued growth.
3. Counsel on balancing the life of faith, establishing priorities, and personal management of time.
4. Release of the mentee for Christian growth, involvement with other mentors, and the acceptance of Christian responsibility and servanthood.

Each mentoring relationship is different. Some last for only a few times of sharing. Others may extend for a year or more. Most important is that you do not become discouraged and fail to meet as long as there is a mutual desire to learn from one another. Guard against allowing a dependency level to develop. We are not professional counselors or psychiatrists, only friends. Be sensitive to the proper time to terminate the relationship, then set a time for closure. Someone has said that mentoring is "preaching in shoe leather," walking the walk and talking the talk. It is like planting without any assurance of the harvest or investing without any guarantee of dividends. Truly, mentoring is sacrificial servanthood in the Spirit of Christ.

Andy's Perspective
We often are so accustomed to doing things our own way that we think everyone ought to do them our way. If you are single, you will fully understand this when you get married! God has designed each of us with unique gifts and talents. When it comes to mentoring another, it is often easy to try and mold the person into a clone of who you are rather than the person God made them to be. Sometimes we do this without even being aware of it.

My mentor does an incredible job of giving me freedom to be me. I have never felt he was trying to shape me into handling life as he would. He listens, guides, discusses, and prays but lets me use God-given gifts. One of the freeing things he does is to give the option to quit meeting if I feel our time is no longer productive. I never feel pressured to have to continue meeting. While always welcoming our times together, he gives freedom for the mentoring relationship to continue or end when needed.

As an example of mentoring, my mentor gives me the freedom to be shaped into who God wants me to be, not what my mentor wants me to be. This may sound like an obvious statement, but as a mentor it is very difficult to keep the balance of giving your mentee guidance yet letting them discover how God has designed them. A mentee who is given the freedom will usually soar to new heights.

Mentoring in Practice

Life Is a Journey

Life is a journey and finding your way requires finding journey mates along with journey guides to help you on your way. This journey we call life is treacherous, and we need others to help us stay on the path. Good wisdom lets us realize that we don't have the journey figured out no matter how many degrees or how many years of experience we may have under our belt. Good sense says we can't make the journey alone. Humility says we can learn from everyone that we come into contact with from the well educated and affluent to the uneducated and poor man on the street. Life is full of teachers if we just look around.

Some of the greatest teachers are often the most illogical. In my life the poor believers in material resources in Guatemala taught me a lot about joy. The little child helped teach me what it really means to love. Life is full of teachers if we will just open our eyes.

Isn't it ironic that those who think they know the most usually know the least? The day we think our education, background, or accomplishments make us better than others is the day we stop learning. The day we think we have it all figured out, have it under control or that we can do it on our own is the day we stop learning and the day we stop living.

Self-reliance is often seen as a positive commodity, but in reality, it is the death of growth. Scripture pushes against the concept of self-reliance towards the need for reaching for the hand of another to be in community. Yet how easy it is to rely on oneself or to be sucked in to believing that with just God and me, I can make it on this journey without any extra help. This concept is not scriptural. God created us to be in relationship with others.

Often past experiences and past hurts cause us to learn not to trust people or push us to become self-reliant. This lack of reaching out to others can come from our family backgrounds, childhood experiences, or experiences in our adult lives. Often it can come from subconscious decisions that we make, decisions that we do not even know about until we dig deep inside ourselves. At some point, Andy made a decision due to seeing his parents, who were pastors, get hurt in the church by close friends. "I made the decision either consciously or subconsciously. Yet the result was a self-reliance and a barrier wall that would let people only get so close to me. For years, I missed the joy and lessons that I could have learned from having close journey mates."

We Need Journey Mates

We all need journey mates—individuals who will pick us up when we fall, who will give us a soft kick in the pants or a hard pull when we are walking into the darkness. We need those who will stumble and search for directions just like us. We need those who will run, walk, and sometimes crawl on this passage of life with us.

If we aren't careful, pride and hurtful experiences can push us to walk life's pilgrimage alone. What we have to make sure is that we are proactive, having people walking along with us and to make sure that we have different types of journey mates alongside of us.

What type of journey mates do we need to have alongside us on our journey?

Spouse: If you are married or aspire to be married, one of the greatest journey mates should be your spouse. Your spouse can teach you, stretch you, and help God shape and mold you as she or he walks through the valleys and on the mountain tops with you. When he made male and female, God knew the strengths that each gender would bring to life, and if we listen closely, God uses our partner to make us into more of who he is.

Accountability Partner: Another type of journey mate we need on our walk is an accountability partner. This is an ally we in ministry often disregard. We can't overlook the importance of such an individual. Howard Hendricks conducted a study of 246 men in full-time ministry who experienced personal moral failure within a two-year period. He found four correlation factors for this group (Farrar 1995, 7, 29–30):

- None were involved in any kind of personal accountability group.
- Each had ceased to invest in a daily personal time of prayer, Scripture reading, and worship.
- Over 80 percent had become sexually involved with another woman as a result of counseling the woman.
- Each had been convinced that moral failure "will never happen to me."

Recently, Andy was on the phone with yet another friend and colleague who had made an unwise decision that cost him his ministry position. We cannot overlook the importance of having individuals of the same gender we can be honest with on this journey called life—accountability partners who can let us know when we are walking off the path, friends who can help us when we are turned around and are lost, journey mates who aren't afraid to ask us the hard questions and make sure we are staying on the right path. If we are going to finish strong, we have to have those who can speak into our life. "In the Christian life, it's not how you start that matters. It's how you finish" (Farrar 1991, 5).

Family of Origin: Other journey mates can be our family of origin. We can learn much from them. We can learn things that we want to carry on and some lessons of what not to do. Families can be great teachers of how to, or how not to, walk life's pathway with our children and spouses. Often we learn how to parent and how to relate to spouses from our family of origin. We need to recognize positive patterns and continue them, and we need to identify negative cycles and break them.

Friends: Other journey mates we need on the journey of life are those we call friends, individuals who support us and walk alongside us. Sometimes we see them regularly, and sometimes we only get to spend time with them every once in a while, but we know they are going to support us and encourage us. Every friend we have in life can help us understand a little more about community and God's design for us to be in relationship with others.

Colleagues: Other journey mates we need to tap into are colleagues in our field. They can be great teachers in life and hopefully they become friends. There is much to learn from those who work in our field or who work with us. We can learn a lot about ourselves, our security or lack thereof, our motives, and our pride or humility from these journey mates. We can learn volumes about what leadership styles are most effective by watching and being around others in our field. Having a humble, I-want-to-learn-from-you spirit can help us discover lessons that we will never learn in a classroom.

Everyday People: A type of journey mate that we often do not utilize is someone we come into contact with in everyday life. This person could be the grocery store clerk, the teller at the bank, the homeless man on the street corner. Every individual we have contact with has a story that can teach us. When we think we don't have anything to learn from certain types of people, we start to slow down on the journey and lose our impact with others.

We Need Journey Guides

In addition to journey mates who walk alongside us, we also need guides. Those who have walked further down the path can help guide us and lead us in the right directions. There are different types of guides that we need to include on the journey. Guides often have to be sought out, and it is our responsibility to find them.

Older Wiser Guides: One of the guides we need is someone who is older and wiser than we are, a person or persons who we respect and can help us grow. Andy notes, "I have sought out those whom I respect, meeting with them and asking questions about leadership and life to help me on my journey. Many of these times have been a single interview where I have just called up someone and asked if I could spend an hour with them. I have benefited greatly from these sessions. Yet the most significant and meaningful learning experiences are when I have a guide that I have to meet with regularly."

Andy's current guide (mentor) is the coauthor of this chapter. Arlo is eighty years old and is well-respected in the ministry world. "Years ago," remembers Andy, "before we ever were in this relationship and lived in different cities, I sought out a short interview time with him. He was full of wisdom. Now we are in the same city, and I initiated a time to meet with him and asked him to be a mentor (guide) to me. Now we meet usually once a month, and we talk about ministry and leadership issues, but most importantly we talk about life. He shares that he doesn't have it all together. He is open that his relationship with his wife isn't perfect and his being real gives me hope. He models what it means to be a lifetime learner. An older wiser guide is an important if not an essential part of the journey."

Books as Guides: Along with a real-life, face-to-face guide, we can use those who are authors as guides when we read their books. Someone once asked whether you would like to spend an hour with someone you really admire and have them pour into you. The speaker went on to say that when you read books, you are spending numerous hours with the author sharing what is on his or her heart. Many authors pour a lifetime of knowledge into those pages. Don't discount the importance of these guides on our journey.

God's Vessels as Guides: Another type of guide is the person that God is using in a mighty way. Some of the greatest lessons we have learned is from seeing those God was using in a mighty way and asking to meet with them. Andy would take his predetermined list of questions and notepad, and sit and learn. For us, these times were incredible times of learning and helped mold and shape some of our style and ministry. Don't be afraid to ask, and be ready to learn.

Growing on the Journey

As you already know, on this journey we need others who can come alongside us and make us stronger. We need journey mates and guides. We need journey mates who are spouses, accountability partners, family, friends, colleagues and everyday contacts. We need guides who are older and wiser, guides from afar who guide us on the journey in their writings and guides who it is apparent God is using in a mighty way. We need each and every one of them, and if we discount or leave one or more out, our development and journey will be hindered. For the sake of the kingdom, let God grow you through all of them.

Conclusion

Mentoring in its varied forms has always been a part of ministry in the church. It is our prayer that you will equip yourself and your people to make use of this excellent tool in the meeting of human need. Everybody needs somebody, and more emphatically, everybody needs the church. Since not everyone will attend the church, we must reach out to them as friends and neighbors, seeking to develop a mentoring relationship. Everyone needs journey mates and everyone needs journey guides. It is essential to our development and growth to be all God has called us to be.

Reference List

Anderson, Keith R., and Randy D. Reese. 1999. *Spiritual Mentoring: A Guide for Seeking and Giving Direction.* Downers Grove, IL: InterVarsity Press.

Biehl, Bobb. 1996. *Mentoring: Confidence in Finding a Mentor and Becoming One.* Nashville: Broadman & Holman.

Clinton, J. Robert, and Richard W. Clinton. 1991. *The Mentor Handbook: Detailed Guidelines and Helps for Christian Mentors and Mentees.* Altadena, Calif.: Barnabas.

Davis, Ron Lee. 1991. *Mentoring: The Strategy of the Master.* Nashville: Thomas Nelson, Publisher.

Engstrom, Ted W., and Norman B. Rohrer. 1989. *The Fine Art of Mentoring.* Brentwood, TN: Wolgemuth & Hyatt.

Farrar, Steven. 1995. *Finishing Strong.* Sisters, OR: Multnomah Books.

Hendricks, Howard, and William Hendricks. 1995. *As Iron Sharpens Iron.* Chicago: Moody Press.

Johnson, W. Brad, and Charles R. Ridley. 2004. *The Elements of Mentoring.* New York: Palgrave Macmillan.

Stanley, Paul D., and J. Robert Clinton. 1992. *Connecting: The Mentoring Relationships You Need to Succeed in Life.* Colorado Springs, CO: NavPress.

Stoddard, David A., and Robert J. Tamasy. 2003. *The Heart of Mentoring: Ten Proven Principles for Developing People to Their Fullest Potential.* Colorado Springs, CO: NavPress.

II.
BECOMING
following Christ into a life in Christian ministry

The life of a Christ follower is an unending experience of life transformation.

"Now the Lord is the Spirit, and where the Spirit of the Lord is, there is freedom. And all of us with unveiled faces, seeing the glory of the Lord as though reflected in a mirror, are being transformed into the same image from one degree of glory to another; for this comes from the Lord, the Spirit" (2 Cor 3:17–18).

What a privilege to metamorphose from one degree of glory to another!

I once knew a student who tried on several different selves before feeling at home with the one that would last—herself in Christ and in the company of the Christ community. She looked for identity in the person of a boyfriend. She looked for herself in the image of well-respected leader. At last, she gained insight into her quest and homed in on who she could become with our Lord and the people of God. It was only there that she found readiness for life, for service, and, in her case, for marriage.

Parker Palmer describes the tale of Rabbi Zusya in these words: "There is a Hasidic tale that reveals, with amazing brevity, both the universal tendency to want to be someone else and the ultimate importance of becoming one's self: Rabbi Zusya, when he was an old man, said, 'In the coming world, they will not ask me: "Why were you not Moses?" They will ask me: "Why were you not Zusya?"'"[1]

Welcome to resources that we trust will aid your discovery of who you may become in Christ Jesus. Blessings on your journey of becoming!

---

[1] Parker Palmer, *Let Your Life Speak: Listening for the Voice of Vocation* (San Francisco: Jossey-Bass, 2000: 11).

CHAPTER FIVE:
Martin D. Grubbs: *Discovering and Affirming Your Approach to Ministry*

"The church is God's welfare office, an institution set up to heal the blind, set free the captive, feed the hungry, and bring Good News to the poor-the original mandate Jesus proclaimed. The church is God's neighborhood bar, a hangout like the television show Cheers for people who know all about your lousy boss, your mother with heart trouble back in North Carolina, and the teenager who won't do what you tell him; a place where you can unwind, spill your life story, and get a sympathetic look, not a self-righteous leer" (Yancey 2001, 67).

There has rarely been a moment as challenging as the present for those who serve in Christian ministry. What a way to begin a chapter. No humor, no easing into it, just put it out there. This is a challenging time for Christian ministry. No, I am not a pessimist, nor am I discouraged. And though depression has been my friend for many years, I am not depressed. I am actually extremely encouraged, optimistic and thankful for the incredible opportunity we have today in the church. In spite of significant changes in the cultural, political, and religious landscape the past twenty years, we are living in a moment of great potential for the church.

Consumerism and the quest for human success have invaded the local church. Even among evangelical, Bible-teaching, conservative congregations, there are a myriad of issues that drive pastors to the offices of Christian counselors. We have tailored worship services to the consumer and have insisted upon drama, multimedia and multisensory experiences. We now serve Starbucks coffee in the lobby (which used to be called the foyer) and run a scaled-down version of Disneyland in the children's wing. We've worked to remove any Christian symbols that might offend the seeker. The traditional church with beams pointed heavenward has been replaced with a remodeled Wal-Mart. I am constantly reminded that if I want to connect with the current generation, I need to get rid of my suits, sit on a bar stool, spike my hair, ride a motorcycle, wear blue jeans, and untuck my shirt. If this is who you are, then I certainly do not mean to be critical. It is not who I am. We'll talk more about this later in the chapter. The rise of the megachurch (which by definition includes the church I pastor) has left many other great leaders in smaller churches feeling insignificant, insecure, and ineffective. And even those who pastor larger congregations feel the need to grow bigger, build more, and equal the latest, greatest show on television. I do not feel any of these trends are necessarily wrong or off base, unless someone is telling you that it is the only way to do effective ministry. It is clearly an effective way to do ministry in some places, but it is not the only way to do effective ministry. It is my desire to help you understand your own approach to ministry, based on your call to ministry, your gifts, your personality, and so on.

Many would look at my situation as the epitome of success. On most high-season Sundays you will find well over four thousand people on a sprawling ninety-acre campus with a building that looks like a shopping mall or junior college, a large staff, no debt, a Christian school; yet how those feelings of inadequacy flood my soul frequently. Don't get me wrong, I enjoy the blessings of twenty-five years in ministry. But you would be surprised at how difficult it is to stay vibrant and fresh, dynamic and exciting. And that is my point. Just when I think I have figured out my emerging approach to ministry, something new and different emerges on the scene that looks to be the next wave in ministry. I don't understand it. I don't relate to it. In fact, I don't even like it, and I would prefer to ignore it.

It took me awhile, but it has been freeing to realize that God has uniquely created us, uniquely gifted us, and will uniquely use us. We need only be all that he has created us to be and to fully prepare for and engage in the challenge he sets before us. Your ministry will not look like Saddleback or Willowcreek or Lakewood or Mars Hill. But it will look like God, and he will do it through you. I want to help you do some self assessment in this chapter. I have prayed that God would help me help you by taking an honest look at yourself. Why are you in ministry? How did you get here? Why

Discovering and Affirming Your Approach to Ministry

are you still in ministry? Knowing who you really are is key to developing your own biblical, theological, and practical approach to Christian ministry. For example, *biblically*, I am a child of God, saved at the age of nine. I have gifts and abilities. I was truly called into pastoral ministry. I did not choose it, nor did I prepare for it. I was told to go to Nineveh and preferred Tarshish. But the last guy that ran to Tarshish spent some time in the belly of a fish, so I felt no need to repeat the lesson. I followed God's call to walk through what Paul called a great door of opportunity (1 Cor 16:9).

Theologically, I am a part of a movement called the Church of God. We believe in extending our hand to "every blood-washed one." We believe in unity. We do not emphasize church membership, rather membership in God's kingdom through Jesus Christ. We believe in free will, women in ministry, and the priesthood of all believers. This theology has shaped both me and my congregation. On a more practical note, we all have a unique personal history that has shaped us. Since I am not a biblical scholar or a theologian, I want to spend my time with you in the practical, nuts-and-bolts side of ministry. Let's dive into these issues.

There are six areas I find critical if we are to be effective in Christian ministry, six issues that help us discover and affirm our unique approach to ministry.

1. Confirm Your Call

Ministry begins with a call. Not a phone call from a search committee in a church. It is a tap on the shoulder from God. You suddenly have this overwhelming sense that God is opening a door and to ignore the door will be an act of disobedience and cowardice. The call will not let you go. You cannot shake it, no matter how hard you try or desire to do so. The call is frightening, and for good reason—ministry is not easy. Regardless of the trappings of success and the fact that being in ministry in the United States is a privilege, the call requires a measure of sacrifice. This call is affirmed by those around you. Paul said to Timothy in 1 Timothy 4:14 (NIV), "Do not neglect your gift, which was given you through a prophetic message when the body of elders laid their hands on you." My call to ministry was validated by spiritual giants in my life at the time. I will never forget Dr. Dale Oldham putting his hand on my shoulder one day before a church service at Salem Church of God in Dayton, Ohio. He looked at me and said, "Marty, I believe God is going to use you to build a great church." That was not my plan at the time, but it shook me, and I never forgot it. My call was confirmed by my dad, my favorite pastor to this day. It was confirmed by a tearful mom, who allowed me to move eight hundred miles from home. The loving people of my church here in Oklahoma City confirmed the call. I had been their associate pastor. They believed God had called me to be their pastor. No matter how skeptical I may have been at the time, to have so many spiritual leaders around me confirming the call of God on my life was quite a gift. Are you called to ministry? Do you have that burning fire in the belly to suit up for the task? Have wise and Godly people around you confirmed this call?

2. Discover Your Gifts

Not only are you called to ministry, but you have been equipped with spiritual gifts that will enable you to function in that call. Paul says in 1 Corinthians 12:7 (NIV), "Now to each one the manifestation of the Spirit is given for the common good." Gifts are not given for your own good or for your own ego or for making an impression; they are given for the common good of the body of Christ. Paul goes on to teach us that there are different kinds of gifts, but it is the same Spirit and Lord and God working in us all. God will use your gifts in ministry, and it is critically important to have a proper understanding of what your gifts are and what they are not.

My primary gift mix begins with the gift of administration. I am highly organized. My secondary gift would be that of pastor, meaning that I am willing to accept responsibility for the spiritual well-being of a large group of people. Partly because of my administrative gifts, I can devise plans and ministries that help people develop and mature as Christians. The third gift in the mix is teaching. Yes, teaching and preaching are not my primary gifts. It has taken me a long time to develop as a preacher, and I still have a long way to go. But at least long ago, I stopped feeling like I needed to apologize for such poor preaching. Even now when I find myself going through files, I will pull out a sermon from ten years ago and immediately feel a need to apologize for saying those things. With preaching as a secondary gift, it means I have to work very hard at the assignment. And it is to this day a very draining and often dreaded assignment.

But God always does something miraculous. He uses the preaching far beyond my plans or preparation. I also lean heavily on a teaching team for the purposes of creativity, planning, and team teaching. There is no reason the church should be held back or inhibited because I insist on doing all the preaching or preparing completely alone for the task. I have found great joy in using my gifts as a pastor, yet at the same time utilizing the gifted people around me to help me be a more effective pastor.

3. Understand Your Personality

The environment in which we are raised shapes us all. If you are raised by positive, affirming, and encouraging parents, chances are good that you will be a secure, positive person. If you were raised by insecure parents or those who did not choose to parent, chances are you have struggled or continue to struggle with insecurity, doubt, or fear. I know so many people in ministry who never received the love and approval of a parent. Some of them to this day have difficulty saying no and doing things that may be met with disagreement. Leading is hard for them, because pleasing is their goal. I have seen many people for whom ministry became the conduit for the love and praise they never got at home. The question must be asked, Are you in ministry for the people, or are the people to minister to you?

Failure to understand our unique personalities can bring disaster in many aspects of life. Even the Bible records personality conflicts. Acts 15 records the disagreement between Paul and Barnabas over John Mark. Paul was not pleased that Mark had deserted them in Pamphylia. Barnabas, being the encourager, seemed quite willing to forget that and take Mark with them on their next journey. Paul perhaps felt he could not take the risk. He had probably read Jim Collins's book *Good to Great* and wanted only people on the bus whom he could count on. All joking aside, this was a big enough issue for Paul and Barnabas to part ways. Was the dispute theological? No. Doctrinal? No. Was some great life principle being argued here? No. It was a simple difference in personality and leadership style.

Growing up in the home of a gifted preacher and pastor, I had to do what most kids do and determine if I believed what I believed because my parents believed it or because I believed it. My home was one of tremendous influence, direction, and encouragement. Yet one of the things holding me back from pastoral ministry twenty years ago was the feeling that I could not do it because I could not preach like my father. Dad was, and still is, a very powerful and persuasive preacher. I am more conversational in my preaching style. Dad was, and still is, a strong leader. He has no fear in blazing trails never before traveled. I am a consensus builder. It is important that you know that my parents have always encouraged me to be myself. It was important that I come to a proper understanding of my own personality style.

Dad entered pastoral ministry at a time when pastors were supposed to be strong, independent, charge-the-hill kind of leaders. Dad grew up in poverty and had to work harder than I can imagine simply to survive. Even at seventy years old, Dad knows only one way to do things: fast and forward. And I mean that as a compliment. Mom and Dad kept my brother and me as their highest priority, even above their own needs at times. Mom and Dad loved us. We were raised in two wonderful and loving congregations. We were taught to work hard. We were encouraged and given a vision of a positive future. But the gene pool and the environment in which I grew up have shaped my personality and view of the world.

My Christian counselor happens to be a very close friend and confidant. It has been a blessing to have someone speak truthfully to me, painful truth at times. But it has helped me confront the truth of who I am. What am I good at? What do I do extremely well? What do I not do so well? In the Paul and Barnabas story, I am much more like Paul. I tend to be blunt, demanding, and impatient. While my intent is never to be unkind, I have often found myself around a Barnabas who had great difficulty with me. It is so important that we come to a clear understanding of our personality makeup, as well as an understanding of those around us. Managing multiple staff members has been the most challenging task of leading a large church, and not because I have had difficult staff. Quite the contrary. I have had outstanding men and women working with me, and we have had very little turnover in our staff during the past six years in particular. But a church staff is like family, and it is very important that staff members understand each other and make allowances for our different personalities and styles. It has been important for me to learn to say, "I'm sorry," as well as, "I forgive you."

Discovering and Affirming Your Approach to Ministry

I strongly encourage pastors to utilize the many personality tests available today. These greatly increase our ability to understand ourselves as well as to help others understand us. These tests point out where you are strong in your personality, where you are vulnerable, and where you are likely to run into problems.

When I became the pastor of Crossings Community Church twenty years ago, I had to ask myself three questions. I had no idea then how key these questions would be in shaping my ministry as well as creating the environment for a growing church. The three questions are:

- Who am I? What are my gifts and talents? What are my struggles and issues?
- Who are the people in my church? What are they like? What do they desire in a pastor and in a church? Where do they want to go?
- Who is my community? Who are the people living around my church and how do I reach them? What are their needs? Am I willing to meet them?

I began answering those questions in my first week as a senior pastor. God gave me not only a great Christian counselor but a few spiritual mentors who helped me get honest about those three questions. God used this process to pave the way for a healthy church.

As your emerging approach to Christian ministry evolves, I encourage you to spend time in the quest for emotional as well as spiritual health. Know who you are. Get comfortable in your own skin. Know your limits. Be fully available for God to use you wherever he so desires.

4. Discern the Culture

Every congregation has a cultural dynamic, even apart from the community in which you have been called to minister. Every family is the result of a cultural dynamic that has shaped them. While you certainly do not need any instruction on understanding cultural turf, we must understand the cultural impact on a church. When I arrived at Crossings twenty-five years ago, it was not unlike many smaller congregations. It was a gathering of about 150 people from all walks of life. The make up of the church had not changed significantly over a fifteen-year period of time. The church was very friendly and very much like a family. There were the typical occasional struggles between those of different economic statuses. As youth pastor, I remember building a particularly strong bridge to one of the elite private schools in our neighborhood. A few of the founding families in the church were a part of this school, and the door was opened for me to go on campus, build relationships with the students, and ultimately see them come to church. Many of these young people were from some of the oil-boom affluent families in our community. Somehow, my parents had raised me in an environment that was not intimidated nor necessarily impressed by wealth alone. I just knew that everyone, rich or poor, needed Jesus. So, I was quite surprised when I discovered a fair amount of discomfort among other kids in the student ministry. These new, private-school, rich kids were making them uncomfortable. Instead of fifteen kids in a classroom on Wednesday nights, we suddenly had forty kids in the gym. I watched the cultural clash between private-school kids and public-school kids. There was a perceived clash between the haves and the have-nots. There were the lifelong church kids and the new kids who had spent little time in church. It was a great lesson for me, because little did I know, it was just the beginning of a very wild ride in pastoral ministry.

We made it through that challenge, and today one of those private-school guys is one of my most trusted staff members. I was there when he came to Christ. I was there when he went to college on a baseball scholarship. I was there when he felt a call to ministry and asked his parents if he could leave the baseball scholarship behind and go to a university where he could pursue that call. I was there when he was a summer intern, every summer until he graduated. He joined our staff as youth pastor right out of college and built that ministry to over 150 kids. I was there when he felt called to Christian counseling, completed his master's degree, and opened the counseling center inside the church. Today, it provides quality Christian counseling to hundreds of our members and is responsible for hundreds of people gathering weekly on Monday nights for help with addiction, divorce, depression, grief, as well as ministry to kids who are going through these things. Two years ago, he felt called to help me as a senior associate–executive pastor. He is a trusted advisor, leader, and friend. But he came to us as a high school student in the midst of a great cultural clash in our church.

You may find it interesting to know that the cultural issues are not as obvious in the larger church. You will find hundreds of people from most walks of life, economic statuses, levels of education, and cultures. I love watching it happen. One Sunday, I looked out over the congregation and saw our lieutenant governor sitting on one end of the pew, and at the other end sat a key employee of our current Democrat governor. They have major political disagreements, which are often played out in the newspapers. But these two men are friends, more importantly, Christians and Christian friends. On another row I see a man who can barely pay his rent sitting next to the man who owns the apartment complex. I have emphasized that when each person walks through the door of the church, it does not matter what they drove up in, how much money they have, where they live, or what they do. It matters that we are all one in Christ. I love watching this work. I see it every Sunday between rich and poor, black and white, Democrat and Republican, mature Christian and baby Christian. This is the way it ought to be.

As church leaders, we must have a clear understanding of the culture of our community, the culture of our church, and our personal preferred cultural comfort zone. My grandfather was a pastor of two congregations at the same time in the cotton fields of South Carolina. He was a very effective pastor. He ministered to the people, made his living in a small business, visited the sick, and always gave them a meaningful worship and preaching experience. They loved my grandparents. In that culture, people parked on the lawn, they did not expect Sunday school classes, and the nursery was typically on the back row of the sanctuary.

We have vibrant congregations in cities of every size and cultural dynamic. If we are to reach the community with the message of Jesus Christ, we must know our community. We must also discern if we are willing and able to reach them. Can we overcome any bias we may have toward them? Some pastors are not comfortable reaching out to professional people. They are intimidated by them. Some pastors are not comfortable reaching out to the so called blue-collar worker. They too are intimidated. I discovered that one of the reasons God called me to pastor the church in

Oklahoma City was that I was completely comfortable with the neighborhood around me. I have never been intimidated around strong, educated, or wealthy people, even though I am none of those. I enjoy leaders, and the stronger the better. But I also highly enjoy people of all kinds, from all places, and can clearly see the work of God in all of them.

5. Find Effective Mentors

The stereotypical male does not like to stop and ask for directions. Men find it difficult to ask for help. And while I hope and pray that many women in ministry are reading this, I can safely say, as a man, that ministers who are men have a great difficulty not only asking for help but acknowledging that they need help. And every pastor needs and deserves help from great mentors.

One of the first things I did as a new pastor was call on two men who had demonstrated the kind of ministry I hoped to imitate. The first one was my dad. I remember a little church in Kingsport, Tennessee, that grew from fifty-five people to nearly six hundred people. At the age of nine, we moved to Dayton, Ohio, where my dad became the pastor of the Salem Church of God. Dayton was a much larger city than Kingsport, and nearly two hundred and fifty people gathered each week in a multipurpose type room for worship. Two years later, a thousand-seat sanctuary was built; and within ten years, the church moved to a new campus with a sanctuary seating nearly eighteen hundred. My dad knew some things about ministry that I would have to pay closer attention to than I had simply growing up around him.

The second pastor I called on was Ray Cotton. Ray was barely a two-hour drive from my front yard. Ray welcomed me to Wichita on many occasions and allowed me to follow him to staff meetings, funerals, hospitals, and then home at the end of the day for dinner. He showed me what could happen when you discovered the needs of the community and began to address them in the church. Ray had an incredible ability to discern the needs and then surround himself with people who could help him reach the city of Wichita. Ray and his wife Janet also demonstrated something very important to Kim and me as a ministry couple: you must be willing to do whatever it takes if you want the church to grow. When I would

Discovering and Affirming Your Approach to Ministry

visit Wichita, I noticed that Ray and Janet's home was always open to the church, which even then was a large church of well over a thousand people. It eventually grew to well over two thousand in attendance, and many of their special events drew upwards of ten thousand people. But Ray and Janet kept their front door open, and their home was a key gathering place for the people of Central Community Church. Kim and I took a cue from them and determined that we would do whatever it took to help our church become a dynamic presence in the community.

It was the fall of 1986. I had been the pastor for nearly a year. We grew from one hundred and fifty to one hundred and sixty-two that first year. One of the things I constantly heard from our people and our leaders was the fact that the church had never grown beyond two hundred. There had been a few times in their history when they got close, but then fell back into the one hundred and fifty range. So I began to do some homework. I started looking around the country to see if anyone was offering anything specifically for the small church, especially one that desired to grow beyond two hundred. And I found one conference. It was led by Pastor John Maxwell, and it was called "Breaking the Two Hundred Barrier." I went to our board and told them that I was completely out of ideas. I suggested we all attend this conference, conveniently held at the Dallas–Fort Worth Airport Hilton Hotel. We took twelve people. It changed all of us, and those twelve people were the key players in a growth pattern that took us to two hundred, and then four hundred, eight hundred, one thousand, twelve hundred, fifteen hundred, two thousand… I had to let my people be inspired by another pastor. I had to let my people hear two days of how-to from another pastor. I had to be content to know that most of the great ideas that would propel us beyond two hundred were not my ideas. In looking back to that conference numerous times these many years later, it stands out as one of the most important steps I ever took to bring good things to my congregation.

John Maxwell is no stranger to anyone these days. I am thankful that I got to know him while he was a pastor in Southern California. He knew my dad from our Ohio days. John connected me to one of his very close college buddies and ministry colleague, Dr. Stan Toler. Stan has been a pastor at two Nazarene congregations here in Oklahoma City, both very vibrant and growing. I remember my first visit to Stan's office. He took me to his study, showed me how he prepared sermons, how he filed illustrations, and how he filed his reference materials. Stan introduced me to another leader in his church, who was also teaching at Southern Nazarene University, located in west Oklahoma City. I spent some time with him and learned a great deal about myself, my personality, and my unique giftedness. Stan also made sure that whenever John was in town, I got to go along.

Six years ago, John introduced me to another close friend of his, Bill Hybels. John wanted him to see our church, so I nervously gave them a tour. That tour of our building opened the door for us to become one of twenty-five satellite sites for the Willow Creek Leadership Summit. That has now grown to over one hundred sites with fifty-four thousand attending last summer. Being a Summit host has meant a couple of meetings a year, not only with Bill Hybels, but with some of the most outstanding pastors in the country. The privilege of knowing these leaders came to me only because I began looking for mentors who would help me through the various challenges of ministry. Each one introduced me to the next one.

I am still asking questions today. As the church has grown, I have stayed committed to finding a pastor somewhere in the country who has moved a similar type church to higher and greater levels. This has been one of the most strategic and valuable steps I have taken in this journey. Next month, I enter a new mentoring relationship with a pastor in Orlando, Florida. I have asked him to meet with me once a month for at least six months. He has agreed to do so. All I have to do is buy a few plane tickets, rent a few cars, stay in a few cheap hotels, but it may be the very key to our church growing from four thousand to eight thousand and beyond.

Allow me to venture from the topic for a moment. Why keep growing the church? Why not be satisfied with four thousand? Can a church really be friendly and personal at eight thousand? To me, the answer is simple. As long as there are lost and hurting people in my town, I have work to do. God is not impressed with the number attending. My ego is not stroked with more people attending. In fact, leading a large church is an extremely difficult and often lonely task. But I have discovered that people really do not need to know me personally. They need to know Jesus personally. They need people to surround them with love and care. They need to be able to confess their sins to one another that they may be healed (James

5:16). They need someone to patiently but diligently help them grow up spiritually. And at the end of the day, they really do not care how many people are around them in the journey. The issue is not how many will I reach, but am I willing to stretch myself, leave my comfort zone, and live up to the potential God has given me and my congregation? If a thousand new people showed up to my church next Sunday, we could handle them. We have room in one of our three services. We have parking spaces available at two of the three services. We still have room in most of our Sunday school classrooms. What does this tell me? We have potential to reach more people. I do not want to be a pastor that prevents a church from reaching its potential. So, I must either learn the lessons necessary to lead us at this level and to the next one, or I need to get out of their way. I prefer to keep learning.

6. Observe Effective Models

Not only have I developed relationships with great mentors, but I have found highly effective models to observe.

On a recent trip to the Netherlands, I met some wonderful pastors. We are preparing for a training conference with EQUIP, John Maxwell's leadership training ministry. What stood out to me was the reality that those pastors had maybe three or four church conferences a year to choose from. In the United States, we have hundreds each year to choose from. These conferences represent dozens of styles and approaches to church ministry. It is often confusing. One will say get rid of the organ and the Sunday school. Another will suggest building the church through the Sunday school. Another will tell you that nothing matters except breaking the church into small groups in the member's homes. Then you have worship issues. Use a printed bulletin or projection screens? Contemporary or traditional? Choir or worship team?

As you come to an understanding of your unique gifts, your unique personality, and the cultural dynamic of your church and community, it is imperative that you guide your church through the discussions that determine your approach and emphasis. Contrary to popular belief, I can show you an effective model in about every style imaginable, and all of them are exalting Jesus Christ, reaching their community, inspiring their people, and growing significantly. Some of these have pipe organs, traditional worship, and the pastor in a robe. Others meet in warehouses, have very edgy music, no choir, no hymnals, and the pastor in jeans. One of the largest and fastest growing congregations in the Church of God is in Bellingham, Washington. Bob Marvel is the pastor. When you stand us next to each other, you could not have two more different people side by side. He is obviously into exercise; I am obviously not. He has a pony tail; I have rarely had hair on my neck, let alone below it. He rides a motorcycle; I chose a Jeep Wrangler—much safer, four wheels, five seats, convertible, as well as off-road capable.

I love Bob Marvel. He is an outstanding, dynamic, and creative pastor. He would be bored to tears in my church, and I would bore his people to death. (These are probably exaggerations, but hopefully you see what I am driving at.) But Bob Marvel understands who he is. He understands his community. He has so effectively reached his community, that based on the percentage of the population he is reaching, he may be the largest church in the country. I find myself wishing I could be as cool as Bob. I wish I were as creative. I wish I were as strong a communicator as he is. Yet God is using both of us, and many more like us, to build great congregations. We have different models, as we also provide different styles for others to observe. But what a disaster would result if I tried to be like Bob or he tried to be like me. Two great congregations would suffer.

Find your unique personality style and match that with similar ministry models that will encourage you and guide you into an effective ministry.

Even though I prefer small groups, we have an extensive Christian education ministry that we still call Sunday school. Even though I prefer contemporary music, our worship service is more of a blend. Why? This is what works best in Oklahoma City. This is our opportunity in our city. One of our key models is Prestonwood Baptist Church in Dallas, Texas. They point everyone in that church to Sunday school. Out of the Sunday school, small groups are formed. Virtually every ministry happens in the Sunday school, such as outreach, assimilation, missions, small groups, and evangelism. They follow up with visitors through the Sunday school. And it works. Nearly twenty thousand people attend Prestonwood, and most of them go to Sunday school. You will find a similar story at South-

DISCOVERING AND AFFIRMING YOUR APPROACH TO MINISTRY

east Christian Church in Louisville, Kentucky. As our church grew, we watched the Sunday school grow, even as small groups struggled. In our situation, we have found that people are more likely to give us two hours on Sunday morning than an hour on Sunday and another hour sometime during the week. So we have seized the opportunity to make Sunday school classes available along with all three of our services.

Five years ago, after moving into our new building, I invited the mayor of Oklahoma City to lunch. He agreed. I asked him to direct me to cities around the country that he thought were similar to our city. He pointed me to a few cities in our region with similar demographics to Oklahoma City. In those cities, I found several very large congregations, and I began to study them. I visited a few of them and came away from that experience with tremendous ideas for ministry.

I caution you to resist the temptation to be exactly like someone else. But always look for what is working in situations that are similar to yours and see what you can learn. Always find someone who is willing to stretch you and make you think. Never settle for mediocrity. Always give it your best.

As I said at the beginning of this chapter, these are challenging days for the church. But there has rarely been a greater opportunity. I believe it is time for the church to perhaps talk less and do more. People have heard about Jesus, but they have not seen him. If the body of Christ will truly study to understand the needs of the community around them and then move into that community with the love and compassion of Christ, the church will become a powerful presence in that community. As a pastor or church leader, God can and will use you. He has called you and equipped you. His spirit empowers you to lead far beyond your abilities. I hope you will prayerfully consider taking the steps to know yourself, to know your church, and to know your community. Do not try to be something or someone you are not. If God has called you, he has called you based on who you are in his eyes. He does not ask you to be something you are not. But he does ask you to diligently shepherd and lead the church. He has done his part. Now it's time for us to step up and do our part.

"Be shepherds of God's flock that is under your care, serving as overseers—not because you must, but because you are willing, as God wants you to be; not greedy for money, but eager to serve; not lording it over those entrusted to you, but being examples to the flock. And when the Chief Shepherd appears, you will receive the crown of glory that will never fade away" (1 Pet 5:2–4 NIV).

Reference List

Yancey, Philip. 2001. *Church: Why Bother?* Grand Rapids, MI: Zondervan.

Chapter Six:
Cynthia Rembert James: *Finding a Placement That Fits*

This chapter is designed to assist ministry students and those with some ministry experience in their search for the right ministry placement. Having served as a graduate professor, pastor, college board trustee, and evangelist, I have seen the look of bewilderment that clouds the faces of recent graduates who are in a total quandary about how to get started. They know that professional ministry is more than just a job or a paycheck; it is where most of them will spend the majority of their waking hours. Consequently, great care should be given to preparation for the actual placement search activities.

The references within this chapter are general so that the concepts discussed can be readily transferred to a number of related disciplines. The narrative content is divided into several broad categories of discussion:

1. The mindset of the minister seeking a placement that fits. This includes a discussion of the roles that motivation, attitude, stamina, and gathering and processing information play in the search process.
2. The methods available for identifying placement options.
3. The measures recommended as part of self-preparation and evaluation of work opportunities.
4. Meeting the mark, which refers to the general disposition helpful to making a final decision.

Section One: The Mindset of the Minister

Ideally, your motivation for finding the right ministry placement should reach beyond the facts of salary, prestige, and convenience. Do not ignore your intrinsic motivation. That knowledge is essential to sustaining you during the job-seeking phase as well as during stormy seasons of subsequent employment. When the minister has appropriate intrinsic motivation, the job-seeking process becomes an enjoyable activity that inspires considerable anticipation.

Behavior will follow attitude. When a minister is required to work longer and possibly harder than would be required by other professions, less internal discomfort exists if the minister is aware of the intrinsic motivations for getting the task accomplished. Self-doubt or resentment will make the search process an unnecessarily miserable experience. On the other hand, the anticipation of being paid to do a task you already desire to do only adds to the satisfaction gained. A minister with a positive attitude toward the vocation will have a significantly more favorable self-perception and motivation for ministry. It has often been said that action stimulates thought. However, the reverse is also true: thought may stimulate action. Engage in careful preparatory thought before launching the actual search for your first ministry placement, but avoid delaying it indefinitely.

Preparation

What might be the nature of such preparatory thinking? The actual job search, like so many other spiritual matters, is not just a destination but a journey requiring preparation. Shaping your thoughts, words, and beliefs to better reflect the Lord's purposes requires the submission of your will. Meditation on the following passages of Scripture, among others, will help you prepare the soil of your heart to hear and receive direction.

> "No eye has seen, no ear has heard, no mind has conceived what God has prepared for those who love him"—but God has revealed it to us by his Spirit. (1 Cor 2:9–10a NIV)

> Many are the plans in a man's heart, but it is the LORD's purpose that prevails. (Prov 19:21 NIV)

"Give ear and come to me; hear me, that your soul may live. I will make an everlasting covenant with you." (Isa 55:3 NIV)

"For I know the plans I have for you,...plans to prosper you and not to harm you, plans to give you hope and a future." (Jer 29:11 NIV)

Henry Blackaby's *Experiencing God* challenges readers to see what God is doing and where God is working and then to dare to join him. Using spiritual disciplines as part of your preparation frees you to get a picture of what God is doing and to see yourself within his plan.

Rick Warren's *Purpose Driven Church* introduces the notion of spiritual surfing. The imagery of surfing spiritually helps us keep our mental and emotional dispositions flexible and simultaneously assures us that we can be carried by the wave of God, rather than being carried entirely by our own sense of self. Your preparation requires recognizing that there is mental and emotional risk-taking involved; a spiritual sense of adventure is required. Go with the wave, or in the words of the old hymn, "where he leads me I will follow."

Nehemiah is an excellent study in the need to think carefully before undertaking a task. Cutting short this process of advance reflection may cause you to make premature choices and abandon your dreams. Anything that has to be brought forth requires labor to do so. This labor of thinking should include a righteous restlessness, a discontentment with letting things remain as they are. As with Nehemiah, careful reflection can effectively foster the kind of brokenness that allows us to access the grace of God.

Discovering God's Will

An appetite for the will of God will fuel your willingness to explore uncharted territory. I vividly recall praying a prayer of desperation one New Year's Eve while waiting for a door of ministry opportunity to open. My New Year's prayer, although faintly breathed, was simply to tell the Lord what he already knew: my desperation for meaningful ministry had reached such a peak that my anticipation for the new year was nonexistent if it did not offer more of an opportunity to labor for souls. I wanted to please the Lord and entertained no thoughts of abandoning the call; however, the status quo had become unbearable. This prayer was not born of frustration or arrogance but rather from a deep yearning that only the Lord could rightly satisfy. This painful prayer of desperation was answered by an unexpected invitation to minister in Scandinavia. The process of discovering God's will is often little more than mental prayers in which we plead and claw our way in search of God's direction.

Formulate what you feel is an effective strategy based on those things that you think are most important in a position. The time spent in preparation for the job search is capable of yielding high dividends: contentment and productivity. Think through the importance of the job placement phase and determine to enjoy the process as well as the acquisition of a position. Magnify the positive aspects of finding a placement that fits rather than approaching the task as if it was so much drudgery. There is a reciprocal relationship that exists between attitude and behavior and between motivation and job placement.

Stamina

As you seek a ministry placement, develop a level of stamina at the outset that will not be readily extinguished—stamina that will enable you to persevere. Stamina refers to one's principal strength, robustness, or power of endurance. In *Be Committed*, Warren Wiersbe describes three responses to trouble: "endure it, escape it, or enlist it. If we only endure our trials, then trials become our master, and we have a tendency to become hard and bitter. If we try to escape our trials, then we will probably miss the purposes God wants to achieve in our lives. But if we learn to enlist our trials, they will become our servants instead of our masters and work for us; …before God changes our circumstances, he wants to change our hearts, reminding us that God's desire is to not make us comfortable but to make us conformable" (Wiersbe 1993, 15).

Stamina is a willingness to meet challenges head on. The story of David and Goliath suggests that the road to stamina is full of slain giants; it is clearly a matter of mastery over opposition (1 Sam 17:8–9). This principle works, regardless of whether it is applied to our own fears or to the negative comments of others. Developing stamina or endurance through exercise of spiritual disciplines develops an inner confidence. Stamina is the result of believing that possibilities for success are only temporarily denied. The desired level of stamina is the point at which we anticipate the mysterious favor of God.

You need to thoroughly evaluate the data about each placement option and integrate it into the whole picture, a mental grid holding all of the data of the target position. This mental grid, for example, might contain the information you've gleaned about the nature of the work environment, the prospect of employment with a specific employer, and your own set of unique circumstances.

Final judgment about a position should be withheld until all of the available information on an open position has been digested. Suspending judgment and avoiding hasty elimination of options will help to prevent you from making decisions based on first impressions and partial knowledge. An intentional approach to the placement process allows you time to reflect prayerfully and listen for the direction of the Lord.

It is important to obtain as much objective input about a position as possible. Without objective input obtained from others, major distortions in judgment are more likely. Identify as many objective measures and people as possible to help you in determining the best placement. The survey material in section three is designed to help strip away layers of complexity and focus on your true interests.

Your mindset as a placement seeker is important. The motivation and the desire to find a placement that fits must exceed the fear of rejection and failure. Many of us hesitate to exert the needed effort out of reluctance and a fear of being turned away. A healthy sense of self releases you to engage in job search activities where your competence is measured against some standard, without threatening your self-worth. Without this, the anxiety caused by the placement search process can debilitate you. Dealing with the uncertainty of your search outcome can often reveal areas in your life where you need to grow spiritually.

Next Steps to Ministry

A balanced approach to the placement search neither limits you to activities that guarantee success nor compels you to constantly pursue options that reflect highly improbable goals. On the other hand, some manageable level of tension is desirable and can be constructive in sustaining the needed focus for the duration of the placement process. Be creative and energetic in your efforts while simultaneously doing both the internal and external work required to maximize your search efforts.

Section Two: Methods

This section suggests plausible places to look as you pursue a ministry placement. The obvious sources include the Internet, libraries, national and regional church offices, local congregations, recently placed individuals, professors, friends, other ministers, the Church of God Ministries Kingdom Ministry Team, search firms, and university placement offices. These efforts can be supplemented by numerous other potential paths to successful placement, including personal interviews, newspaper searches, volunteer work, unpaid internships, mission trips, and self-promotion.

Based on my research, the most productive leads appear to come from contacts within the church, either personal contacts or organizational representatives. These people tend to have inside knowledge about possible positions and about what the church or agency is looking for; they may also give you greater opportunity to speak to individuals who have firsthand knowledge about positions in which you are interested.

Self-promotion

The matter of self-promotion is delicate but it can be particularly helpful to our discussion of the highly competitive placement search. Self-promotion does not have to be affronting; when handled prudently, it can convey an attractive degree of self-confidence. I once saw a book in an airport newsstand titled *Lions Don't Need to Roar*. While "roaring" is unnecessary, it can be helpful in ensuring that your presence is not overlooked. If job seekers are not convinced of their own value and efficacy, it is difficult for them to convince others.

The goal of self-promotion is not to gain popular acceptance but to make a memorable first impression. One method is developing original phrases or acronyms that will intrigue the listener or reader and foster interest in your application. Or you may include audio or video presentations that are simple and to the point, without overselling. There are occasions when it is helpful to send a photograph with your resume. For pastoral positions or other church positions, when family is an important element of the position, I have found that it is often helpful to include a photograph.

Self-promotion is not so much in what is said but more in one's awareness of opportunities to make a positive impression. The point is to control the image that you are communicating as much as possible. As a job seeker, you should know what image is desirable and determine which of your characteristics enhance that impression as well as which ones detract. Attention to detail beyond mere dress helps. Consider your facial expression, the positioning of the shoulders, arms, legs, hands, and feet—these are all significant image makers. Self-promotion is a matter of using every available acceptable means to express confidence and believability.

Often, self-promotion is a matter of having the courage to risk what others will not. Your willingness to risk can be an indication that you have the makings of a true leader. Self-promotion highlights positive distinctions enough to stand out while literally trying to blend in. Self-promotion does take courage. This is the type of courage that will point out overlooked or unpopular points of view or dare to be innovative and save the organization money with a new idea. Folks admire people with guts, when exercised with wisdom.

As you seek a ministry placement, consider these questions as well: Have you developed a set of healthy protocols to use when faced with rejection? What authentic self portrayals do you wish to project as part of the interview process? These and other questions deserve an in-depth response.

Listening for God's Voice

To some extent this information-gathering phase is a research assignment. It can feel very much like being trapped in a dense forest and trying to find a pathway out. An orderly process for collecting information about

Next Steps to Ministry

your various placement options can minimize your feeling of being overwhelmed. Many of the skills that characterize the resourceful employee are also the skills needed in the search process. As with all information gathering, keen observation skills, curiosity, and organized thinking lead to the best results. No one can totally envision the unpredictable turns in a placement search, but learning how to focus on relevant bits of information and how to pursue a hunch differentiates the successful seeker from all others. But finding the best placement must, of necessity, include listening for God's voice.

Everyone will not have the same experience in hearing the Lord's voice. But it is my contention that the Lord is always speaking, though perhaps not in audible ways, trying to communicate his will to us. We have not been left to the whims of a capricious Creator who forsakes his creation. The spiritual disciplines—especially prayer, fasting, and Bible study—calibrate our hearts to hear the voice of the Lord. Isaiah speaks to us: "Give ear and come to me; hear me, that your soul may live. I will make an everlasting covenant with you" (55:3 NIV). Some individuals discern the Lord's will for their lives through an inner sense of knowing. Others rely on impressions gained from the Scriptures. Still others describe more mysterious occurrences resembling those found in the New Testament. Doctrinal postulations have no place here, but I recommend that you develop an intimate knowledge of the Lord and come to recognize God's intentional involvement in your life. The ways in which God leads us may vary, but it is time spent leaning into the Lord's presence through worship, prayer, and practice of spiritual disciplines that acclimates us to divine activity.

Not unlike our understanding of Communion, the work of ministry may be viewed as a sacramental offering. The ministerial call is more than a job; it is symbolic of how the Lord's mercy includes us in God's plan to advance the kingdom of God on the earth. We are called to act in God's stead. We are servants in another's house. We wear the priestly garments. These and endless other metaphors help us to locate our place in the body of Christ.

Our contributions are needed, but it is not about us. We have to expend a certain amount of effort, but we have to relinquish control to the Lord. This posture of leaning into the will of God in order to serve in ministry reminds us that ministry is not an ordinary vocation. Just as the ministry placement is more than a mere placement, so the search is more than a mere search. We simultaneously look for a position while also being called to serve a particular people in a particular place at a particular time. What can sometimes feels like a jigsaw puzzle to us is, in fact, a sacred unfolding of the Lord's carefully laid plans for us.

So while we discuss methods of searching, we paradoxically confess that all does not depend on our search for a placement but also on our willingness to hear and be led of the Lord. The things we search far and wide for and the things we need are most often already within our grasp, but we cannot see them until we receive the enlightenment to recognize them.

Section Three: The Measurement

The survey questions included in this section are intended to help you formulate a concept of the position and placement best suited to you. Each seeker brings particular skills, interests, and experience to the process. Gathering information using all of the means discussed is essential to being able to give honest and clear responses to the survey questions. The process of asking and responding to these questions should lead you to understand which positions are compatible with your self-expression and vocational talents. The placement must be a fit with who you are and who you are called to become. The sense of fit is partially an internal phenomena. There should be a rightness about the choice. You should feel a compatibility and a sense that you are approaching or have arrived where you are supposed to be.

But we must resist looking for a foolproof method or seeking to package the voice and will of the Lord. There is and remains a role for faith and trust. At first blush, some marriages appear to have been made in heaven, but there comes a day when the realization hits that marriages are worked out on earth. Similarly, after following the dictates of good judgment, you have to come to the realization that your job must be worked out by bringing every skill and ability to bear. What if you choose a job that initially appears to be heaven-sent but turns out to be a nightmare? In this event, pride and ego should not prevent you from reevaluating your decision and making an effort to change things.

Unlike many surveys, this one does not attempt to categorize the job seeker into some rigid type. Rather, these survey questions are offered to help you look into the nooks and crannies of potential positions and to closely examine yourself and your expectations. This information gathering can reveal areas that require further questioning and thought on your part.

Finding a Placement That Fits

Directions: Respond to these questions as a way to organize your thoughts about a new ministry placement. The survey questions do not all fit into discrete categories. Some combine considerations of various categories.

Category 1: The Organization

> What is the mission statement of the organization offering the ministry position?
>
> How does this position fit into the organization's mission statement?
>
> Have you developed questions to help you understand the dynamics of the organization?
>
> Have you seen a full job description? An organizational chart?
>
> What type of organizational structure do you prefer?
>
> What image do you have of the organization? What is the public's image of the company?
>
> Does the organization assume the costs, if needed, for relocation, childcare, and training?
>
> What is the pay schedule? What are the built-in opportunities for pay increases? (Also pertains to category 5.)

What opportunities exist for training (internal and external to the company)? What kind of financial support does the agency offer for training? (Also pertains to category 3.)

When are evaluations conducted, and by whom?

What is contingent upon evaluations? Are they directly related to salary?

What is the compensation package, including benefits, associated with this position?

Are the compensation package and the expectations for this position comparable to similar positions in other organizations within the same general geographic area?

Is this organization respected by the professional organizations representing the position you are seeking?

Category 2: The Position

To what other opportunities do you see this position leading? (Also pertains to category 4.)

What would make a position of this type your absolute number one choice over all other similar positions?

What one factor could you not tolerate in this position?

What factor(s) would you be willing to tolerate? (Also pertains to category 4.)

Within the organization, what other positions similar to your top choice would you find satisfying? (Also pertains to category 4.)

Who is currently in this position that you can interview? (Also pertains to category 3.)

What type of work environment best suits you? (Also pertains to category 5.)

Does the work environment of this position meet your expectations? (Also pertains to categories 4 and 5.)

What physical or other accommodations do you need?

What are the posted hours of the position? What kind of hours might the position actually require?

In order for you to do your best work and for you to be the most comfortable, what kind of management style should the person you report to have? (Also pertains to category 5.)

Have you viewed your potential work space?

Does this position fail to meet or exceed your salary needs? Desires? (Also pertains to category 4.)

Does the position offer opportunities to build professional relationships or friendships within the organization?

Category 3: Your Preparation

What type of training does the position require?

How have you prepared yourself for this position?

What additional preparation might be needed to make you more marketable?

Are there opportunities for further training, either inside or outside the organization?

Category 4: Your Present and Your Future

What position do you most desire?

What motivates your desire to work in this position? (e.g., money, spiritual giftedness, discernment)

Which of your core values would be enhanced by this position? (Also pertains to category 5.)

Where would you like to be and what would you like to be doing in three, five, and ten years?

If this position requires that you move, what changes would you have to make in order to adjust to a new location? (e.g., climate, lifestyle, culture, language)

Category 5: Tangibles and Intangibles of This Opportunity

What about this position will you likely find most satisfying? What will you likely find least satisfying?

Which core values would be in tension with this position?

How important to you is the title of the position?

If applicable, which type of management style do you tend to employ? Is that style compatible with this organization's work environment?

What kind of commute would this position require?

What adjustments would members of your family need to make if you accepted the position?

Further Research

The goal of this final phase is to obtain as broad a familiarity with employment opportunities as possible. Every ministry context has nuances that do not make it into the textbooks and the classroom setting, but these are readily known to those individuals who work in that area of ministry. So, one tactic to use as you seek a ministry placement is to work closely with a successful practitioner in your desired discipline. Having a mentor or role model who is actively engaged in the selected field helps you to keep abreast of current issues affecting placement opportunities and trends. Interviews with practitioners in your discipline help you incorporate what is open knowledge about the field into your thinking.

The best placement is one that is capable of sustaining your interest over a long period of time. Be alert to the following factors: Might a particular placement be an emotional trigger likely to hinder performance in the long run? Positions which bring particularly painful past experiences to the surface or which present you with an opportunity to grind an ax are best avoided. In choosing a placement, choose one that is personally meaningful but which does not cause you to become overinvested emotionally.

Equally important is that you find a placement that allows you to demonstrate some independent mastery. Few people are content over the long term to just do a task; most desire to eventually exercise ingenuity and creativity in their position. If that is your desire, the appropriateness of the job fit should be evaluated early on. Different positions will offer more or less opportunity for individualizing the work.

What is the Lord requiring of you? That is the overriding question. Sometimes the answer to this question is elusive. It is often helpful to start a "hunch box." This is a collection of three-by-five cards that briefly list good ideas and strong hunches about places to check for employment, people to see, or Scriptures to read for encouragement. It might even include a vision statement of how you see yourself doing ministry at some future point. A hunch box is a tangible way of expressing your faith and confidence that God is up to something in your life—something good and something wonderful is coming to pass.

Section Four: Meeting the Mark

Ministry cannot be reduced to precise formulas because the full range of divine mystery is in operation. Remember that you and your ministry belong to the Lord. Remain sensitive to God's leading as you search the Scriptures for guidance. In the midst of your thorough efforts, maintain a dependence on the Lord for help and direction. Finding a placement that fits with the Lord's plan for your life and your willingness to receive it is a faith journey not unlike the other aspects of our Christian pilgrimage. Faith is what will allow you to receive with joy whatever the Lord permits because you trust that God has good plans for your life. Finally, it is most important to set pride aside and to not despise your meager starts. If you do not follow the flow of the Lord's Spirit, you will never know the extent of God's grace.

Reference List

Blackaby, Henry, and Claude V. King. 1994. *Experiencing God*. Nashville, TN: Broadman & Holman.

Egan, Gerard. 1986. *The Skilled Helper: A Systematic Approach to Effective Helping*, 3rd edition. Monterey, CA: Brooks/Cole Publishing.

Fast, Julius. 1976. *Creative Coping: A Guide to Positive Living*. New York: Morrow.

Hirsch, Peter. 2002. *Success by Design: Ten Biblical Secrets to Help You Achieve Your God-Given Potential*. Minneapolis, MN: Bethany House.

Power, Bruce P., ed. 1985. *Church Administration Handbook*. Nashville, TN: Broadman Press.

Sourtherland, Dan. 1999. *Transitioning: Leading Your Church Through Change*. Grand Rapids, MI: Zondervan.

Warren, Rick. 1995. *The Purpose Driven Church: Growth without Compromising Your Message and Mission*. Grand Rapids, MI: Zondervan.

Whiteley, Richard C. 2001. *Love the Work You're With: Find the Job You Always Wanted without Leaving the One You Have*. New York: H. Holt.

Wiersbe, Warren W. 1993. *Be Committed*. Wheaton, IL: Victor Books.

Chapter Seven:
Rand & Phyllis Michael: *Working with People: A Case Study in Effective Communication*

Scott was excited about his plan for reorganizing the youth ministry at the church where he had just begun to serve as youth pastor. His vision was that each teen would have an adult mentor; the teens would be divided into small cell groups with the adult mentors facilitating Bible study and sharing. He would eliminate the weekly large group meetings and instead concentrate on the small groups. He was sure this would revolutionize the teens' lives and transform his ministry as well. He presented his plan to the Parents' Advisory Council. With his PowerPoint slides to illustrate the new youth ministry configuration, Scott spoke about the value of this new structure and shared his passion. When Scott finished his presentation, he solicited questions and comments. He was stunned: although some parents were supportive of the proposal, many other parents expressed their displeasure at such a radical reordering of the youth ministry.

"Our kids are doing great with things the way they are."

"You can't just come in here and impose your agenda on us and our teens."

"Are you trying to get out of handling the large group? That's what a youth pastor is supposed to be able to do."

These were just some of the comments. A vote was taken; the plan was defeated. Scott left discouraged, hurt, and angry. What had he done wrong?

Scott was fortunate to be on the staff of a seasoned senior minister, Pastor B, as Carol Bell was appreciatively known. Carol had a reputation for her ability and skills in working with people. The next morning, Scott scheduled an appointment with her. As he sat in Carol's office and told her what had transpired the night before, he was aware of her giving him her full attention. Carol's gaze was calm and steady; she maintained eye contact with him, without staring. Because of the pain he was experiencing, she set aside the issue of his not discussing with her his plans before the meeting with the parents. She realized that what he needed now was a supportive presence. She would at a later time address the need to talk with her about his visions. Her face reflected the dismay he was feeling as she nodded and spoke brief comments at strategic points along the way, such as "Uh-huh," "Yes," "Sure," "That sounds difficult." She even echoed a few of his own words. He talked about his initial exhilaration for the reorganization. Pastor B's focused response to Scott's emotions was, "So you were excited about your new plan but now are hurt and discouraged." Feeling heard and acknowledged, Scott quickly exclaimed, "Yes!" This one word was rich in nuance.

Carol's listening fostered Scott's sharing his frustration and recounting the tone of the meeting as he had experienced it. Along the way, she checked her understanding and, in the process, conveyed to him her caring concern. She used a bridge statement: "Let me see if I understand what you are saying," and then continued, "You are hurting about what happened at the meeting. You thought your plan would bring transformation. That it was something the teens need and that the parents would eagerly accept; yet, to your surprise, at least some of the parents were critical of it. Am I hearing you correctly?"

"You are!" said Scott.

In a tone that conveyed compassion, Carol queried, "Anything else?"

In response to this gentle but clear invitation, Scott talked until his whole story was told. Pastor Bell then asked him "I'm wondering…what do you think you might like to do at this point?" Scott was already feeling better; why? Because he had been experiencing the power of "care-full" listening. What may seem artificial or even like clichés in writing were experienced by Scott as deeply encouraging, helping him to regain his balance.

"I need to spend some time thinking about what I could have done differently with the parents. After that, perhaps we can meet again to strategize the next steps."

Scott's experience illustrates how important communication skills are in ministering to other people. His time with Pastor B gave him a good model for the strength of "reflective listening." Had he met with parents in one-on-one conversations, and in small groups, really hearing their concerns, he would have realized that some of them were not ready for such a significant change at this point in time.

What were the listening skills Pastor B exhibited? There are six of them, and all of them reflect the spirit of James 1:19, "Let everyone be *quick to listen*, slow to speak, and slow to anger." In this mindset, the listener puts his/her own concerns and questions on hold and pursues hearing the speaker's issues. Agreement is not the goal; understanding is.

The first skill is that of *listening with one's total presence*. The listener focuses attention on the content, the nonverbals (i.e., posture, facial expressions, energy), and the paraverbals (i.e., tone, volume, and speed of speech). The listener's own body language is an external sign of the internal choice to listen. Turning toward the speaker, leaning forward, and giving steady (but not intense) eye contact exhibit the listener's commitment to giving full attention. The listener's intention is to receive the other person and the message or concern.

The second skill accompanies the first. It is called by many names; Pastor B referred to it as *encouraging*. Using this skill, the listener acknowledges the other's experience by such nonintrusive but clear responses as nodding and repeating fragments (i.e., words, brief phrases) to show that the listener is tracking with the speaker. Examples from Pastor B are "Uh-huh," "Yes," "Sure," and "That sounds difficult."

The third skill is what may be called *microparaphrasing*. This demonstrates that the talker has been understood. Microparaphrases are made along the way while listening. They may be just one sentence to let the speaker know that the listener is following the story, or they can be more than one sentence so that they reflect back portions of the speaker's story in the listener's own words as it unfolds. While sounding simple, it can be challenging to find the balance between not interrupting on the one hand and on the other not sitting passively. An example from Pastor B is, "So you were excited about your new plan but now are hurt and discouraged."

The fourth skill can be named *soliciting more information and/or more of the story*. This skill seeks to encourage the speaker to tell the full saga as she or he sees it. The listener encourages more speaking with open-ended questions, such as "Anything else?" or "Is there more?" It is crucial to use an inviting tone of voice.

Macroparaphrasing is the fifth skill. When listeners macroparaphrase, they repeat in their own words the core of the speaker's points or story. The listener is careful not to add or subtract anything. The listener asks for confirmation or clarification of the summary. An example from Pastor B is, "Let me see if I understand what you are saying. You are hurting about what happened at the meeting. You thought your plan would bring transformation. That it was something the teens need and that the parents would eagerly accept; yet to your surprise, at least some of the parents were critical of it. Am I hearing you correctly?"

After the listener has fully heard the speaker's story and the speaker is satisfied that there is no more to be told, the listener may use the sixth skill, which is *asking open-ended questions*. These help to fill in missing information and clarify unclear parts. Pastor B's open-ended question was, "I'm wondering…what do you think you might like to do at this point?"

Using listening skills may feel quite awkward at first. Most people do not hear good examples of them when they first learn to communicate as children. Few people take the time in their adult lives to learn and apply these skills. But they are absolutely essential in effective interpersonal relationships, especially as one is involved in ministry. If one could choose only a single skill set, listening would be a wise choice.

A person engaged in ministry also, however, needs to be able to speak with clarity and precision in a spirit of *agape*. Paul in the epistle to the Ephesians emphasizes the strength of words when he says, "Do not let any unwholesome talk come out of your mouths, but only what is helpful for building others up according to their needs, that it may benefit those who listen" (Eph 4:29 NIV). Jesus' words, recorded in Matthew 12:34, support the idea that when one speaks, one reveals his or her inner being: "...out of the overflow of the heart the mouth speaks"(NIV).

Scott realized that, along with listening skills, he needed to learn better methods of talking so that the parents and teens with whom he worked might better understand his spirit and motives. Meeting with Pastor Bell for strategizing, he confessed that he did not know how to speak for himself while also respecting others. Pastor B shared what she had learned in a communication class during her preparation for ministry. She recalled entering the class thinking that speaking for herself was a selfish activity and that her focus should only be on the other person. Her teacher and mentor had made the point that responsible and responsive communication must include ways to disclose aspects of oneself. Letting others know what she was thinking and feeling was really an unselfish act so that people did not have to guess about her awareness and viewpoints. Scott asked her if she could teach him what she had learned. Following are the self-disclosure principles and skills she shared.

First, is the necessity to use what are popularly called *I-statements*. Employing the personal pronoun *I* is the core of this process. Rather than speaking for others or trying to hide oneself, a self-responsible person relates his or her own experiences and consciousness. Again, Pastor B exhibited this skill when she said to Scott, "I do have some time today to share what I have learned about communication. I have another appointment in an hour, so I want to accomplish as much as we can in the time we have. Then I would like to schedule another time next week for us to meet again. Does that work for you?" She modeled communication that allowed her to speak for herself but also inquired about the other person's needs.

The other skills for speaking build upon the foundation of self-responsibility. *Revealing information taken in through one's senses* lets the listener know what one has seen, heard, touched, tasted, or smelled. Giving the data upon which one has based his or her interpretations prevents one from speaking as if those thoughts are reality. An example from Pastor B might be, "I see that it is 12:30 and that is the time at which we agreed to be finished for today." Or she might say, "When I heard what you had

Next Steps to Ministry

to say about your meeting with the parents, I felt sad for you." What she has also done in the preceding statement is to add a *statement of emotion* to her documenting of the sense data of hearing. *Expressing thoughts or interpretations* is another invaluable skill as one speaks. Self-responsible speakers are always clear that these thoughts are theirs and not the only way to view a situation. In fact, it is quite useful to structure a statement in the following manner: "Currently my thinking is…," "I believe that…," or "Currently, my understanding is…" Sometimes the people to whom one ministers may want to hear an interpretation that is a final word, an authoritative conclusion. A good dose of humility and the realization that each person only has a piece of the truth will help the one who ministers to avoid giving his or her interpretation as the "truth." God is indeed the author of all truth, but human perspectives (even those of people engaged in ministry) fall short of being on a level with God's understandings.

Two more skills round out the list of effective speaking. *Declaring desires* brings out one's intentions into the open. Saying, "Here's what I want… What do you want?" allows the other individual to feel valued while knowing where the speaker is coming from. *Describing choices and behavior*, whether past, present, or future, allows one to demonstrate that one is aware of his or her own actions and takes responsibility for them. The following are some examples: "Oh, I interrupted you." "I'm watching the clock because I have a plane to catch." "I am available for lunch tomorrow. Are you free?"

After Scott had spent time with Pastor B learning and practicing the skills for listening and speaking, he began to implement them in his dealings with both his youth and their parents. His first action was to call another meeting of the Parents' Advisory Council. Rather than trying to move the parents into action, he began by saying that he wanted to listen to them, to hear their hopes, satisfactions, and concerns about the youth ministry program. However, before that, in light of the prior meeting, he wanted to share with them the process he'd gone through in contemplating the reorganization just so they would know his heart and intentions. As he spoke to the parents, he used I-statements, sharing what had gone into his plan for reorganization. He talked about his experiences and thoughts since that meeting, including his training in communication skills. After speaking, he then invited the parents to talk with him about their thoughts, feelings, concerns, and hopes about the youth ministry. He carefully used the listening skills as each one shared. After making sure the parents on the council had been able to tell their whole story, Scott paraphrased what they had said and thanked them. Before adjourning the meeting, Scott told them that the next thing he would like to do would be to schedule a time for talking with and listening to each of the other parents and to collect their ideas for what would help create a more responsive youth group. As he incorporated their thoughts into his future planning, he hoped that he and they would become co-creators of a strategy that all could feel a part of. As he envisioned the future, he realized that talking with and listening to the teens would strengthen his approach as well. With his new skills in his tool kit, he was ready for the challenge.

While talking and listening techniques are invaluable when working with people, one also needs to understand how to deal with conflict. As long as people have differing thoughts, feelings, expectations, and styles of relating, there will be conflict. Scott's conflict with the parents of his teens started him thinking about how often dealing with conflict was a part of ministry. He felt guilty about his feelings of anger toward the parents, but also anxious about their anger toward him. Thoughts and questions kept whirling in his head: "Shouldn't Christians also live out the other part of James 1:19, 'be slow to anger'? And what about that passage in Ephesians 4:26 about not letting 'the sun go down while you are still angry' (NIV)?"

It was back to Pastor B's office for some more resourcing for Scott. Again, she helped him with some new concepts for getting along with people.

When persons have differences, sometimes those differences are heated up into disagreements. Anger is often generated in the disputing parties. It is important to realize that anger is a God-given emotion, one that people have for their own protection in response to actual or perceived threats—physical, psychological, or relational. Anger gives one physical energy to either stay and fight or run away as fast as possible. Of course, in most instances, anger is not expressed in ways that are helpful for physical or relational health. One rendering of Ephesians 4:26 might be, "When you are angry, do not let it become sin for you, but deal with it in a way that is constructive rather than destructive. Do not let your anger build up over time and become resentment, because this gives the enemy an opportunity to defeat you."

Some of the not-so-helpful ways that people have learned to express anger include (1) *to deny that one is angry;* (2) *to distance oneself* from the person with whom one has the disagreement; (3) *to detonate and vent the anger* on another person; (4) *to divorce* oneself finally from the person. These stances usually are learned in childhood and feel as if they come naturally. However, they have been learned, and they can be unlearned. A helpful process for dealing with anger is (1) *to admit it*, using I-statements disclosing, not blaming or attacking (e.g., "I am upset about what just took place"); (2) *to ask for help* in dealing with the anger from the person with whom one has the disagreement (e.g., "I would like your help to work through this situation"); and (3) *to allow time for each to speak and listen* to one another around the issue.

At this point in the teaching, Scott became energized: "Wow, this is the first time I have heard anyone explain anger and conflict to me that gave me a strategy for dealing with it. I can see how helpful it could be for my wife and me to practice the steps above when we are in conflict."

Pastor Bell replied, "Oh, indeed, it is quite helpful, not only in ministry settings, but also in our intimate relationships. However, we still haven't discussed how to negotiate the actual issues. Anger is such a forceful emotion that it must be dealt with first before anyone will be willing to negotiate."

Pastor B shared several options for negotiating areas of conflict and working out a solution to a disagreement. The first one, *giving a free gift*, takes place when one person in the conflict agrees to do what the other person wants. It must truly be *a free gift*, done willingly and without resentment. Individuals may share with each other on a scale of 1–10 how important their viewpoint is; if one is more heavily invested in his or her viewpoint, the other may defer to that person. The second option is *compromising*. In this method of negotiation, each gives something and gets something. Most compromises are not fifty-fifty; many will be seventy-thirty or some other ratio. But each person is satisfied with the arrangement. The third choice is *agreeing to disagree agreeably*. With some issues, a decision does not have to be made immediately; thus, a person can put it aside for a time, making sure not to lay the relationship on the line over this one challenge. A fourth method is to *co-create a new possibility.* People who choose co-creating will brainstorm other ways of dealing with the challenge and together come up with a new strategy.

As Scott pondered how he could employ these approaches when working with parents and teens, he realized that he was feeling new energy and enthusiasm rather than the discouragement that had been plaguing him since that tense meeting several months before. Although he was aware that there would continue to be challenges, he also felt renewed in his commitment to "pursue peace with everyone" (Heb 12:14).

Reference List

Adler, Ronald B. 2004. *Interplay: The Process of Interpersonal Communication*, 9th ed. New York: Oxford University Press.

DeVito, Joseph A. 2005. *Messages: Building Interpersonal Communication*, 6th ed. New York: Allyn and Bacon.

Hedahl, Susan K. 2001. *Listening Ministry: Rethinking Pastoral Leadership*. Minneapolis, MN: Fortress Press.

Lawyer, John, and Neil Katz. 1985. *Communication Skills for Ministry*, 2nd ed. Cartersville, GA: Kendall/Hunt Publishing.

Miller, Sherod, and Phyllis Miller. 1997. *Core Communication: Skills and Processes*. Evergreen, CO: Interpersonal Communication Program.

Miller, Sherod, ed. 1991. *Talking and Listening Together: Couple Communication 1*. Evergreen, CO: Interpersonal Communication Programs.

Savage, John S. 1996. *Listening and Caring Skills in Ministry: A Guide for Pastors, Counselors, and Small Groups*. Nashville, TN: Abingdon Press.

CHAPTER EIGHT:
Christina T. Accornero: *Living into the Call*

As I have made transitions into a variety of ministry contexts over the years, I have found myself coming back, over and over again, to Paul's letter to the Romans. It seems that as I continue to live into the call of God on my life, I find myself seeking God for insights and a deeper understanding of what Paul was saying to the church in Rome. I find myself stuck, in particular, in chapter 12, where Paul exhorts his sisters and brothers to place their lives before God. Eugene Peterson interprets it well in *The Message* and begins the chapter with, "So here's what I want you to do, God helping you: take your everyday, ordinary life—your sleeping, eating, going-to-work, and walking around life—and place it before God as an offering...."

Placing my life before God "as an offering" has taken me on an amazing journey of daily living with intention and a desire to question, learn, inquire, seek, and understand God's heart from many contexts of ministry. Thus I come to this piece of writing with a title, "Living into the Call," giving name to my lifelong journey with God.

This year is my thirtieth year in ministry—ministry with mission organizations, churches, educational institutions, and many individuals that God has moved across my path. I have known about my call into ministry as a preacher, teacher, leader, and administrator for a long time, but it has only been in recent years that I have fully understood how I have been living into that call. As a young Christian, I was so eager to please and do my best for God and the church that I rarely thought that what I was doing was a long process. I could only see the ministry before me—the needy people, the work to be done each day, the Scriptures to study, and the sermons to prepare. Life in each of my ministry contexts was consuming, full, challenging, and at times so overwhelming. I could not meet the needs of everyone, nor could I solve all the problems of the sinful world before me. I tried so hard to work the long hours, sacrifice my personal time and family time for the church, put off vacations until the time was just right—but it never was—I was so weary in my well doing. From my perspective, of course, it was all the sisters and brothers that were wearing me out. I was just the best overachiever that God had ever called into ministry, so I just needed to be called somewhere else where I could fully use my gifts.

As a young child, I had learned to perform well for my dad's approval and to make the grades academically. As a top athlete, I drove myself to be the best on the court and to train the hardest to get the affirmation from the coach and the crowd. As a young Christian, I was on the fast track to be the best Christian I could be. Somewhere along the way, I realized that what God was asking of me was a "living into" a call on my whole life, not just a job assignment for a few years. I realized that all these years I had been thinking in terms of a call to a particular ministry context for a particular time. My friends and I would talk about our "call" to a certain church or to study at a seminary or to a leadership position at the ministry headquarters or other callings. Sure we knew that we had made a lifelong choice to follow Christ, but we never talked about how we were living into our call, how we were ordering our lives for the long haul. We were just too busy and too focused on the immediate to understand what was needed to sustain us. The call thus became a series of good or bad ministry assignments. We worked with great people and some very difficult people. We found that leading a church was great and very difficult at the same time and that some of those brothers and sisters were sometimes like the distant cousins that nobody wanted to see at the family reunion. If we prayed and sought God for change, maybe we would be called somewhere else.

Through my work with churches and mission organizations over the past few years and through conversation with many Christian leaders from around the world, I have become increasingly aware of how we need to help each other live into our calls through stewardship and spiritual discipline.

Into the Call to Be Stewards of God's Love

Stewardship is a general calling for us all as caretakers of what God has given each of us to do and to be. As Paul says in Romans 12, "Readily recognize what God wants from you, and quickly respond to it." We are called to be stewards of God's love, serving those whom we lead by helping them reach their maximum potential. As we are blessed, so we are to bless others. It seems that God's continuous purpose, as seen through the Old and New Testaments, has been just that simple. God has consistently and continuously given good things to us and asks that we be stewards of those gifts, of that love, for the purpose of blessing others.

Jesus modeled for us a life where peak performance was a process toward wholeness, not perfection. It seems that it is here, in the interpretation of following Christ as a journey toward perfection, that we get so burned out in our life work in ministry. As Christians, we follow his example with a passion to become the best that we can be, given over to Christ both in our personal lives and intent on one purpose. We are very simply called, however, just to be a steward of God's love to others who do not know that love—to reach a hurting world with God's love (Matt 28:19–20). As we cultivate an exceptional relationship with Christ, we are to give to others what God has given to us. We are to seek to know how we might best use those gifts through God's grace and for God's glory. The challenge is in being real and genuine and in being stewards of God's love. The challenge is not in the performance.

As I began my search to find the best working definition for the word *stewardship*, I found many writers focusing on the narrow concepts of tithing, pledging, budgets, and other money matters. The word seems to bring to mind all of those yearly talks about fund-raising and faith promises. However, as it is traced through the Old and New Testaments, stewardship takes on a much more complex meaning. In the light of the gospel, it takes on a meaning of relationship, friendship, purpose, and partnership.

T. A. Kantonen expresses it clearly in his foreword when he states, "If stewardship can be shown to be vital Christian faith in action, revealing its power to transform all areas of life, then it raises the hope that here may be the beginning of a new awakening and renewal, a new coming of the

Spirit. The fulfillment of this hope demands a greater depth in our approach to stewardship, an exploration of its full potentialities in the light of the theology of the Christian gospel" (1956, viii). Examples are seen in both the Old and New Testaments: the steward had general charge of the business of the house, and special care of the heir. This is referred to in Galatians 4:2, where the word elsewhere rendered "stewards" is translated "governors." The office is a very ancient one. Abraham had a steward, Eliezer (Gen 15:2; note also Gen 24:2). The steward was generally an old faithful slave, though sometimes free men were so employed. The honorable position of the stewards is seen in the fact that they were considered to be rulers over the household (Luke 12:42). Their duties are also referred to in the parable of the laborers (Matt 20:8).

In the Old Testament a steward stands out in the figure of Abraham. In Genesis 12, God sets the agenda clearly for all who will follow—Abraham is blessed in order that he might in turn be a blessing (v. 2). In Abraham's great-grandson Joseph, we see another outstanding example of stewardship. When Joseph is sold to the Ishmaelites and then brought into Egypt (Gen 37–47), there unfolds a series of events that brings him into a close relationship with the pharaoh. He is made manager of the pharaoh's household, and because of his good management, he becomes a trusted representative of the pharaoh's name. Joseph had no idea that he would be reunited with his family in the future and that his position with the pharaoh would be the salvation of his people. Kraybill, in *The Upside Down Kingdom*, illustrates the type of steward that we see in Joseph when he states that:

> We who manage land and people are not owners. We are stewards accountable to God, the true owner. We dare not use land and people selfishly to build economic pyramids, create social dynasties, or feed greedy egos. Giving the land a vacation in the sabbatical or seventh year fits this understanding. Since the land is the Lord's, it shouldn't be abused—on the seventh year it's given back, restored to God, its original Owner. Natural, human and financial resources are, very simply put, God's. These resources are ours only on loan. As short-term stewards of them, we are accountable to God for their proper use and care. (1990, 95)

After Joseph, there are numerous examples of people who used their gifts and blessings consonant with God's mission in the world. But as I have studied the different personalities throughout the Old Testament, I have come to appreciate the ministry of Nehemiah the most. He is usually spoken of from the standpoint of the great leader, which he was, but my interest here is in his life as a steward—he was not about performance.

For me, Nehemiah represents the ordinary person who is called by God into a leadership position, having been prepared for this role by serving as a cupbearer in the king's court while in exile. Nehemiah seems to mirror a pattern similar to that of Abraham, Joseph, Esther, Ruth and others who were called out of their ordinary circumstances to serve God in a specific and special way. They all seemed to have a deep compassion for God's people. And they each responded out of that love to become the stewards that God needed for such a time as this (Est 4:14). They all seemed to have teachable spirits, humble hearts, and an unselfish, modest, and authentic way of approaching people, and they were living into their call—a lifelong journey.

When the concept of stewardship is developed in its New Testament contexts, it implies more than trusteeship and responsibility. It contains also the idea of partnership. The relation between master and servant gives way to the relation between friends working together for the realization of a common purpose.

We are created with a purpose, and as that purpose is revealed through our life's journey, we see the Lord intervening in our lives in surprising ways. Throughout the New Testament, we are challenged by the lives of the sisters and brothers in the early church. What are we doing with our talents? Have we oiled our lamps? Have we watered the vine and grown fruit? Stewardship keeps us from being shaken loose and keeps us on the journey. When we focus on being stewards of God's love, the call is so very simple. The focus is on what God would have us do with the love that has been poured into our lives. We have a place to start with each individual we meet, in each ministry context—no performance required, just being the steward.

Into the Call to Spiritual Discipline

Throughout the Old and New Testaments, God teaches us by means of the stories of individual lives. God chooses to show us ordinary people and their daily struggles and victories. Their stories are our stories. We all know the Ruths, Deborahs, Johns, Peters, and Marys—and we can learn from their examples, just as if they were walking with us today. We can see in the lives of these real stewards both a model for living and a very way of being. They were disciplined in their attitudes, in their thinking, and in their actions.

It seems that one of the keys to living into our call can be found in how we discipline and order our lives. Marjorie Thompson, in her chapter in *The Pastor's Guide to Spiritual Formation*, asks, "Are we ordering our lives to catch the wind of grace?" (2005, 142). The call of God, when it is ordered toward grace, becomes the full sail that carries us through the troubled waters. Think of a sailboat with its main sail unfurled to catch the fullness of the wind—picture it catching the wind of grace. Does grace fill your sail? Is your life driven and ordered by grace, by the love of God?

In the Romans 12 text, Paul challenges the church in Rome in a similar manner: "I'm speaking to you out of deep gratitude for all that God has given me, and especially as I have responsibilities in relation to you. Living then, as every one of you does, in pure grace, it's important that you not misinterpret yourselves as people who are bringing this goodness to God. No, God brings it all to you. The only accurate way to understand ourselves is by what God is and by what he does for us, not by what we are and what we do for him" (Rom 12:3 MSG).

Like the sailboat that positions itself to catch the fullness of the wind, our lives can be intentionally positioned to be fully moving in the grace of God. As a spiritual discipline, the way that we make daily choices in our habits, our attitudes, our perceptions, and in our actions determines whether we will move forward in our call.

Think with me for a minute or two about that statement, that daily choices determine whether we will move *forward* in our call. Do you agree? Let me tell you a bit about how I came to make such a statement.

A number of years ago, I remember being very discouraged about what I was doing in life and ministry. I was disappointed with everything around me and found myself complaining all the time. It took a good friend to say, "So what are you going to do about it?" My friend helped me look at my habits, my attitudes, my perceptions, and my actions. We talked together each day for three months; this friend made a commitment to stay with me in this process and help me really assess what was going on. At the end of the three months, I came to the conclusion that my daily choices were keeping me from reaching my full God-given potential.

- **Habits:** Were all of my habits affecting how I was growing as a Christian and how I was responding to God's call? No, but what was getting in the way of moving forward? I saw that I complained a lot about being tired and overweight, but I was not willing to change my eating or exercising habits. I would say that I was not reading or writing as much as I wanted, but I would not turn off the television and pick up the books. God was trying to prepare me for a move into a very active community where a new level of energy would be needed and where I was to begin teaching and writing more, but I was not ready to make daily choices for better eating, sleeping, and exercising habits.
- **Attitudes:** Each day my choice had been to start with a negative attitude and complain about everything. I was looking for someone else to blame. I was the victim, the one who was not realizing the call and not getting prayers answered. In talking through the issues with my friend, I began to see that my attitudes were laying a foundation for failure each day. I was not able to accurately assess my circumstances or get through a day without criticizing someone. Most importantly, however, I was so focused on myself that I was not able to make a positive contribution to anyone else.
- **Perceptions:** Wow, had my world view changed. My friend helped me see that as I started to complain more and see the negative side of things more, I also started to move from an optimistic, positive person to one who could not start a day without being negative. I got out of bed with aches and pains. I was not happy with my job so I did not look forward to going each day. I set myself up for a bad day with the first choice I

made in the morning. I was not preparing myself for the day that God had given me. As a result, I could not even hear or see what God was doing around me.
- **Actions:** Finally, my friend helped me to realize that I had become sedentary and had pulled away from people emotionally. I still went to church, participated in ministerial gatherings, sounded really good with my colleagues, but I was not present. I was too busy wondering why God was not moving mountains for me. My daily choices were to meet my needs. When did I get so self-centered?

Since that time, I have been asking whether my life is positioned through daily choices to catch the fullness of the wind of God and whether my life is intentionally positioned to be fully moving in the grace of God.

Into the Call to Serve a Hurting World

As I have been on this journey with the Romans 12 text, I have noticed that my awareness of God's grace has become heightened. Conversations have turned to thankfulness more often lately, as I am more aware of what a privileged life I lead. I recently sat with a colleague over lunch talking about the last few years of life and ministry. We have both traveled to many places—to Europe, Asia, Africa, and throughout the United States and Canada. We were aware of God's grace in travels, in bringing people across our paths, in a healing touch on a variety of health concerns, and in the many ways that God had allowed us to respond freely to grace, free to be ourselves, to be real in our particular ministry contexts.

I've been living for weeks since in the portion of the Romans 12 text that says, "Love from the center of who you are..." (v. 9 MSG). Who am I at my center? How do I respond daily to divine grace? How do I make God's love real for others? Where do I need to go deeper with God? What are my daily intentions toward God and toward others?

When I began this journey with God thirty years ago, it was a very dramatic change from the first twenty-five years of my life. I was surprised by the immediate changes in lifestyle, in anger, and in the sense that I had come out of a very long tunnel that seemed to be leading nowhere. I did not know much about God's grace, but I responded with a clear choice to move in God's direction. As a young Christian, I was instructed carefully in a performance gospel that taught me to worry about how I measured up to all those visibly "successful" Christians that I saw in the big churches or at retreats or on TV or in my local church—the ones who always looked so good and always seemed to get all their prayers answered.

God has called me to a vocation of personal and social holiness—to be a virtuous, ethical, and trustworthy person who continually connects life and learning through Jesus. My calling has been consistent over the years, but in a variety of circumstances. I have always been a leader, administrator, and teacher—that is my calling—but I have also been asked to work and minister in a variety of contexts.

I have been talking recently with my faculty colleagues at Asbury Theological Seminary about spiritual formation and "rules of life," about the call of God. One of my colleagues, Dr. Steve Martyn, summarizes well this idea of sustaining the call of God as he talks about the daily commitment to responding to God's call. For each of us, the daily choice is to seek the heart and will of God through:

- Devotional Living—practicing the spiritual disciplines of prayer, Scripture reading, worship, and formative listening to the voice of God—and living out the reality of that devotion by bringing the love of God to a personal community and to a hurting world.
- Relational Strengthening—nurturing primary relationships in life and intentionally seeking opportunity to strengthen others.
- Serving Vocationally—managing well the spiritual gifts and talents, the physical life, and the material goods that God has given in order to fulfill the calling to particular ministry contexts.

Across the years and through a variety of ministry assignments, God has taught me to fix my eyes on the path of Jesus, to use my particular gifts and talents to their fullest, and to only be me. It gets more exciting each year as I trust Jesus more and more to handle my life. In reality, the call is to Jesus—nothing more, nothing less. We then get to live out that call in a variety of vocations and contexts, helping others live into their call.

The good, the bad, and the ugly of these past thirty years, however, have taught me about a real God who shows me real grace on a daily basis. I have tried to quit many times, because working with the brothers and sisters in the church is just too hard. But here I am, still seeking, still growing and still living into my call as a minister of the gospel of Christ. I pray that you and I will continue to learn to position our sails to take in the fullness of a divinely inspired life that is grounded in the reality and authenticity of God's love and grace.

Reference List

Block, Peter. 1993. *Stewardship: Choosing Service over Self-Interest.* San Francisco, CA: Berrett-Koehler Publishers.

De Pree, Max. 1997. *Leading without Power: Finding Hope in Serving Community.* San Francisco: Jossey-Bass.

Hagberg, Janet O. 1994. *Real Power: Stages of Personal Power in Organizations.* Salem, WI: Sheffield Publishing.

Helgesen, Sally. 1995. *The Web of Inclusion.* New York: Currency/Doubleday.

Hesselbein, Francis, el al, eds. 1999. *Leader to Leader: Enduring Insights on Leadership from the Drucker Foundation's Award-Winning Journal.* San Francisco: Jossey-Bass.

Kantonen, Taito Almar. 1956. *A Theology for Christian Stewardship.* Philadelphia, PA: Fortress Press.

Kouzes, James, and Barry Posner. 1987. *The Leadership Challenge: How to Get Extraordinary Things Done in Organizations.* San Francisco: Jossey-Bass.

Kraybill, Donald B. 1990. *The Upside-Down Kingdom.* Rev. ed. Scottdale, PA: Herald Press.

Lincoln, C. Eric, and Lawrence H. Mamiya. 1990. *The Black Church in the African American Experience.* Durham, NC: Duke University Press.

Neidert, David. 1999. *Four Seasons of Leadership.* Provo, UT: Executive Excellence Publishing.

Nouwen, Henri. 1989. *In the Name of Jesus.* New York: Crossroad Publishing.

Ortiz, Manuel. 2002. *One New People: Models for Developing a Multiethnic Church.* Downers Grove, IL: InterVarsity Press.

Sanders, Cheryl J. 1997. *Ministry at the Margins: The Prophetic Mission of Women, Youth, and the Poor.* Downers Grove, IL: InterVarsity Press.

Senge, Peter M. 1999. *The Dance of Change.* New York: Currency/Doubleday.

———. 1990. *The Fifth Discipline: The Art and Practice of the Learning Organization.* New York: Doubleday/Currency.

Sumner, Sarah. 2003. *Men and Women in the Church: Building Consensus on Christian Leadership.* Downers Grove, IL: InterVarsity Press.

Thompson, Marjorie J. 2005. Making Choices: Developing a Personal Rule of Life. In *The Pastor's Guide to Personal Spiritual Formation*, ed. William Willimon et al, 139–148. Kansas City, MO: Beacon Hill Press.

Willhauck, Susan, and Jacqulyn Thorpe. 2001. *The Web of Women's Leadership: Recasting Congregational Ministry.* Nashville, TN: Abingdon Press.

Wright, Walter C.. 2000. *Relational Leadership: A Biblical Model for Leadership Service.* Waynesboro, GA: Paternoster Publishing.

CHAPTER NINE:
Fredrick H. Shively: *Continuing Education in Ministry*

A young ministry student, returning to his or her seat clutching a newly received diploma, thinks, "At last! I am finished preparing! Now I am ready to begin my ministry!" The truth is that this student has only begun to prepare for this awesome task of ministering to others.

Definition of Continuing Education

If ministry in today's world is to be adequate to the challenge, the minister must be well-prepared. If ministry is to keep pace with changes in society, the minister must grow in preparation for this task. This calls for continuing education in ministry. A physician friend of mine once said that he had to be reeducated completely three times throughout his medical career to stay current in medicine. Can this be any different for the ministry?

Nathan Pusey defines Christian ministry simply as "service on behalf of the Lord" (1978, 42). I like to define ministry as openness to the good news of God's love (the gospel) so that that good news comes through the individual's personal set of gifts in order to effect good in the lives of others at the point of their real needs. The capacity to recognize one's spiritual gifts and to utilize those gifts for good develops over a long period of time. When Jesus said to Peter and Andrew at the Sea of Galilee, "Follow me, and I will make you fish for people" (Mark 1:17), he implied that continuing preparation to serve effectively was necessary. When the apostle Paul wrote that "in it [the gospel of God] the righteous of God is revealed from faith for faith" (Rom 1:17a), he implied that faith is dynamic and must grow throughout one's life. Because changes throughout one's life are inevitable, the need for personal and professional growth in ministry is essential.

Mark Rouch, in *Competent Ministry: A Guide to Effective Continuing Education*, gives this definition: "Continuing Education is an individual's personally designed learning program which begins when basic formal education ends and continues throughout a career and beyond. An unfolding process, it links together personal study and reflection and participation in organized group events" (1974, 16–17). Please note the words *designed*, *program*, and *organized*. Catholics define it as "learning after ordination" (Stewart 1974, 126). Although one learns much from life's experiences, intentional planning for continuing education in ministry is vital. It is a lifelong process. It is intentional, not haphazard; open, not closed; flexible, not rigid. Ultimately, responsibility for this education is personal. Built upon a strong base of undergraduate and, hopefully, seminary education, this growth in learning draws from many sources and is done in many different settings. When I graduated from college, I was but beginning my education. After seminary, I felt many times more ready to serve effectively, yet I had much more to gain.

This approach to education recognizes that what is adequate in one generation may not be adequate in a later one. New questions arise from changes in worship, changes in the world, current biblical and theological scholarship, and even new understandings about the church. At the heart of this learning is staying alive to inevitable changes. As a young minister of music and worship, I could not have anticipated the flood of changes that have taken place in the practice of worship in the church in my lifetime.

Necessary elements for adequacy in continuing education include opportunities to reflect upon experience and learning, built-in accountability to others, openness to challenging and stretching ideas, building upon one's strengths and confronting one's weaknesses, and purposefulness. All of these result in personal and spiritual growth.

Resources for Growth

Resources for growth in ministry exist in many settings, some so close they may not seem obvious. They are both formal and informal and provide both personal and professional growth. A logical place to begin is with **college and seminary.** A strong base for learning can be found in a university that provides a variety of majors and programs while at the same time allowing for concentration in Bible, theology, and ministry. Double majoring in college can help to broaden one's base. Even after graduation, formal classroom experiences are available for ministers, whether or not one seeks additional academic degrees. Today's and tomorrow's ministers must be well educated. **Seminars** are provided by churches, denominations, colleges and universities, ministry agencies, and charitable organizations. A minister should investigate all available possibilities and schedule those that are most appropriate. Negotiating a continuing education benefit with one's employing congregation or ministry agency to make possible attendance at such seminars is wise. In the initial development of the Center for Pastoral Studies at the Anderson University School of Theology, we incorporated the use of continuing education units (CEUs) to help people track their growth plans.

In most communities, **libraries** are available; ministers may have access to public as well as university and seminary libraries. They may find it advantageous to regularly schedule several hours or even a whole day discovering the resources available. Some ministry friends have scheduled a week or a year away from the parish, exploring the resources of a good library. While serving a congregation in Oregon, I benefited greatly by visiting the wonderful library of the Dominican Order's Mount Angel Abbey. It was the only place I have ever seen an actual bookworm. It had eaten its way through an ancient book and had died on page 989.

One of the best resources for growth can be found in a **colleague group,** a small group of five to eight people who meet regularly to study together, to build mutual support and to hold each other accountable.[1] It takes time to build a group that can serve this purpose, but once a level of trust is developed, it can serve very well for both personal and professional growth. A group may choose to study a book together, invite resource persons to visit, or access such persons by way of the media. A conference telephone call may bring nearly anyone in the world into such a group.

Another proven resource for growth is a mature person who might serve as a **mentor.** Regular meetings and other communication with a mentor can build accountability and offer modeling needed for growth. Robert Clinton defines mentoring as the process by which a person sees leadership potential in another person and is able to influence that person in the realization of that potential (1988, 130). A mentoring relationship may be formal or informal. I have often met informally with personal friends in ministry who have served as mentors to me.

It is good for ministers to develop a **personal reading list**. This reading should include books and articles specifically related to professional growth. A beginning reading list for continuing education is included with this chapter. Such a list should also include a wider reading list of both nonfiction and fiction for learning and enjoyment. Finding time to read for pleasure in addition to professional growth is more difficult for me, but it is an important part of a well-rounded education.

Increasingly, **media resources**—TV, videos, CDs, DVDs, and the Internet—are available for personal use. Materials of this kind include presentations, speakers, and seminars. Another possibility involves **clergy and laity** meeting and learning together. Ministers can gain much from non-clergy persons.

Sometimes personal learning can be best accomplished through **counseling**, in which one gains helpful personal insights. One's life can be enriched greatly also by taking **lessons** in music, drama, or languages. In nearly every community, **wellness programs** or physical development facilities are available, often with guidance and instruction in health and physical fitness.

Another way to learn is **travel**. There is no substitute for visiting developing nations to learn more about the true nature of a world of poverty. Many churches and other religious organizations offer group travel experiences of this kind. When one combines visiting such a country with a service project, learning is enhanced.

Stages of Education

Several authors[2] outline stages of lifelong learning for ministry. These include, of course, early education in school, church, and home, as well as a broad-based undergraduate education that includes major(s) and minor(s) and a possible first internship in ministry; graduate study including further practical experience in ministry; a first position, especially including the first three years, followed by an intentional plan of lifelong learning. Key points along the way include the first three years in ministry, the first seven years in the same position, midlife adjustments, the preretirement stage, and retirement.

It can be very helpful for a minister to be given sabbaticals for retooling, refreshment, and spiritual growth. These, too, should be negotiated at the time of employment. National endowments[3] and other programs offer possibilities for sabbaticals. The ministry is one profession in which growth in skills and wisdom should continue throughout one's ministry. That person should be at his or her best later in life.

Growth in Competencies

To accomplish skill development in the necessary competencies for success in ministry there is no substitute for actual experience in those competencies. While it is helpful to observe outstanding preaching, one can learn to preach only by doing so. This ability can be enhanced by supervision from a skilled and experienced preacher. This need for experience is true for all of the skills in ministry, including teaching, worship leading, outreach ministries, pastoral care, and administration. One may not be gifted in every area, but general growth in each area can serve a very useful purpose. Specifically, in pastoral care one needs to learn to listen and to know how to recognize real emotional, psychological, and spiritual problems. Clinical pastoral education (CPE) programs sensitize persons to the needs of others. In administration, one needs to understand group dynamics in order to know how to work with groups. Knowledge of parliamentary procedure, developing mission statements, and setting and reviewing budgets are all skills expected of ministers.

There are other, more specific, personal competencies. One vital skill is maintaining strong family relationships in the midst of a busy ministry. Parenting skills and strengthening one's marriage enable one to find great meaning. Seminars such as Marriage Enrichment, Marriage Encounter, and other denominational programs are available for ministry couples. What does it profit a minister to build a huge congregation while losing touch with spouse or children? Seminars are also available for unmarried individuals who can also benefit from personal growth and further development of relational skills.

Personal Competencies

Included in other personal competencies are understanding the culture in which one lives, the Scriptures, congregational life and culture, and the wider church world. One may develop skills in problem solving and the enabling of others to live together in harmony—reconciliation skills. The development of skills in technology and a wider knowledge in many fields can enhance personal enrichment and effectiveness in ministry.

Maturing into Leadership

I have yet to have a congregation that I served ask me what my grades were in college. They have wanted, rather, to determine what I know about the Bible and Christian life, whether or not I am able to communicate clearly, whether I can work effectively with people, and whether or not I love them.

Carnegie Calian includes a report from the Readiness for Ministry survey taken by member schools of the Association of Theological Schools in the United States and Canada. The findings of this survey were that people of all denominations are seeking ministers who (1) serve without regard for personal gain, (2) have personal integrity, (3) are examples of generosity and belief in the gospel, (4) display competence in ministry skills, (5) can build community, (6) are insightful counselors, (7) can think theologically, (8) remain calm in stressful situations, (9) are willing to admit mistakes and recognize the need for continuing growth (Calian 1977, 4–5).

While growing in personal faith, a minister needs to develop a philosophy of ministry that includes methods by which decisions are made. One essential attribute in ministry is speaking the truth in love (Eph 4:15), knowing how to face problems with a positive attitude, and being willing to be confronted when necessary. Ministers often score high on defensiveness scales in psychological exams. To learn to face oneself honestly and even to accept criticism enables one to grow spiritually and to enable others to do the same.

A minister can develop healthy habits of growth through a disciplined use of careful reflection upon experience. A disciplined life is built upon personal reflection, a careful meditation upon one's actions or experiences in order to gain insight. Thomas Swears lists four steps in growth: *repetition* of reading or of an affirmation, which guides the mind; *concentration*, leading to a singleness of purpose; *comprehension*, which enables clear perception of reality; and *reflection*, which brings forward the true significance of what is being learned. Critical reflection enables one to grow spiritually, to become more like Christ, to live more faithfully, and to serve more responsibly (Swears 1991, 85, 11).

One great aid to critical reflection is journaling. Journaling is more than keeping a diary; it includes more than facts and information. It includes careful reflection upon experiences. It cultivates a relationship with one's own soul and ultimately a relationship with God. John Sanford calls journaling "the most inexpensive form of psychotherapy I know." He goes on to compare a journal to a container that holds water. Without the container, the water spills and escapes from us. The journal enables us to hold onto a major part of our inner lives (Sanford 1965, 111).

Growing and maturing in Christian leadership enables a minister to face and overcome one of the most serious problems: ministry burnout. Ministers are particularly susceptible to burnout. John Sanford (1991, 5–15) explains why:

- The job of the ministering person is never finished.
- The ministering person cannot always tell if his work is having any results.
- The work of the ministering person is repetitive.

- The ministering person is dealing constantly with people's expectations.
- The ministering person must work with the same people year in and year out.
- Because he works with people in need, there is a particularly great drain on the energy of the ministering person.
- The ministering person deals with many people who come to her or the church not for solid spiritual food but for "strokes."
- The ministering person must function a great deal of the time on his "persona."
- The ministering person may become exhausted by failure.

By understanding the causes of burnout in ministry, a person may confront and overcome these causes. As one combines an active imagination with meditation and prayer, the minister understands oneself and envisions solutions much more readily. This growth in insights into oneself and others and the nature of the role of ministry itself can lead to a wisdom that is much greater than technique and skills.

One of the people who has influenced me the most through his writing is Henri Nouwen. In the introduction to his timeless *Creative Ministry*, he writes:

> If God does not become more and more a living God to those who minister to the people of God every day, He will not be found in the desert, the convent, or the silent hours either. If professionalism is to be prevented from degenerating into a form of clerical manipulation, it has to be founded on the deep-rooted spiritual life of the minister himself [herself] as it develops out of his constant care for those he works with. (1978, xxiii)

The Continuing Challenge

Robert Clinton (1988, 196–97) summarizes this task of lifelong learning in ministry with three challenges:

Challenge 1: When Christ calls leaders to Christian ministry he intends to develop them in their full potential. Each of us in leadership is responsible to continue developing in accordance with God's processing all our life.

Challenge 2: A major function of all leadership is that of selection of rising leadership. Leaders must continually be aware of God's processing of younger leaders and work with that process.

Challenge 3: Leaders must develop a ministry philosophy that simultaneously honors biblical leadership values, embraces the challenges of the times in which they live, and fits their unique gifts and personal development if they expect to be productive over a whole lifetime.

Getting Started

Having a plan for continuing education is very important. Getting started into that plan is more important. What can a person new to ministry do to begin this process? One easy step is to read. I urge the person to read widely. What books should a person begin with? Every experienced minister would have a unique list. Mine would include (1) something from Henri Nouwen, like *The Wounded Healer* or *Creative Ministry*; (2) a book on ethics, like Dietrich Bonhoeffer's *Ethics* or William Willimon's *Calling and Character: Virtues of the Ordained Life;* and (3) a book to stimulate biblical study, like *Engaging the Powers* by Walter Wink or *The Meaning of Jesus* by Marcus Borg and N. T. Wright. A book like *The Call to Conversion* by Jim Wallis would also stimulate much thinking.

In addition, I recommend that the new minister look for a program that would maintain a steady list of teachers in his or her consciousness. A good example is that which is provided by the Center for Christian Leadership, directed by David Neidert through the Anderson University School of Theology. This center offers twenty-five different self-study courses that one can do at one's own pace. These courses include books, work books, tapes, and DVDs written and developed by faculty and former faculty of the school. Examples of programs available are an Introduction to the Bible; a study of the Book of Acts, *The Widening Witness* by Fred Shively; and a theological primer, *Beliefs that Guide Us*, by Gilbert Stafford. A number of these courses are also available in Spanish.

This is but one example of many such programs available to the minister who wants to continue growing throughout one's life of service. The element of the desire to grow is perhaps the most important aspect of lifelong learning. If that student clutching the diploma will be intentional in pursuing continuing learning, he or she will be better and more and more productive as the years go by.

Endnotes

[1] One program that places Church of God ministers into such groups is the Sustaining Health and Pastoral Excellence (SHAPE) program administered by Church of God Ministries.

[2] See Rouch, Clinton, and Stewart, for example.

[3] The Lily Endowment runs two programs: the National Clergy Renewal Program (www.clergyrenewal.org) and the Clergy Renewal Program for Indiana Congregations (www.indianaclergy.org).

Reference List

Anderson, Ray S. 1997. *The Soul of Ministry: Forming Leaders for God's People.* Louisville, KY: Westminster John Knox Press.

Bartlett, David L. 1993. *Ministry in the New Testament.* Minneapolis, MN: Fortress.

Calian, Carnegie Samuel. 1977. *Today's Pastor in Tomorrow's World.* New York: Hawthorn Books.

Clinton, J. Robert. 1988. *The Making of a Leader: Recognizing the Lessons and Stages of Leadership Development.* Colorado Springs, CO: NavPress.

Coles, Robert. 1993. *The Call of Service: A Witness to Idealism.* Boston: Houghton-Mifflin.

Leonard, Juanita Evans. 1989. *Called to Minister, Empowered to Serve.* Anderson, IN: Warner Press.

MacDonald, Gordon. 2003. *Rebuilding Your Broken World*. Nashville, TN: Thomas Nelson.

Messer, Donald E. 1989. *Contemporary Images of Christian Ministry*. Nashville, TN: Abingdon Press.

Nouwen, Henri J. M. 1978. *Creative Ministry*. Garden City, NY: Image Books.

Pusey, Nathan M. 1967. *Ministry for Tomorrow: Report of the Special Committee on Theological Education*. New York: Seabury Press.

Rouch, Mark. 1974. *Competent Ministry: A Guide to Effective Continuing Education*. Nashville, TN: Abingdon Press.

Sanford, John A. 1965. *Ministry Burnout*. New York: Paulist Press.

Stewart, Charles William. 1974. *Person and Profession: Career Development in the Ministry*. Nashville, TN: Abingdon Press.

Stone, Howard W., and James O. Duke. 2006. *How to Think Theologically*. 2nd ed. Minneapolis, MN: Fortress Press.

Swears, Thomas R. 1991. *The Approaching Sabbath: Spiritual Disciplines for Pastors*. Nashville, TN: Abingdon Press.

Switzer, David H. 1979. *Pastor, Preacher, Person: Developing a Pastoral Ministry in Depth*. Nashville, TN: Abingdon Press.

Taylor, Charles W. 1991. *The Skilled Pastor: Counseling as the Practice of Theology*. Minneapolis, MN: Fortress Press.

Warlick, Harold C., Jr. 1982. *How to Be a Minister and a Human Being*. Valley Forge, PA: Judson Press.

Witham, Larry A. 2005. *Who Shall Lead Them? The Future of Ministry in America*. Oxford: Oxford University Press.

III.
DOING

basic responsibilities of a life in Christian ministry

It sounds simple to say, "Just do it."

Pastoral ministry calls for an artistry that engages the whole person. The sections of this book: being, becoming, and doing, while meant to be helpful are somewhat artificial. Being a Christ follower, becoming our Lord's servant, doing the acts of Christian ministry are all of a piece. It is not possible to separate them and ourselves as neatly as the divisions of this volume may suggest. Indeed, we do not want to do so, for we serve as whole persons. Who and what we are carries a powerful impact upon how our doing is received.

At the age of fourteen, Ian Pitt-Watson read a book on dancing. He studied its contents carefully. He went through the suggestions it made before a mirror. It all seemed awkward and contrived. And then it happened:

> Then one night at a party a nice girl who knew of my difficulty said, "Come on, try it with me." So I did, and to begin with I felt even more of a fool because I was so awkward and she was so full of grace. Then something strange happened. A little of her grace seemed to pass to me and I began to get the feel of it. For the first time all I had learned in the book began to make sense, and even the painful practice in front of the mirror began to pay off. What had been contrived now became natural, what had been difficult now became easy, what had been a burden now became a joy--because at last I had got together what I

was thinking and what I was doing. In that moment I experienced a kind of grace, and it was very beautiful.[1]

We pray, dear friend, that a similar grace will meet you as you arise to walk with our Lord in a life in Christian ministry. May you experience yourself and bring to those whom you serve, great joy, as you learn to step in rhythm with the One who has been called the Lord of the Dance!

---

[1] Ian Pitt-Watson, *A Primer for Preachers* (Grand Rapids, MI: Baker Books, 1999), 102–103.

CHAPTER TEN:
David E. Markle: *Care for Souls*

This chapter takes a wide-angle look at the care of souls. Indeed it will approach the subject from perceptions about what a healthy Christ-centered community values, how that community structures time and people together, some hoped-for outcomes in individual lives, and finally, some wisdom on loving persons well at those significant moments of life—birth, baptism, marriage, and death. Another way to say it is that we will look at how the Christian community approaches people within and around itself, what arenas of participation it most values for its members, and how we may care for one another most fittingly at those gateway moments of life.

Some who believe in the necessity and possibility of "new birth" or "birth from above" identify only one or at most two peaks in Jesus' teaching. I will highlight three of them. Before you read on, think about the high points of Jesus' teaching from your point of view. What words stand out as especially formative in shaping a healthy community of Christ followers?

A Three-Peaks Approach to Life and Ministry

The snow-capped peaks of the Cascade Mountains[1] provide one of the delights of the landscape of the Pacific Northwest. Stretching from southern British Columbia, through Washington and Oregon, to northern California, these slumbering (sometimes waking) volcanoes highlight the topography of this picturesque region.

Next Steps to Ministry

While living in the Portland area, we became familiar with a number of meteorological terms associated with rainfall and sunshine, at times the lack of the latter. However, the term we most enjoyed in Portland described a picture-perfect day where one could see for miles and miles—literally a five-mountain day. I would like to identify three Cascades peaks with three of the high points of Jesus' word to us. I am working from the assumption that optimal health is found in Christ-centered community and in a Christ-follower's soul when that community and its people are living in dynamic relationship with these words from Jesus.

The grandeur of Mount Hood looms large over the Portland skyline. Located approximately sixty miles east of the city, Hood retains a beautiful conic shape and provides year-round skiing and other recreational opportunities for residents and visitors. What God created, humankind complemented with the beauty and craftsmanship of Timberline Lodge, built by the Depression-era Civil Conservation Corps. A fascinating feature of Timberline's story is that only a few skilled crafts persons and artisans labored on the job. Most of the workers were unemployed persons from the streets pressed into service to secure food and a livelihood. Their artistry gives witness to the glory of human life in the image of our Maker.

So I associate Mount Hood with the Great Commandment of our Lord:

He said to him, "You shall love the Lord your God with all your heart, and with all your soul, and with all your mind." This is the greatest and first commandment. And the second is like it: "You shall love your neighbor as yourself" (Matt 22:37–39).

The glory of God is most clearly seen in life that honors God and other people with steadfast love.

South and east of Salem, Oregon, near Bend, one may find a cluster of three mountains called Sisters. Now most often called simply North, Middle, and South, these three were once known as Faith, Hope, and Charity. These stratovolcanoes may be imagined to remind us of life in community.

An essential facet of our health as Christ followers is the embrace of the Christian community. Another is the adoption and incarnation of a Chris-

CARE FOR SOULS

tian ethic in home, family, workplace, and neighborhood. At the center of them all is the embrace of our Lord Jesus himself, knowing the Christ as Savior, following his Spirit daily as our Lord.

That life of discipleship occurs in us as we engage the Christ life together with other followers of Jesus. That life becomes contagious to the lives of our colleagues and friends as it continually penetrates the varied facets of who we are becoming in Christ Jesus.

And so, I imagine the view of the three Sisters Mountains as an indicator of the disciple-growing, disciple-making life depicted in the Great Commission:

Now the eleven disciples went to Galilee, to the mountain to which Jesus had directed them. When they saw him, they worshiped him; but some doubted. And Jesus came and said to them, "All authority in heaven and on earth has been given to me. Go therefore and make disciples of all nations, baptizing them in the name of the Father and the Son and of the Holy Spirit, and teaching them to obey everything that I have commanded you. And remember, I am with you always, to the end of the age" (Matt 28:16–20).

These two words from our Lord are the "peaks" most commonly identified as we seek to honor Jesus' teaching by shaping our community life by his priorities. Yet a third peak may be identified that fills out a more holistic picture of our Lord's care for the people of the world.

Our final Cascade peak for review is my personal favorite, Mount Saint Helens. Saint Helens is a broken mountain. In the cataclysmic explosion of Sunday, May 18, 1980, at 8:32 AM, she lost more than one thousand feet of elevation. Saint Helens is a recovering mountain. The vista of virtual "moonscapes" restored by the creative genius of the natural order is breathtaking. It is a miracle of life from ashes.

Fifty-seven people are known to have perished on that Sunday morning decades ago. David Johnston, a USGS geologist who had predicted the eruption, is memorialized by the visitor center nearest the crater and by his final words as the fury engulfed him, "Vancouver, this is it!" Irascible Harry Truman, pink convertible and all, lost his life due to his refusal to leave his beloved Spirit Lake Lodge. A number of lives were spared because their tree-planting crew worked the south slope that bright Sunday morning rather than the north slope that the eruption scarred.

Brokenness in the hands of a loving God holds potential for the birth of great compassion. So, I allow Mount Saint Helens to suggest to me the great compassion of our Lord:

> "Then the king will say to those at his right hand, 'Come you that are blessed by my Father, inherit the kingdom prepared for you from the foundation of the world; for I was hungry and you gave me food, I was thirsty and you gave me something to drink, I was a stranger and you welcomed me, I was naked and you gave me clothing, I was sick and you took care of me, I was in prison and you visited me.'" (Matt 25:34–36)

Our aim is lofty, our aspirations of the highest order. We desire, with the help of God, to shape a community of God's people that provides holistic care for the world and her peoples. The mandate to make disciples becomes wedded together with the charge to "visit the sick…feed the hungry…clothe the naked." No more segmentations of our compassion for others is desired! We are sent forth into the world as ambassadors of the living Christ to love God with all that we are as we love our neighbor holistically in dimensions of physical, emotional, mental, spiritual, and community need.

Viewing the three peaks of Jesus' word to us together may help to shape a more holistic community and Christ followers with a better rounded care for the persons who journey with them in this world. What would a three-peaks approach to ministry mean in your local fellowship?

Healthy Living in Christian Community

Where were you on the morning of Tuesday, September 11, 2001? I had just come from an uplifting breakfast with twenty-five to thirty pastor's prayer partners when I heard the stunning news of the terrorist attacks in Washington, DC, and New York City. A question not often asked but of interest is, Where were you on Sunday, September 16, 2001? More Americans than average were found in a house of worship. Our own congregation (usually around five hundred people at that time) swelled by one hundred persons on that occasion.

We were working our way through the *paraclete* passages of John 14–17 in that season. My message that day reflected the passage. Out of the ashes of 9/11 had arisen scores of heroic stories; some like Father Mychal Judge's (who himself was killed as he pronounced last rites on a victim) we knew, but others are known only to God. There were three hundred plus firefighters and more than forty police officers who lost their lives. That week, I had been fortunate to overhear a conversation between two women of distinction and service in our community. Their conversation summed up my message for September 16, 2001: Sister Cook said, "Life is real." Sister Pistole replied, "And God is good." And I said, "We will trust God."

Thank God that every Sunday is not September 16, 2001, but a significant opportunity to provide care for souls occurs each Sunday morning (or Saturday night) in your local church. The exciting yet sometimes grueling opportunity of bringing the riches of God's eternal Word to bear upon the vexing and challenging conditions of human life in community face each preaching pastor and worshipping community each Lord's Day.

In recent decades, we have crafted worship in the key of sensitivity to the seeker and at times in the key of praise. What would worship look like in the key of care? That is, care for all the people that God is entrusting to your ministry, both today and tomorrow. While a concern for numerical growth in the community of faith holds import, such concern needs to be held in dynamic tension with health-related issues of the body. Max De Pree aids the focus of a caring leader: "The measure of leadership is not the quality of the head, but the tone of the body. The signs of outstanding leadership appear primarily among the followers. Are the followers reaching their potential? Are they learning? Serving? Do they achieve the required results? Do they change with grace? Manage conflict?" (De Pree 1989, 12).

The Psalms provide a rich resource for tapping into the varied tapestry of human experience, both in terms of God's rich presence and in God's palpable absence: Psalms that lead us from sites of despair to lands of victory; from deep lament to resolute faith; from failed human response to the unending assurance of our Lord's steadfast love.

I sometimes grow weary in my work as a pastor. But I have yet to weary of the joyful discipline of discovering afresh what God is revealing to us through the Word and laboring with the people of God to understand what that Word means for our journey with God today.

Expressing care for the people with whom we share the worship experience grows from a fundamental shift in motivation. I have yet to meet a pastor who did not want to do a good job in proclaiming God's word, shaping worship that provided meaningful avenues of response by God's people, and set an atmosphere where healthy love for God and others matured. For me, it has been a liberating experience to move from a potentially self-centered motivation that may be expressed by the question, How am I doing? to a more externally-focused motivation that asks, How are we doing?

Our prayers move from a focus upon ourselves and our performance to ones more like these: "Lord, grant the word that our community most needs this day!" A prayer of old takes us beyond a self-centered focus to one that expresses the heart of a community that is getting well: "Lord, grant the measure of success that will most give you glory. Amen."

The healthy Christ follower finds meaningful expression and participation in the worshiping life of a local body of God's people. As Paul prepared to leave the saints at Ephesus, he gave witness to his ministry among them in one of the more poignant New Testament passages:

You yourselves know how I lived among you the entire time from the first day that I set foot in Asia, serving the Lord with all humility and with tears, enduring the trials that came to me through the plots of the Jews. I did not shrink from doing anything helpful, proclaiming the message to you and teaching you publicly and from house to house as I testified to both Jews and Greeks about repentance toward God and faith toward our Lord Jesus" (Acts 20:18b–21).

The apostle's practice exemplifies caring ministry in two arenas of life together: (1) He held nothing back that would be for their good as he taught and led them in public; this would be a parallel to our large group gatherings in community for worship and teaching. (2) He also taught them from house to house; that is, in the smaller group where we know and are known, they experienced intimate, soul fellowship captured by the word *koinonia*.

In this chapter, I take the position that care for souls occurs best in a holistic approach to ministry that heeds and expresses Christ's Great Command and Great Commission in vital relationship with the descriptive lifestyle of the Christ community we find in Matthew 25:31–40, what I like to call the Great Compassion.

Now we move into those key contexts of Christian experience that shape the healthy soul. Here again we identify three of them: the large group or worshiping community, described above; secondly, the small group, house group, or circle of care; and finally, the ministry activity of the Christ follower both within the Christian fellowship and to the wider world.

As a college senior, my life was transformed by an experience of community led by Pastor Rick Pressell. Though I was not a regular participant at Park Place Church of God as a student, I was invited to join a group of about a dozen students aimed at personal and spiritual growth through affirmation. Though we did not know one another well at the outset, the group process walked us through exercises of history giving, self-identification of strengths, and affirmation of same by one another. In a few weeks, we attained a high level of trust and comfort with one another. The experience yielded a dramatic impact upon my self-image. This group called forth abilities that I barely knew were resident. They named potentials that I may have hoped for but would have been hesitant to claim. This small group changed my life!

I have participated in multiple small group settings since that time. For me, none has been better than that one, illustrating the truth that life change happens in small groups.

Next Steps to Ministry

In the booklet *Beginnings: Six Sessions to Become a Support Group*, Lyman Coleman provides a picture of the process that a small group traverses to experience community. He utilizes the picture of a baseball diamond to depict the process (Coleman 1987, 9):

- First base: Telling your story to one another—your childhood, your journey, your hopes, and your dreams for the future.
- Second base: Responding to each other's story with positive appreciation and affirmation.
- Third base: Going deeper in your story—your present struggles, roadblocks, anxieties and where you need help from God and the group.
- Home plate: Genuine support group.

Elsewhere, Coleman describes home plate as *koinonia*, or "deep soul fellowship."

Participation with the Christ community in life-giving, life-expressing worship and participation with a smaller circle of persons in soul fellowship holds fertile promise for life transformation.

Kelli Lander brought vibrant life and energy to our community at Warner Pacific College when she came to our small college as a freshman. Participation in on-campus life had been at a low ebb. Kelli and her classmates helped revive a vital spirit of community among us. She enrolled as a major in religion and Christian ministries and expressed strong interest in missions.

As her academic advisor, it became my responsibility to interact with Kelli about her course schedule and progress toward life goals. A year or so into her course of study, she decided to change her major to health and human kinetics. Though our department "needed" more majors, it was apparent that Kelli needed to follow a different course. I readily acceded to her request. This new major along with preparation to teach in secondary classroom would provide a teaching credential for Kelli.

She retained her interest in missions and so enrolled in a course using the materials from Perspectives on the World Christian Movement[2] from the U.S. Center for World Mission in Pasadena, California. I had the privilege of facilitating the course, and we enjoyed the presence and insights of Kathi Sellers, a Church of God missionary on home assignment from Costa Rica. About a dozen of us made the journey together. Since I had not taken the course myself prior to this time, I felt that I had as much to learn as the students.

In my view, the class became as much like a small group as any academic course that I have taught. The conversation, interaction about life-changing topics raised by the course, and personal applications held deep significance. A lay couple, Rick and Jeri Kemmer, who participated that semester, went on to serve in Africa.

In time, Kelli married a young electrician from her home congregation, Ben Shular. After Kelli's graduation, she and Ben took up life responsibilities in Vancouver, Washington. Some time later, I encountered Ben and Kelli at a gathering for missionaries in Indiana. I was elated to learn that Kelli and Ben had applied to serve as missionaries in Africa. One year after that, during the North American Convention of the Church of God, Kelli and Ben were commissioned to Africa.

Life change happens in small groups. And that change directs us toward service to Christ in the church and in the world.

Both *who* God makes us in Christ and *how* God made us as people give shape to our service to Christ. The apostle Paul writes:

Now there are varieties of gifts, but the same Spirit; and there are varieties of services, but the same Lord; and there are varieties of activities, but it is the same God who activates all of them in everyone. To each is given the manifestation of the Spirit for the common good (1 Cor 12:4–7).

For by grace you have been saved through faith, and this is not your own doing; it is the gift of God-not the result of works, that no one may boast. For we are what he has made us, created in Christ Jesus for good works, which God prepared beforehand to be our way of life (Eph 2:8–10).

As we make this journey with Christ and with the people of God, the shape of our service is formed and informed by the persons that we are:

Do not give to the poor expecting to get their gratitude so that you can feel good about yourself. If you do, your giving will be thin and short-lived, and that is not what the poor need, it will only impoverish them further! Give only if you have something you must give; give only if you are someone for whom giving is its own reward (Dorothy Day, cited in Palmer 2000, 48).

There is one additional thread that informs our *diakonia*. That thread is the need of the community. Our spiritual gift is for the common good. Our vocation is aimed at the world's deep need. Here, we get beyond ourselves to serve the need of the community that surrounds and supports us and the world dying for the bread of good news.

The need for Christ followers to penetrate and leaven Western culture has never been greater. The opportunity to shine as Christ's light is distinct. The need for salt that preserves and flavors is crucial. The outcome of our life in the Christ community may take varied expression.

Arenas of Service in the World

The Bible asserts that Christ followers are built together as "a spiritual house, to be a holy priesthood, to offer spiritual sacrifices acceptable to God through Jesus Christ" (1 Pet 2:5). This priesthood of all believers affirms that each follower of Christ holds potential for service to the world in the name and spirit of Christ. Our lives are to express a call to leave the kingdom of darkness for God's marvelous light (1 Pet 2:9). Each believer, regardless of occupation may do their work as unto the Lord giving glory to God.

Diehl, in his book *Ministry in Daily Life*, examines four aspects of our lives in which we seek to allow the glory of God to shine through. The first arena is occupation. Occupation has to do with that role in which we invest most of our time. During our most active years this role may metamorphose from life as a student to the role in our work place to our most significant time investment in retirement.

Work, though in many ways now distorted by the fall, is a gift from God given prior to sin's entry into the human condition (see Gen 2:15). In our occupation, we have the greatest opportunity to bring glory to God and to serve the good of our neighbor. Obviously, baser pursuits may mar our efforts. Frederick Buechner suggests that "vocation is where my deep joy meets the world's deep need" (1993, 119). That person is doubly-blessed who enjoys the favor of expressing their vocation through their occupation.

Dorothy Sayers speaks to the story of good work done in response to God's great love in Christ: "…work is not, primarily, a thing one does to live, but the thing one lives to do. It is, or should be, the full expression of the worker's faculties, the thing in which he finds spiritual, mental, and bodily satisfaction, and the medium in which he offers himself to God" (1949, 53).

A second arena of concern and involvement is our life in home and family. For many Christ followers, this is an area of great challenge and struggle. Those who pursue a life in Christian ministry are not exempt from the struggle. Indeed, our quest to give priority to our spouse and family may be complicated by the demands of a great cause, expansion of the kingdom of God.

A daughter of a world Christian leader who is at peace with her father's priority on ministry at the cost of his family said to me recently, "Near the end of his life, my father said to me, 'My one regret is that you never had the opportunity to know your father.'" These poignant words speak volumes about one father's regret and one daughter's loss. However, they are not alone.

The provision of a consistent day off apart from parish responsibilities, regular focused times with a spouse, a priority upon the needs of our children is the bare minimum for building health in relationship to home and family.

While it is not uncommon to conceive of a call to serve God in pastoral ministry or in another particular line of work, it is rare to hear a person speak of his or her call as a husband or wife, a father or mother. Priority attention to the persons of this most important arena of our living will set a worthy example for others and enrich the living of our families immeasurably. It is not possible to attain quality time with others apart from a sufficient quantity of time invested with one another.

Next Steps to Ministry

A third arena is that of service in one's own community. The challenge to think globally and act locally calls us to consider strategic service in our own neighborhood. The reality that the world has come to us in North America for education or employment or simply with hope for a better life provides opportunities to be on mission without ever leaving our own home area. The strategic priority of the needs of children in our time heighten the possible meaning of one hour each week given to a child as a tutor, a reading buddy, or a mentor of some other description. Caring for others and their needs is a significant expression of the good news, but it is also a means of attaining and maintaining health in one's own soul.

A fourth arena of service is that of service to church and the world. 1 Corinthians 12:7 places the gifts of the Spirit in proper relationship to the community of faith. Gifts, of course, are given for the benefit of another more than our own satisfaction (see 1 Cor 12:4–7). The purpose of our giftedness in the Christ community is the common good. A prayer to pray early and often in our journey with Christ is one that yearns to be of greatest use for the kingdom of God.

As we are concerned for the wholeness of our people, we shepherd a concern for the wholeness of the expression of their lives in the world: occupation, home and family, neighborhood, church, and world.

That we should hold such widespread concern for God's people and for God's world is to be expected given the gospel. Each of us holds responsibility and presence as Christ followers in each of these arenas. Some may expend most of their time or energy in one or two of them. Yet we each hold potential to make impact for Christ in each arena.

The care of souls not only has to do with the care of the particular individual placed before me, but also in shaping the character of a community that lives in readiness to express the varied facets of gospel presence (loving, witnessing, serving) in terms of holy love (for God, for one another, for the least and the lost). This spirit and life and ethos must be shaped in communities of faith that are themselves growing toward health: in the corporate worship of God, in the multiplication of healthy circles of people experiencing soul fellowship, and in growing Christ followers who will serve God's kingdom in their occupation, in their family, in their community, and through their church.

A healthy community grows peoples with concern for the whole person. The varied dimensions of Christ's mandate for the world find expression in their common life and ministry.

One of the pitfalls that we face in pastoral ministry is to seek to use persons to meet our needs to run an effective program. Here, our concern shifts to a primary focus on the well-being of the servant of God. We grow in concern for the serving person's intake of spiritual nourishment in worship and in small group as well as fit expression of her graces and gifts in service to church and world. How would you measure the health of the people of your church and the range of your community's service to Christ in the world?

Meeting the Lord at Gateway Moments

Our journey through life is marked by gateway passages to a new chapter in our journey with God. One of the unique privileges of a life in Christian ministry is the high honor of walking in intimacy with the people of God at these moments. Faithful ministry at these junctures aids spiritual birth, growth, and development and provides the platform for further life-giving ministry with the persons involved.

Birth

As November 22, 1963, and September 11, 2001, are days etched indelibly on my memory due to national tragedy, Friday, November 12, 1982, is there due to personal and family joy. Just after noon in a Catholic hospital in suburban Detroit, our Iranian-born obstetrician-gynecologist chided the nun present at our daughter's birth with the words, "The priest has a daughter." There are several particular moments of that chilly fall weekend that stand out in my memory, but none more so than the moment when I moved to the warming tray where our newborn lay and extended a finger that she squeezed with all the might of her delivery-room grasp.

Next Steps to Ministry

Such moments are alive with the presence of God and the sense that one has been witness to a miracle. A visit by a pastor that expresses and embodies the care of a whole community makes it easy for the parents to express the thanksgiving within their hearts. That opportunity and need for connection with God is just as present when all is not well and a little life hangs in the balance.

This is an appropriate time for me to say to you, that as a pastor of a community of God's people, you hold a noble trust. In a very real sense, you embody the presence of that community's concern and joy with the family of the newborn. Secondly, you embody the presence of the Christ with them. I urge you to hold and exercise that trust with respect and with care. It is only yours for a time. You stand as ambassador of the Christ in this life situation. Your servanthood and willingness to call the newborn's family to a closer walk with Christ across the bridge of relationship is strategic. Effective service at this gateway moment sets the stage for future ministry to be welcomed, appreciated, and maximized in the lives of those that you will serve.

To the discerning spirit, the life moment of becoming a parent is a ripe opportunity for spiritual growth. Midst the demands of through-the-night feedings, diaper changes, and energy now re-directed to the welfare of a new life, God comes to call to a new level of consecration to the Kingdom. The true paradox of parenting as a moment of spiritual growth is seen both in what one is called to pick up and what one is called to place in the hand of God.

At our daughter's dedication, we recognized that we now held a weighty responsibility in living Christ before her and teaching her the faith by deed and word. At the same moment, we recognized that the little one who grasped my finger so tightly in the delivery room belonged to another with hands larger, firmer, and more able than ours. And so, we placed her life in the hand of the Father. That moment of surrender held within it the seed of every surrender of her life to the care of the Lord since that day.

Deuteronomy 6:4–9 unpacks the opportunity and responsibility of the faithful parent: "Hear, O Israel: The Lord is our God, the Lord alone. You shall love the Lord your God with all your heart, and with all your soul, and with all your might. Keep these words that I am commanding you today in your heart. Recite them to your children and talk about them when you are at home and when you are away, when you lie down and when you rise. Bind them as a sign on your hand, fix them as an emblem on your forehead, and write them on the doorposts of your house and on your gates." A ministry that not only calls parents to take up the responsibility of forming faith in their little ones but also provides tools and equipping for doing so, will be highly valued by parents on the journey of faith.

"Parents have both extraordinary influence and extraordinary responsibility in the religious education of their children. Not only may moral virtues be taught early, such as courage, honesty, prudence, compassion, and temperance, but also intellectual virtues, habits of consistency and of looking for good evidence, habits of order and precision of thought. These are basic patterns that can be engendered more effectively by parents than anyone else" (Oden 1983, 146).

Baptism

Recall with me the time of your baptism. What meanings stand out most prominently for you? Baptism in water reflects our intent to follow Jesus throughout life. The experience communicates the burial of an old life and resurrection to new life. It is an act of witness to others that Christ lives in us. By following Christ in baptism, we identify ourselves with the Christ community, the church; further, as with our Lord's experience, we make ourselves available to God to fulfill the service to others that God intends for our living.

One might summarize baptism as an act reflecting the experience of new life and expressing the intent to follow Christ in a servant life. Psalm 2:7 and Isaiah 42:1 most likely lie in the background of the Father's word of approval for his Son: "You are my Son, the Beloved; with you I am well pleased" (Luke 3:22b). As Jesus' baptism comes at the threshold of his earthly ministry, our water baptism stands as the moment when the Christ follower answers the call to a servant life.

One may see the rhythm of healthy Christian living in active participation with other believers in worship, fellowship, and service. Again, here, at baptism, that same rhythm of health is discerned: we receive new life from our Lord, and we express the grace of that life in service to others. Working with persons at the moment of baptism provides a fresh opportunity not only to explore the dimensions of life now received but also to explore how that shared life from Christ will be poured out in the world.

Where baptism is conceived of as response to God's call to all his children to serve, revisiting one's baptism becomes a reencounter with the first flush of our love for the triune God: the sacrifice of Jesus for us, the warm presence of God's Spirit who woos us to life and service, the security of God's care and superintendence of our life for good purpose. These combined facets of our Lord's care for us lay bare our motivation to love and to serve our God.

Water baptism thus experienced, at any age, becomes a living paradigm of warm experience with God that gives rise to grateful service to the Savior!

Marriage

Marriage is the good gift of God for a lifelong covenant of love between a man and a woman. Marriage provides the most searching examination of one's soul and character. Daily, a mirror is held up to our behavior and attitudes through the intimacy of relationship with our beloved. Again, we encounter a life gateway rich with possibilities for spiritual growth, strewn with pitfalls wherein relationships often founder and die. One of our strategic opportunities in pastoral ministry is to serve premarital couples with credible and faithful counsel. In part, this counsel aims at the prevention of unrealistic expectations; positively, it aims at the formation of healthy patterns of communication. The overall yield of faithful premarital work is, at its best, the opportunity to continue a close, helping relationship with the couple as they progress in their marriage. The commitment to a check-up visit three to six months after the wedding is one of the more strategic steps a pastor may take in providing excellent care for newly married couples.

The scripture instructs us that in marriage, "a man leaves his father and mother and clings to his wife, and they become one flesh" (Gen 2:24). A life of growing intimacy will be aided by the discovery of as many expectations as possible prior to marriage. These unspoken assumptions range from the mundane to the sublime: Does one squeeze a toothpaste tube from the end or the middle? Will we seek to have children? If so, how many? Money, sex, and in-laws remain perennial topics of potential conflict: Who will manage our money and why? How often do you anticipate the joys of sexual intercourse? What role will your mate's parents play in your life? In his or her life? In our life together? The same set of questions for relationship applies to your own parents. These few questions are meant to be suggestive of a range of topics that you will want to address in a series of premarital conversations.

Over time, you will discover resources to aid your ministry with premarital couples. Currently, I am finding resources prepared by Drs. Les and Leslie Parrott of Seattle Pacific University[3] to be of consistent quality with relevant and helpful content. As you become aware of couples in your congregation or community with healthy marriages, you may want to structure a mentoring role for them with a premarital or newly married couple. Well-placed matches of this kind will complement your work with the couple in multiple ways: the opportunity to interact with another person(s) about faithful marriage, an additional model for marital health, a multiplied circle of concern for the new couple.

It is primarily your responsibility as officiating minister to see that the ceremony retains the character of a service of Christian worship. The inclusion of appropriate music that honors God and elevates the meaning of marital love, acts that include and call the congregation to active, ongoing support of the couple, and words of scripture specially chosen and crafted for this particular occasion will heighten the couple's special day.

Death

The pattern that emerges in healthy, caring Christian ministry is that competent and caring service at life's gateway moments yields an open door to further ministry when life's inevitable challenges and opportunities unfold. Each of you will need to discover a pattern of service that fits who you are. Regardless of personality or working style, our ministry of faithful presence provides foundation for all that follows. We embody the presence and blessing of Christ and the community of faith at life's special moments. This is a particular uniqueness of a life in Christian ministry.

Yesterday, an older woman in the life of our congregation went to be with the Lord. Her husband, a very expressive man, spoke of the experience as being "flooded" by the care of his family, the medical personnel, and our church. He named family members and beloved friends that circled his wife's death bed. When he came to me, his words reflected the role of the pastor in embodying the presence of the congregation: "Through you, the whole church is here."

Ministry with dying persons and with the loved ones who surround them provides particularly fertile opportunity to experience and share the love of Christ. Awareness of the stages of response to one's own death was given classic expression by Elisabeth Kubler-Ross (1969). She identified five stages that are commonly, though not always, experienced. The stages identified included: first, denial and isolation; second, anger; third, bargaining; fourth, depression; fifth, acceptance. As you walk closely with another in an experience of death, you will be able to identify evidences of these stages of work toward acceptance. Knowledge of such matters is not given for the purpose of labeling another but in order to calibrate our ministry with them according to where they are living.

One priority to keep in mind when death comes is to aim at a brief time of presence with the family as soon as possible. As your presence signifies the presence of Christ and the Christ community throughout life, this is even more palpably felt at the time of death.

In preparation for a memorial or funeral service, I have found it helpful to schedule a time with intimate family members to invite their memories and stories of the life of the one who has died. Such stories, occasionally shared at the service by a family member or woven into the pastor's remarks, lend fresh insights into life as this person has lived it. You do want to comfort the family and friends, but they must recognize the person of whom you speak.

I regard the invitation to officiate at a funeral as an opportunity to proclaim the good news of Christ in terms of the life now completed. I attempt to open myself to a particular word of scripture that may capture some facet of the essence of this person's life with God. In most cases, I am addressing a life lived with Christ. Regardless of whether the life has been lived with Christ, the presence of our Lord and a word that speaks to the particular situation is always present. It is our assignment to listen for the Spirit's leading in bringing a word from God that this person's life helps to reveal.

Care for loved ones following death happens best in a community that knows and is involved meaningfully with one another prior to the passing. Here again, the benefit of living in meaningful fellowship in a class, group, or circle of people shines forth. The opportunity for the body of Christ to open arms and hearts and to meet practical needs (for presence, for food, for transportation) at this strategic moment is a significant opportunity to fold another into life with Christ.

Ongoing recovery from grief is personally experienced and does not always fit to a universal calendar. Nonetheless, in the initial grieving period, it is crucial to encourage expression of emotion, both tears and whatever anger is present, in settings that are safe and with persons who are enabled to understand. The healthy expression of emotion clears the way for the griever, over time, to come to terms with the loved one's death and to accept the reality of their passing. Many describe the experience of grief in terms of ocean waves that come unbidden and with varying degrees of strength. As one moves through the process of grief in a healthy manner, the waves will subside over time.

Ultimately, having come to a place of acceptance of the death, the grieving person now finds fresh opportunity to invest time, emotion, and energy in new ways and people. Though life will never be the same again, a page has been turned and a new chapter of living with God and with others is now possible. Large decisions of change in one's life (selling a home, moving to another city, marrying again) are typically inadvisable until after one has grieved well and fully. The Christian community, by intentional ministry, in small group life, and through direct relationship of pastors and caregivers may facilitate greater health in the lives of those most directly affected by death.

A Context for Care of Souls: A Healthy Community of God's People

This essay aims to place the care of souls in the context of the faith community, a balanced and healthy one where persons may experience God's grace in a full way and share that grace with others in a manner that is fit both to the giver and the receiver. The fact that we never fully arrive here in this life need not deter our efforts to that end. And it serves only to heighten anticipation of that day when our faith shall be sight and we find ourselves at home in the city of God:

Then the angel showed me the river of water of life, bright as crystal, flowing from the throne of God and of the Lamb through the middle of the street of the city. On either side of the river is the tree of life with its twelve kinds of fruit, producing its fruit each month; and the leaves of the tree are for the healing of the nations. Nothing accursed will be found there any more. But the throne of God and of the Lamb will be in it, and his servants will worship him; they will see his face, and his name will be on their foreheads. And there will be no more night; they need no light of lamp or sun, for the Lord God will be their light, and they will reign forever and ever (Rev 22:1–5).

May God speed our efforts to build communities where souls receive Christ's care and lives are made new!

Endnotes

[1] For information from the United States Geological Service on these mountains, see http://vulcan.wr.usgs.gov.
[2] The Web site is www.perspectives.org.
[3] See Reference List.

Reference List

Bonhoeffer, Dietrich. 1954. *Life Together: A Discussion of Christian Fellowship.* Translated by John W. Doberstein. New York: Harper. [Small Groups]

Buechner, Frederick. 1993. *Wishful Thinking*. San Francisco: Harper.
Coleman, Lyman. 1987. *Beginnings: Six Sessions to Become a Support Group*. Nashville, TN: Serendipity House. [Small Groups]
De Pree, Max. 1989. *Leadership Is an Art*. New York: Doubleday. [The Church]
Diehl, William E. 1996. *Ministry in Daily Life: A Practical Guide for Congregations*. Bethseda, MD: The Alban Institute. [Ministry of the People of God]
Donahue, Bill. 1996. *The Willow Creek Guide to Leading Life-Changing Small Groups*. Grand Rapids, MI: Zondervan. [Small Groups]
Ferguson, David. 2004. *Relational Foundations: Experiencing Relevance in Life and Ministry*. Relationship Press. [The Church]
Frymire, Jeffery W. 2006. *Preaching the Story: How to Communicate God's Word through Narrative Sermons*. Anderson, IN: Warner Press. [Preaching]
Haugk, Kenneth C. 1984. *Christian Caregiving: A Way of Life*. Minneapolis, MN: Augsburg Publishing House. [Caregiving]
Icenogle, Gareth Weldon. 1994. *Biblical Foundations for Small Group Ministry: An Integrative Approach*. Downer's Grove, IL: InterVarsity Press. [Small Groups]
Jackson, Edgar Newman. 1957. *Understanding Grief: Its Roots, Dynamics, and Treatment*. New York: Abingdon Press. [Caregiving]
Kubler-Ross, Elisabeth. 1969.*On Death and Dying*. New York: MacMillian. [Caregiving]
Oden, Thomas C. 1983. *Pastoral Theology: Essentials of Ministry*. San Francisco: Harper and Row.
Palmer, Parker J. 2000. *Let Your Life Speak: Listening for the Voice of Vocation*. San Francisco: Jossey-Bass. [Ministry of the People of God]
Parrott, Les, III, and Leslie Parrott. 1995. *Saving Your Marriage Before It Starts: A Marriage Curriculum for Engaged, About-to-Be Engaged, and the Newly Married*. Grand Rapids, MI: Zondervan. [Relationships]
———. 1997. *Mentoring Engaged and Newlywed Couples: A Small Group Video Curriculum for Recruiting and Training Couples*. Grand Rapids, MI: Zondervan. [Relationships]
———. 1998. *Relationships: How to Make Bad Relationships Better and Good Relationships Great*. Grand Rapids, MI: Zondervan. [Relationships]

Next Steps to Ministry

Pitt-Watson, Ian. 1999. *A Primer for Preachers.* Grand Rapids, MI: Baker Books. [Preaching]

Sayers, Dorothy L. 1949. Why Work? In *Creed or Chaos?* New York: Harcourt Brace and Company: 46–62. [Ministry of the People of God]

Schwarz, Christian A. 1996. *Natural Church Development: A Guide to Eight Essential Qualities of Healthy Churches.* Carol Stream, IL: ChurchSmart Resources. [The Church]

Trueblood, Elton. 1961. *The Company of the Committed.* New York: Harper. [Ministry of the People of God]

———. 1975. *The Common Ventures of Life: Marriage Birth, Work and Death.* New York: Harper. [Caregiving]

United Methodist Church (U.S.). 1992. *United Methodist Book of Worship: Pastor's Pocket Edition.* Nashville, TN: United Methodist Publishing House. [Relationships]

Warren, Rick. 1995. *The Purpose Driven Church: Growth without Compromising Your Message and Mission.* Grand Rapids, MI: Zondervan. [The Church]

Other Resources

Stephen Ministries. http://stephenministries.org [Caregiving]

Chapter Eleven:
Steven L. Rennick: *Equip for Ministry*

The Story

His name was Orville. He was just past middle age and balding, and had false teeth and a bit of a paunch, a little belly. And he drove one of those terrible 1970s-era long-nosed Plymouths. Me? I was a fifteen-year-old teenager with a full head of hair and all my teeth. I played tennis, umpired farm-club baseball, and (most importantly to me) had a 1965 Mustang. Furthermore, he was a pastor, a preacher at a local church. Me? I was not from a church-going family, was still overcoming some of the more obvious habits of my life that were not on a church-approved habit list, and leaned toward a free-spirited attitude and approach to life. We were as much of an odd couple as Jack Klugman and Tony Randall.[1] Yet somehow something strangely unusual grew between us, and because of him, my life was shaped and changed forever. How can that be?

On the surface, no one would have connected us. There were plenty of other adults and even teens in whom Orville could have invested his life. And for my part, he seemed far from the normal role models of that era—action hero Indiana Jones and baseball players George Brett and Reggie Jackson. But as so often is the case, life is not lived out on the surface level, but on a much deeper level.

I had been a Christian for less than a year. It was a tumultuous transformation that was much more at a just-beginning stage rather than a nearly-complete stage. I had struggles with drinking, cussing, attitude, and actions. Yet there was burning within me a spiritual desire—a hungering

Next Steps to Ministry

and thirsting for something more than life was offering. I was finding this in my relationship with Jesus Christ and in connections (fellowship) in the church. Relationships were forming, and I was being formed by them. I had experienced what I knew was a certain calling to Christian ministry. I went to my pastor, Orville, and shared this with him. His response was not to discount the validity of the call. Rather, he confirmed it. He reassured me that God does indeed call people, even people like me, to ministry and that part of his own calling and role as a pastor was to equip people for ministry. I was amazed.

Orville offered to meet with me in an ongoing basis. Not just this one time to discuss what had brought me to him, but also to meet together, pray and study together, and actually "do ministry" together.

My internal response was something like, "Me? Him? Together?" I knew that it wasn't my idea—it was his—and that it wasn't at my initiative—it was his. What I didn't know then was that it wasn't only my opportunity—it was his as well.

Orville and I began to meet together every Saturday morning. We did so for nearly one and a half years. I seldom knew in advance what we would be doing. I would go to his office at the church around eight o'clock or so. We would sit together and talk. He would ask me about my week, school, and life. He would ask me about my Bible reading. What had I read that week? How often had I read? What was I learning from the Bible? What questions did I have from this reading and learning? We would just sit together and talk. We would talk for a few minutes at the minimum. But as time went on, we would talk more and more, sometimes for an hour or more. He drilled into me that I needed daily Bible reading, study, and prayer. These were the primary sources of my spiritual nourishment. Indeed, from Orville's perspective (which became my own), I needed to nourish my soul with the Bible and prayer every day even as my own physical body required healthy, daily nourishment.

After talking together, Orville would ask me to pray with him. He would open up his life. He would ask me to pray for him as a husband and as a father. His wife Ruth was a wonderful lady, and he was very blessed to be married to her and have her as a partner in ministry. We would pray for her, especially for her health as she had a recurring heart condition. We would also pray for their children. They were all older than me. Several had made and were making decisions in life that were not in line with their parents' faith. In fact, Orville and Ruth were raising one of their own grandchildren. Orville trusted me. I could feel it. I knew that because he openly shared with me his own life. I was amazed.

He would ask me how he could pray with me. He did not talk but would listen to me as I talked about my own life, my own family, my own struggles, and my own occasional victories. He would allow me to share week by week as much or as little as I chose. He discovered that I often took a little while to figure out how to express what I wanted to say. He was patient with me. He knew that I did not have the language, words, or terms to convey my life experiences. I was learning to talk about faith out loud, even when I did not realize it. After I had shared, and he had often asked probing, but not intrusive, questions, we would pray together. Our prayer positions would change from week to week. Sometimes we went into the sanctuary and would kneel at the altars. Sometimes we would kneel right there in his office. And most often we would just bow our heads and pray where we were seated. Our prayer times would sometimes be short with each of us praying one time. At other times we would pray longer, taking turns praying, always praying out loud. I was amazed.

Our activities together were never chosen by me. Orville would have things to do, and we would do them. They were not personal things. This was not casually hanging out or just accomplishing his own errands, like picking up dry cleaning or washing his car. Rather, these were the things he did as a pastor. He would take me with him. On the way, we would talk about where we were going, who we would be seeing, what the setting and discussion would likely be, and what he was hoping would happen.

These were often visits to people. Sometimes it was at a hospital where I would, at first, mostly sit and watch. Over time, he would invite me into the conversation. He would include me in the discussion. After I had witnessed him reading scriptures of encouragement to patients/parishioners, on later visits, he would ask me to read my choice of encouraging scriptures. Praying was always a part of these visits. And as it was with the reading of scriptures so it was with prayer: at first I watched him do it, and then he would invite me to participate. It was the common occurrence that once we were in the parking lot, he would talk with me about what we had just done, why we had done it, how important it was to the person, and even how God was pleased by such things. He would affirm the ways I had done things, things I had said, or the care I had expressed by my presence and prayers. He would help me to know how to compassionately care for people in more than one way, to think about other ways to be the presence of Christ to a person. I had never before had such thoughts. I was amazed.

Other visits were with people in their homes. I learned that these visits were often unpredictable, both inside and outside of the house. Once when we were outside of the city limits on a country road, we visited a family who had recently attended a worship service. On the way to the car, Orville tossed the keys to me. He told me that I could start the car. I couldn't believe it. I was only fifteen and didn't have my learner's permit yet. He let me sit behind the wheel of his car and start the engine. Then he got in on the passenger's side and told me that we were only going down the road about a quarter of a mile to the next house to visit and, "Why don't you drive us there?" All of a sudden it didn't matter that this was a long-nosed Plymouth and not a '65 Mustang—I was behind the wheel. Talk about amazed!

One Saturday morning following our normal discussion of Bible readings and prayer time together, Orville told me we were going to visit a lady whose adult grandchild came to our church; she had asked for him to come visit. He sensed that God was preparing her and us for an important visit. We prayed for her and our visit together. We drove to her house, and she warmly welcomed us in saying, "I've been waiting for you to come." Orville asked her why she had been waiting and she said, "Because I need someone to pray with me. I need to get my life right with God." We talked for a few minutes, and I remember Orville saying, "You know, we don't need to talk to one another as much as we need to talk to God about this." So, all three of us knelt down on our knees at her couch as she prayed for God's forgiveness and for a new life in Jesus Christ. Orville also prayed and he asked me to pray for her too. He informed her that the next day was Sunday and that he would like to share this very good news with the entire church in the worship service. She agreed, and we made plans about how this wonderful step of faith would be shared openly with everyone

Equip for Ministry

in the Sunday morning worship service. He told her that the angels were rejoicing, and we were too. She agreed. She was rejoicing, and she looked forward to tomorrow. The next day I arrived at church in time for Sunday School. I was a little bit early, but I was excited about this wonderful story that was about to be told in the worship service. When I went to see Orville, I was told he had just left in a hurry. There was an emergency and he was on his way to the hospital. I found out that the emergency was that this lady had died early that morning. Orville had gone to be with the family. In the informal setting of the fellowship hall, I began to tell the story of what had happened the day before in her home. Other people gathered as I was telling the story and I had to start over again to get them caught up. The word was spreading to people as they arrived for Sunday School, and I honestly cannot remember how many times I told that story again and again. I spoke of God's grace and timing. I thought of what a privilege was mine to be a part of God's work. And, yes, I was amazed.

These regular, weekly meetings went on for about one and a half years. Orville accepted a calling to another congregation, and our departure from one another was filled with many tears. I still have a scar on my left arm from a deep gouge I received while loading up the moving truck with Orville and Ruth's wooden furniture. Because of Orville's time with me, I had read of the young man Timothy in the New Testament. I had read those two letters that bear his name time and time again. Orville and I had discussed them repeatedly. In our departing words from one another, Orville told me, "You have been my Timothy." The Bible was not just a book to be read, filled with static statements and inert ideas. The Bible was alive in my life. Even in our good-bye, I was amazed.

The Reason

Why would Orville invest his Saturday mornings for a year and a half in an unchurched teenager? Why would he take the time to talk with me about the Bible, what I was reading, what I was learning? Why would he open his own life to me? Why would he allow me to share my life with him? Why would he pray with me week after week? Why would he take me with him to hospitals and people's homes? Why did he do all of this?

175

Next Steps to Ministry

He told me, and he showed me. He had me open my Bible and read aloud these verses. (I would encourage you, the reader, to also read these verses out loud.)

> It was he [Jesus] who gave some to be apostles, some to be prophets, some to be evangelists, and some to be pastors and teachers, to prepare God's people for works of service, so that the body of Christ may be built up until we all reach unity in the faith and in the knowledge of the Son of God and become mature, attaining to the whole measure of the fullness of Christ. (Eph 4:11–13 NIV)

Orville explained to me that one of his responsibilities as a pastor was to equip people for ministry. He said that it was not only a biblical responsibility but also a privilege to share his life with others. This dual responsibility and privilege resulted in others entering into and enjoying Christian ministry. And this is available not only to pastors but to everyone who would participate. He said that the job and role of the pastor was not to do all of the work of the ministry but to equip others to do the work of the ministry. Indeed, his job was primarily to enlist, equip, and empower as many people as possible to actively participate in ministry. And in fulfilling his biblical responsibilities as a pastor, he enjoyed helping others discover the joys of ministry—of serving others in the name of Christ.

Orville and I discussed Jesus' own teaching methods with his disciples, how Jesus never set up a blackboard in the front of the room and led boring lectures. Rather, he shared his life with the disciples. They would often pray together. Jesus would openly discuss with them as long as they wanted to talk. They shared their lives together. This is seen throughout the four Gospels and is explicit in readings from Mark:

> As Jesus walked beside the Sea of Galilee, he saw Simon and his brother Andrew casting a net into the lake, for they were fishermen. "Come, follow me," Jesus said, "and I will make you fishers of men." At once they left their nets and followed him. When he had gone a little farther, he saw James son of Zebedee and his brother John in a boat,

> and they left their father Zebedee in the boat with the hired men and followed him. (1:16–20 NIV)
>
> The apostles gathered around Jesus and reported to him all they had done and taught. Then, because so many people were coming and going that they did not even have a chance to eat, he said to them, "Come with me by yourselves to a quiet place and get some rest." (6:30–31 NIV)
>
> They went to a place called Gethsemane, and Jesus said to his disciples, "Sit here while I pray." (14:32 NIV)

This type of closely intertwined, shared life was not just for Jesus and the twelve disciples. Rather, this is the example that the New Testament lifts up for all learners in the ministry. Orville pointed once again to the relationship between Paul and Timothy: how Paul was the older, more experienced one of the two, and how much Paul trusted Timothy. Paul entrusted the church in Ephesus to the care and leadership of Timothy (1 Tim 1:3). As with Jesus and the disciples, so also Paul and Timothy had obviously been very open with one another because Paul knew just the right words of encouragement to share with Timothy, such as:

> Don't let anyone look down on you because you are young, but set an example for the believers in speech, in life, in love, in faith and in purity. Until I come, devote yourself to the public reading of Scripture, to preaching and to teaching. Do not neglect your gift, which was given you through a prophetic message when the body of elders laid their hands on you. Be diligent in these matters; give yourself wholly to them, so that everyone may see your progress. Watch your life and doctrine closely. Persevere in them, because if you do, you will save both yourself and your hearers. (1 Tim 4:12–16 NIV)
>
> I thank God, whom I serve, as my forefathers did, with a clear conscience, as night and day I constantly remember you in my prayers. Recalling your tears, I long to see you, so that I may be filled with joy. I have been reminded of

your sincere faith, which first lived in your grandmother Lois and in your mother Eunice and, I am persuaded, now lives in your also. For this reason I remind you to fan into flame the gift of God, which is in you through the laying on of my hands. For God did not give us a spirit of timidity, but a spirit of power, of love and of self-discipline. (2 Tim 1:3–7 NIV)

These two passages illuminate the closeness of the personal relationship between Paul and Timothy, and these words illustrate a shared life. I experienced this biblical pattern first in my own relationship with Orville and then came to understand it even better through the words of the Bible. This is why Orville invested his life in me. And even after more than twenty-five years have passed, I am still amazed.

The Method

For some reason, we often think that for something to be effective, it must also be correspondingly complicated. However, as with many other areas of life, becoming equipped for ministry does not require unnecessary complications.

It would have never occurred to Orville that what he was doing needed to be complicated. Indeed, he viewed his actions not as a new idea but as an ancient approach to teaching, learning, and equipping (not a bad definition for *discipling*). His thought would probably have been something like, Why don't more people just read these scriptures and apply them to their lives? Why don't more people just do what is so evident and plain in the Bible? Even after all of these years later—I am amazed.

I don't remember that Orville ever said it in quite the same way as I am about to write, but this is Orville's method written down in as succinct a way as I know. There are four simple steps to teach anyone anything. I know this sounds simplistic—and maybe it is—yet it is seldom done. This is simple. Anyone can do it, and you can teach anyone anything if you will adopt this life-changing approach.

4 Steps to Teach Anyone Anything
1. You come and watch me do it
2. You come and help me do it
3. I'll come and help you do it
4. I'll come and watch you do it

First, Orville simply asked me to come and watch him do life and ministry. He openly shared his life with me, and I shared my life with him. We discussed the Bible and life together. We prayed out loud and openly with and for one another. We did ministry together. We visited people. At first, I watched him do it. He would discuss it with me. He wanted me to know what he was doing and why he had done it. He allowed me to be present and observe.

Next, Orville asked me to help him in these visits. He would ask me to do a single part of a hospital visit. He would do this more than once. He would discuss it with me until I was more comfortable with it. Then he would ask me to do something else. At first, this was just being there, then talking with the person, then reading scriptures of encouragement to a person, and finally praying out loud with the person. Orville helped me to first see what to do and to then do each aspect of a visit, step by step, guiding, and coaching me along the way. What was he doing? He was helping me to do it.

Then he would allow me to take the lead on a visit. He would talk me through this in advance. We would discuss the visit together and then do the visit together. He would go with me. He would be there and would help as was appropriate and needed. But it was clear that I was actually taking the lead while he was present to help me have a good, caring, compassionate visit.

Finally, Orville would watch me and observe a visit. He would smile, make short contributions to a conversation, and afterwards affirm and encourage me. This did not happen quickly, but it did take place, methodically unfolding over time. I did not know all of this was happening at the time. In fact, it was only with hindsight that I caught the simple yet comprehensive approach to equipping for ministry.

These four steps happened in other areas as well, including preaching, teaching, administration, planning, time management, and more. They always took place in the context of a shared-life relationship connected to what we were actually doing together.

The Result

It was only a year later after Orville moved away that I went to college to officially study and prepare for ministry. When I arrived, I was at first shocked and over time saddened to see how few young men and women had experienced any level of becoming equipped for ministry. It seemed as though many local churches and pastors assumed that this was the college, university, or seminary's responsibility. I arrived at college already well established in the basic disciplines of the Christian life (daily Bible reading and prayer) and experienced in many aspects of ministry. When these discussions arose in class, I did not relate from an ethereal, some-day-maybe thought but from an already-experienced-and-ready-to-learn-more position. Formal studies were not separated from the real world, but they helped to frame my experiences even as my experiences informed my studies.

The result of being equipped by Orville and pursuing formal studies was a powerful combination. I experienced what some might call the best of both. But my experience should not be the exception to the rule. The shared-life experiences I had with Orville should be a normal part of equipping people for ministry, whether it is through a small group like the twelve disciples or one-on-one like Paul and Timothy. Either way, the same four steps can be applied. And the result will be another person, or better yet another group of people, enlisted, equipped, and empowered for ministry.

And this is something we do not seek for ourselves alone but also to pass on to others. Jesus was clear with the disciples in Matthew 28:19–20 that this is for everyone: "Therefore go and make disciples of all nations, baptizing them in the name of the Father and of the son and of the Holy Spirit, and teaching them to obey everything I have commanded you. And surely I am with you always, to the very end of the age" (NIV).

And Paul, too, wanted to make sure that Timothy continued this close, shared-life approach to preparing others for ministry. He was explicit in 2

Timothy 2:2: "And the things you have heard me say in the presence of many witnesses entrust to reliable men who will also be qualified to teach others" (NIV).

The Bible is clear. This method and its results are to be passed on, repeated over and over again "until we all reach unity in the faith and in the knowledge of the Son of God and become mature, attaining to the whole measure of the fullness of Christ" (Eph 4:13 NIV).

The Payback: Pay It Forward

How could I ever pay back Orville for what he has done for me? It would never be an amount of money. And even before Orville died some years ago, nothing I could have done for him would have been sufficient. Rather, it is the multiplying effect of enlisting, equipping, and empowering others for ministry—in effect, paying it forward—that is the only fitting response or "payback" that I could ever offer. Thus, in my own life, I have sought to provide what Orville gave so willingly to me to others.

His name was Scott. I was a young youth pastor in Fairfax, Virginia. He was a thirteen-year-old young man with a tender heart and an earnest desire. He became very involved in our youth ministry. He was willing to take on new challenges and leadership roles. As time went on, we spent more and more time together. He would help lead various aspects of our weekly youth group gatherings. And as we spent time together, I told him of Orville. And the simple, uncomplicated four steps to teaching anyone anything began to be repeated yet again and again.

I was asked to do several Christian education conferences in our area. My response to these invitations was to not go alone. Rather, I prepared the sessions in outline and would go over them with Scott. I would ask his input and help. He would lead various aspects of the conferences, his eyes alive with excitement. I watched his skills, abilities, and confidence grow. Here was a fifteen-year-old teenager standing up front in rooms filled with adult teachers, and he was the teacher. He would teach new methodologies and fresh approaches for Christian education. And many times, his presence, his unique voice, and his own contributions were the things that people talked about the most.

Next Steps to Ministry

Scott became one of the most ardent leaders in our youth ministry, always willing to take on the next challenge. He went away to college and earned a degree with a major in education and a minor in Christian ministry. Today, he serves as an elder in his church, with oversight of both the youth ministries and the missions programs of his church. And the only thing I would ever want for him to do is to continue to do for someone else, indeed, for many others, what I have attempted to do with and for him.

In my current ministry assignment, I have the responsibility for weekend teaching and preaching for our worship celebrations. Rather than approaching this task alone, I am sharpened greatly by working cooperatively with our Teaching Design Team of five people. We range in age from twenties to sixties, and we are anything but clones of one another. We are three men and two women. One of us is single. One of us has grown children. One of us has children still in the home. Two of us are married and without children. And one of us holds dual citizenship in two countries, and neither of those countries is the United States. Yes, we are diverse.

Monthly, for two to four hours, we gather together. We pray with and for one another. Together, we work on our weekend teaching and preaching schedule. We brainstorm series. We potentiate topics together, bringing each of our own best ideas and efforts to the task we share in teaching and leading our congregation in six different weekend worship services. And we sharpen one another. No one assumes the role of teacher. Each one is a disciple, a learner of Jesus Christ, and together we experience the ongoing leadership of the Holy Spirit. Yes, my role is to convene this group and occasionally to keep us on task as several of us are rather long-winded storytellers. But together, as with a one-on-one relationship, we are being enlisted, equipped, and empowered for ministry.

Indeed, many times we are caught up with the keen sense that what we are doing is so much more than the sum total of our own individual contributions. We are living these words: "He who has an ear, let him hear what the Spirit says to the churches." The Spirit says this seven times in Revelation 2:7, 11, 17, 29; 3:6, 13, 22 (NIV). Why does the Spirit repeat this message again and again? Perhaps because God wants to be sure that the disciples of Jesus Christ will hear clearly this important message.

My desire is that this chapter will be a bit like the seven-times-repeated phrase of Revelation. It is God's desire to enlist, equip, and empower everyone possible into the ministry that God has for each one and for everyone. The method is uncomplicated, and the challenge is ours. May we hear what the Spirit says and do what the Bible teaches "until we all reach unity in the faith and in the knowledge of the Son of God and become mature, attaining to the whole measure of the fullness of Christ" (Eph 4:13 NIV).

May it be so. Amen!

Endnotes

[1] See www.tonyandme.com.

Reference List

Anderson, Keith R., and Randy D. Reese. 1999. *Spiritual Mentoring: A guide for Seeking and Giving Direction.* Downer's Grove, IL: InterVarsity Press.

Easum, Bill, and Dave Travis. 2003. *Beyond the Box: Innovative Churches That Work.* Loveland, CO: Group Publishing.

Hybels, Bill. 2002. *Courageous Leadership.* Grand Rapids, MI: Zondervan.

———. 2004. *The Volunteer Revolution: Unleashing the power of Everybody.* Grand Rapids, MI: Zondervan.

Manning, Brennan, and Jim Hancock. 2003. *Posers, Fakers, and Wannabees: Unmasking the Real You.* Colorado Springs, CO: NavPress.

Maxwell, John C. 1993. *Developing the Leader within You.* Nashville, TN: Thomas Nelson.

McLaren, Brian. 2000. *The Church on the Other Side: Doing Ministry in the Postmodern Matrix.* Grand Rapids, MI: Zondervan.

Miller, Donald. 2006. *To Own a Dragon: Growing Up Without a Father.* Colorado Springs, CO: NavPress.

Nouwen, Henri. 1989. *In the Name of Jesus: Reflections on Christian Leadership.* New York: Crossroad.

Ogden, Greg. 2003. *Unfinished Business: Returning the Ministry to the People of God.* Rev. ed. Grand Rapids, MI: Zondervan.

Next Steps to Ministry

Stevens, R. Paul. 1999. *The Other Six Days: Vocation, Work, and Ministry in Biblical Perspective.* Grand Rapids, MI: W. B. Eerdmans.

Stoddard, David A. 2003. *The Heart of Mentoring: Ten Proven Principles for Developing People to Their Fullest Potential.* Colorado Springs, CO: NavPress.

Tillapaugh, Frank R. 1982. *Unleashing the Church: Getting People Out of the Fortress and Into Ministry.* Ventura, CA: Regal Books.

Trueblood, Elton. 1961. *The Company of the Committed.* New York: Harper.

CHAPTER TWELVE:
Steven Lewis: *Contextualizing the Gospel*

Sallie McFague suggests, "Theology is always hermeneutical, always concerned with how the gospel can be translated or understood-grasped-by people" (2002, xviii). Professional theologians attempt to speak the gospel in context to the larger Christian audience; however, theology is not a discipline exclusively reserved for professional theologians. Pastors are theologians who speak the gospel in the context, translating the timeless message of gospel for their community and congregational cultures. Translators, however, must understand both the culture in which they live and the culture to which they speak or risk miscommunication and perhaps alienation from those they hope to reach. Contextualization is central to the translating process and vital for ministry in the twenty-first century, but it is not an easy task.

The apostle Paul was a master at contextualization. He approached the Stoic philosophers and intellectual Athenians through conversations about their Unknown God (Acts 17:16–34). Paul affirmed Athenian religiosity as he walked around their objects of worship and then used a part of their religious culture, the altar to the Unknown God, to speak to them about his understanding of the one true God. He used Athenian culture to elaborate his message and thus translate the conversation into a familiar jargon. He preached the gospel in the context of the culture.

Twenty-first-century pastors must be part theologian, part sociologist, part cultural anthropologist, part preacher, and all-around caregivers. Pastors are often well trained to preach the gospel, exegete a biblical text, or design a worship service; however, clergy remain generally unaware and uninformed as to how one speaks to, and understands the culture in which they live. This chapter articulates some of the challenges that the church faces in its attempts to contextualize the gospel in postmodernity and develops a methodology that will enable the church to speak in a relevant way to the culture. I propose story, symbol, and place as a basic methodology to explore individual spiritual journeys as well as congregational and community cultures.

Story, Symbol, and Place Method

Story, symbol, and place are universal components of the human condition and are central to an emerging postmodern spirituality. Everyone has a story expressed in symbol and located both in metaphor and in a particular geography. Stories are central to the human experience. Our stories reflect our journeys, struggles, celebrations, discoveries, and explorations. Stories are filled with symbols that represent significant points, events, and experiences on the sojourn. Symbols aid us in telling our stories while pointing beyond themselves to a greater reality and a deeper meaning. Symbols communicate in ways words cannot. They capture the imagination while expressing passion and pain, joy and jest. Stories and symbols are located in places, geographically and metaphorically. Location is vital to a story line and the symbols that grow out of stories. Rural or urban, mountain or desert, West Coast or Midwest, location affects how experiences are processed, symbolized, and articulated. Phillip Sheldrake suggests, "The concept of place refers not simply to geographical location but to a dialectical relationship between environment and human narrative. Place is space that has the capacity to be remembered and to evoke what is most precious" (2001, 1). A spiritual desert and mountaintop experience are metaphorical places. These places generate stories and symbols that are woven into the fabric of our greater narrative. The story, symbol, and place methodology will help us contextualize the gospel while we face the many challenges that lie ahead for Christianity.

Challenges

The church faces a number of challenges in its current context that must be recognized and addressed if we hope to speak the gospel in the twenty-first century.[1] According to Wade Clark Roof, American society has become a "spiritual marketplace" (1999). In this marketplace, individuals strive for self-fulfillment and actively construct religious identities that are malleable and multifaceted. This process often blurs the boundaries that separate one faith tradition from another. For seekers in this marketplace, spirituality is more important than religion (Roof 1999, 33–35). How does the church speak to this spiritual marketplace? How do we speak to generations of young people who have grown up outside of faith communities, who do not share basic Christian assumptions, who do not know basic Bible stories, and who are unfamiliar with religious language? How do we speak to generations who have grown up in church (many Boomers and Xers), but who have consciously left organized religion and yet embraced various forms of spirituality? These questions cannot be answered in the confines of this chapter. They deserve far greater attention than can be given here. Two general points, however, are foundational to the questions: the modern-postmodern debate, as it relates to the church, and the inability of the church to embrace and practice theological reflection. These two elements, the modern-postmodern debate and theological reflection, work together. The challenges facing the church require serious theological and spiritual reflection, which must be conducted within the context of postmodernity.

Reflection

Theological reflection is essential to engage the modern-postmodern conversation. "Reflection is the act of deliberately slowing down our habitual processes of interpreting our lives to take a closer look at the experiences and at our frameworks for interpretation."[2] Postmodernity simply offers a new framework for interpretation. This framework, however, presents challenges for North American Christendom. A postmodern framework displaces the authoritative and organizational structures that interpret religious experiences and replaces them with individual experiences interpreted through reflection and community.

Reflection is a fading part of American culture, and spiritual reflection is a lost art among many Christians. In a sound-bite society, true reflection, sitting with an idea, a thought, an experience, an event, is getting lost in the race to spin stories and interpret events for the masses. Spiritual reflection not only requires an ability to sit with our thoughts and experiences but also an ability to listen for and interact with the Spirit of God. Spiritual reflection is sacred listening, the ability to open one's self to the movement of God, to listen for the voice of God and in turn to speak the words of God to the world. These elements lie at the heart of the prophet voice. The loss of spiritual reflection accounts, in part, for the loss of the prophetic voice in our culture. Spiritual reflection enables us to speak the gospel contextually, to be sensitized to the culture, and to listen to the Spirit of God. We must recover the art of spiritual reflection if the church hopes to address the modern-postmodern tension.

Spiritual reflection and the contemplative arts are beginning to emerge among evangelical and mainline denominations alike. The New Monasticism movement is one example of reclamation of spiritual reflection among evangelical Christians.[3] Sitting with God, listening for the movement of the Holy Spirit, and meditating on the teachings of Jesus have become common practices for many Christians. Spiritual formation programs and classes are becoming standard in many Protestant colleges and universities. The increased interest and practice of spiritual reflection will enable the church to speak with an increasing relevance to the modern-postmodern debate.

Modern-Postmodern Debate

One can find the label *postmodern* on just about anything. The term *postmodern*, which originated in the world of architecture, has been overused, referring to everything from works of European and American philosophers to worship styles of start-up gatherings in storefronts. Philosophically, postmodernism refers to the criticism of the power of reason to solve human problems, to discover essential truths, or to establish definitive meaning. For many evangelicals, including the storefront pastors, postmodernism represents the use of contemporary pop culture to frame ministries. The upside of this approach is the attempt to contextualize the gospel via pop culture; however, the downside is its failure to engage deeper theological issues. It simply dresses modern theology in postmodern packaging.

Philip Sheldrake reminds us that postmodernism, at best, is thoroughly contextual, which allows it to cope more easily than modernity with distinctive wisdom of particular traditions (1998, 8). The contextual nature of postmodernity opens the door for the church to engage in creative conversations about twenty-first-century ministry. Postmodernity, however, requires deeper theological reflection along side of creative expressions of ministry. *Postmodernity* will be utilized in this context to refer to cultural tendencies that highlight experience versus logic, spirituality versus religion, mystery versus certainty, and the centrality of community to life and spirituality.[4]

The church, steeped in modernity, has mastered the religious and yet struggles to communicate the spiritual to postmodern generations, who question the relevance of organized religion. Bridgette O'Brien's worship experience consists of composting, recycling, and daily five-mile runs. Isaac Bonewits talks to his ancestors, the spirits of nature, and other deities on a regular basis (Adler 2005, 56). Postmodern spirituality stands in stark contrast to modern religion with its structured worship and liturgy. In the current culture, people are more likely to identify themselves as spiritual (79 percent) rather than religious (64 percent) (Adler 2005, 50). If one listens to National Public Radio's "This I Believe" series on *Morning Edition* or strikes up a conversation at a Starbucks, it is easy to discover how quickly people flee from the word *religious* and embrace with pride their spirituality.[5] Recently, *Newsweek* magazine featured a special report on spirituality in America (Adler 2005). The stories and statistics revealed an ever-increasing diverse spiritual culture that has grown well beyond traditional Christianity. Postmodern thinking does not place faith in doctrine, institutions, systems, or structures. Faith is founded in individual experience, nurtured through relationships and played out in community. The question before us is this: Can and will traditional Christianity contextualize the gospel for the twenty-first century? And if so, in what ways?

The modern-postmodern debate among Christians will continue for some time. The debate is being played out among evangelicals through the works of Brian McLaren and the late Stanley Grenz, through Tony Jones and the Emergent moment[6], and through *Relevant Magazine* and Web sites like Spencer Burke's www.theooze.com. *Christianity Today's* cover story for its September 2005 issue was titled "The New Monasticism: A Fresh Crop of Christian Communities Is Blossoming among the Urban Poor." The article explored a growing trend among young evangelicals to form intentional communities in poor neighborhoods and contextualize the gospel among the homeless. Scott Bessenecker suggests that young evangelicals are looking to commit themselves to something much more radical than the suburban faith of their parents (Moll 2005, 46). Younger generations of Christians are rejecting the health and wealth gospel. How the church will face the challenges of postmodernity is yet to be determined. The form of Christianity that will emerge in the twenty-first century that will remain true to the gospel and respond to the culture, continues to be revealed. The debate will continue and intensify as individuals and groups attempt to contextualize the gospel in postmodernity.

I offer one approach to contextualizing the gospel in the postmodern context: story, symbol, and place. It does not address all the problems inherent to the modern-postmodern debate. In a way, it avoids or circumvents some of the problems and refocuses attention on the individual spiritual journey as a common meeting place for spiritual conversations. An individual, however, is related to a community and perhaps a congregation. With this in mind, each section will explore individual, community, and congregational elements of story, symbol, and place.

Story

Stories are universal to the human experience. We have been telling stories since the beginning of time. "Stories link past, present and future in a way that tells us where we have been, where we are, and where we could be going" (Taylor 1996, 1). As children we were told fairy tales, family stories, and in some cases biblical narratives. At death, eulogies represent a summation of our life stories framed into the confines of a memorial service. The film *Final Cut*, starring Robin Williams, develops around the implanting of a video device in embryos to record the stories of their lives. The implant records every moment of the person's entire life, nothing hidden and nothing secret. At death, the implant is given to a "cutter" who edits the stories into a short narrative for a final memorial service. One's entire life would be reduced to a twenty- or thirty-minute presentation.

Individual Stories

We are a collection of stories, most of which go untold. Everyone has a story, and that story is woven into the stories of hundreds, even thousands of other people. Daniel Taylor reminds us "we cannot live our story alone because we are characters in each other's stories" (1996, 3). The interwoven nature of our stories is why we must provide places, and spaces to share our narratives.

Personal narratives are vital for our spiritual journey. We need to provide safe space to tell our stories, especially the stories of God's activity in our lives. Once upon a time, testimonies were vital parts of worship. People would tell their stories of God working in their lives, or articulate their struggles to discover God amid difficult times. The storytelling allowed the community to be involved in the individual's story. The stories encouraged, offered hope, invoked support, strengthened faith, and built community.

There are many ways to express one's story. Body art is a growing means that some people use to express their personal narrative. Body art aids some individuals in telling their stories of faith and divine encounter. Tragedies, struggles, and other transforming events are being expressed through tattoos. For some, tattoos reflect the spiritual dimension and interpretation of events as a part of their inward spiritual journey. For others, tattoos are conversation starters that may invite dialogue about one's spiritual journey or attempt to "evangelize" another.

We need to listen and reflect on one another's stories, receiving people as they are, where they are, and invite them to experience genuine Christian community. Genuine Christian community is not judgmental, but gracious, compassionate, and authentically interested in others. Postmodern Christian communities must invite others to tell their stories while encouraging them to listen to the stories of Jesus and discover themselves in the biblical narratives. This narrative approach invites others to be transformed by Christ and not to simply conform to one specific religious or denominational interpretation of the stories.

We must be cautious of the modern temptation to advocate a single interpretation of the biblical narratives. One of the miracles of Scripture is its ability to speak in fresh and new ways to seeking individuals searching for a deeper connection with God. The power of the Spirit of God surrounds the texts, inspiring the reader. The biblical stories are human stories, age-old stories that continue to be lived out in a twenty-first-century context. Scriptural narratives connect our stories with the biblical stories of God's interaction with humanity, and guide us as we struggle to understand and draw closer to God.

The Bible is filled with stories of individuals and communities journeying with God. These stories reflect excitement, confusion, anger, grace, blessings, and struggle. The people of the Bible understood the world and interpreted events in a way that we have long since lost, but their stories reflect themes central to the human condition. They go well beyond the limitations of geography, gender, ethnicity, and time. These stories reveal people's journeys with God at their best and worst. They are powerful stories that draw us into the experience and require us to struggle with their truths. We are challenged to place our stories alongside the biblical and classic narratives to discover how God may be working in and through us in our context.

Community Stories

Individual stories are often shaped by and lived out in community. Communities have stories rooted in history and rich with meaning. In the same way the church needs to encourage and cultivate individual storytelling, it also needs to know the community stories to contextualize the gospel. There are different types of community stories each having different effects on one's ability to contextualize the gospel. The ministry of a congregation is affected by the closing of a General Motors auto plant that once was the foundation for area employment. The selling of large portions of farmland over the last few years to make way for the growing housing developments and the dying of the old neighborhood in the inner city as populations shift are factors that impact the direction of congregations. Some stories reflect deep wounds of a community's history, like the deaths of a group of soldiers in one national guard unit from the same small town. Perhaps the community was once divided over issues of race or busing, where the "other side of the tracks" had deeper meaning than a simple cliché. These types of stories require careful exploration. One is hopeless to contextualize the gospel without understanding the wounds of the past.

Community stories form identity and are vital to the revelation of the community's future. Community stories can shape the context for the church's ministry. Perhaps the church needs to encourage and facilitate a ministry of reconciliation. Maybe a focus should be placed on healing relationships or recovering after the loss of jobs to the community.

Some community stories are often woven into the fabric of congregations for better or worse. Sunnyside United Methodist church in Portland, Oregon, was known in the community for its ministry to the homeless. Its Wednesday night dinners attracted a large number of homeless people looking for a hot meal. Recently, some members of the community attempted to take legal action to prohibit the church from continuing its ministry. Empty bottles of alcohol and used needles too often littered the areas surrounding the church, and the community grew impatient with the process. The story of the congregation and the story of the community were woven together and in conflict. Not all congregation and community stories are negative; many are positive expressions of joint work, like Habitat for Humanity, community food programs, and shelters. If congregations want to be a community church, they must learn the stories of the community and commit to ministry in the neighborhood.

Congregational Stories

Congregations are rich with stories that are deeply rooted in the identity of the church. One of the first things a new minister should do after arriving at a new congregation is to learn the stories of the church. What stories do people highlight about the church and what versions of the stories emerge as you listen to people? The answers will determine how ministry will unfold in the future. When one hears, "We have never done it that way before," it is a way of saying that there are no stories in the congregation's past that allows them to reference a new program or ministry. As a pastor dreams and reflects on God's direction for the congregation, it is important to remember to connect the plans and visions to the stories of the past. Congregational stories not only reveal the identity of the church, but also reveal the key points of conflict and potential.

Symbol

Jesus used a number of symbols to communicate his message: a mustard seed, a lost coin, a vineyard, and many more. The items were familiar to his audience and easily used as symbols. "A symbol is a story told by a familiar sign that may be read at a glance" (Webber 1927, v). This quote from F. R. Webber is simple but true. American culture is filled with familiar symbols from the flag to the golden arches. Dominant symbols can easily be recognized and associated with their deeper meaning. However, symbols can become so prevalent in the culture that they go unnoticed. Christianity has a deep history of rich symbols that invoke universal identification such as the cross or crucifix, and yet many of its symbols go unnoticed even by believers. Symbols connect us to stories and represent a key element of a greater narrative. They play vital roles in our journey through life and function as signposts that allows us to immediately transport to the times and places of importance. The loss of symbols can result in subtle but significant changes in the spiritual culture.

The seeker sensitive movement of the '80s and '90s removed a number of historic symbols from churches: pulpits, wall crosses, hymnals, communion tables, pews. One of the consequences of these actions has been the search for symbols to represent both individual and community spiritual journeys. Body art, crucifixes worn by evangelicals, and Orthodox icons in dorm rooms and living rooms have increased over the last few years. A growing number of young evangelicals are attending Catholic and Orthodox services seeking a symbolic and textured means of celebrating their spirituality. In addition, the secular but spiritual folks who use spiritual symbols as expressions of their spirituality are making it easier to begin contextualizing the gospel in postmodernity.

Some cultures are very intentional about symbolism and consciously incorporate symbols into every day life. Some clothing carries specific religious meaning: a robe, a special type of head covering, or veils covering the faces of women. The biblical culture was filled with symbolism. Biblical characters represented their encounters with God by piling up rocks at a sacred place, removing the foreskin of males, placing a snake on a pole, and carrying an ark, having a meal with bread and wine, and so on. These symbols embodied great stories that continue to be told thousands of years after the events have past. Symbols are powerful means to communicate those things that people hold as important and sacred. Can Christianity breathe new life into ancient symbols while cultivating new symbols growing out of the experiences of the people? To contextualize the gospel in postmodernity, the answer must be yes.

Individual Symbols

Individual symbols can reveal a lot about the person. A person who drives a Cadillac SUV and wears designer clothes may or may not be aware of the symbolism expressed in their daily lives. What symbols are important for a person? How do they use or displace symbols? Do they have specific religious or spiritual symbols that are significant to their lives? Becoming sensitive to the symbolism in the culture and community is central to contextualizing the gospel.

For the last five years I have been researching intentionally spiritual body art as a symbolic expression of individual spiritual journeys. Tattoos have become a part of mainstream culture for movie stars, rock stars, and a growing number of Christians. A spiritually significant tattoo struggles to be birthed from within the imagination before ultimately finding expression on the body. The type of symbol, its location, and the number of tattoos received are all vital parts of the individual's ongoing story. Tattooing as storytelling is not a product of postmodernity. For centuries, the Samoan culture has used tattoos as a means of expressing one's ongoing story. Body art has simply opened some people to new avenues of spiritual expression. These avenues include symbols, metaphors, and images that aid in the articulations of the spiritual journey. Some Christians see tattoos and quote Leviticus 19:28, which declares that one should not tattoo the body. But for a growing number of people, tattoos are not some form of graffiti on the body, but symbols of their religious and spiritual commitment. Many start with a simple fish symbol to represent their Christian commitment and later add other tattoos to reflect different aspects of their spiritual journey.

There are a number of symbols that individuals use to express spirituality. Intentionally spiritual body art is just one growing expression. Ancient symbols—icons, historical depictions of saints, portraits of Jesus—can be found on tee shirts with social comments like "Jesus was Homeless." Religious artwork, albeit by amateurs, hangs in storefront coffee shops and churches to express individual interpretations of the faith journey. A growing number of Christians are using icons and candles to create sacred spaces for prayer and Scripture reading. Postmodern Christians are becoming more aware of the individual symbols that represent their spirituality.

Next Steps to Ministry

Community Symbols

In Portland, Oregon, Pioneer Courthouse Square stands at the heart of the city and is referred to as Portland's living room. The square is a symbol of community for Portland. It is a place for small events, street preachers, and protesters of everything, as well as a place to have a cup of coffee, eat lunch or read a book.

Community symbols often represent shared experiences: losses, pride, overcoming adversity, commemorating an event, etc. The Oklahoma City Memorial is a beautiful symbol of remembrance, and in a strange way, a symbol of pain and peace. There is a series of chairs there that represent those who lost their lives on the day the Murrah Federal Building was bombed. The small chairs represent the children who were in the daycare located on the first floor of the building. The taller chairs represent the adults who died in the bombing. The reflective pool, which lies where the street once was, invokes stillness and peacefulness. The entire area of the memorial invites visitors to spend time in reflection.

Community symbols are often local and not always obvious to outsiders. They invite conversation and facilitate storytelling. It is important to seek out community symbols, inquire about their meaning, and discover how to connect and relate to the community in a deep way. Community symbols may be closely related to congregational stories.

Congregational Symbols

Congregational symbols can be both implicit and subtle. Implicit symbols are easy to identify, along with the unwritten rules that surround them. For example, the pulpit Bible, often placed on the Communion table, symbolizes the centrality of the Word of God, authority, history, and tradition. Relocating the pulpit Bible to a new location may invoke some strong emotions. This is a good sign that you have encountered a significant symbol in the life of the congregation. Implicit symbols have wonderful stories surrounding them, stories that sometimes involve conflict as well.

Sometimes symbols clash. Symbols of one generation may conflict with the symbols of another. Numerous congregations have struggled to incorporate technology into worship spaces. Installing large screens to allow projection of music, scripture, announcements, and sermons perhaps tops the list of conflict over congregational symbols. Many sanctuaries were not designed to accommodate the new technologies of the late twentieth century. The conflict comes when the new technology, symbolic to a younger generation, covers the wall cross that had been the focal point to the sanctuary, symbolic to an older generation.

Implicit and subtle symbols can conflict with one another. The wall cross is an implicit symbol. It is a central image of Christianity and connects the congregation to a deeper history and tradition. The screen that descends from the ceiling and covers the wall cross is a subtle symbol. The screen does not connect the congregation to any historic Christian symbol or invoke a deeper meaning. The subtle nature of the screen as a symbol goes virtually unnoticed, but with a little reflection, one can see the subtleties of this symbol. The screen represents the new, progression, and an attempt to be relevant to a technological, contemporary culture. Congregational symbols can be the most difficult to deal with as one attempts to contextualize the gospel.

Place

All stories and symbols are located in places, geographical or metaphorical. "The meanings of places unfold in stories, myths, rituals, and in naming" (Sheldrake 2001, 6). I cannot overemphasize the importance of place for contextualizing the gospel. While contextualizing the gospel is a universal need, it requires local application. Forms of ministry that are effective in the Midwest do not always work on the East Coast. Contextualizing the gospel in Seattle, Washington, may look quite different from ministry in Evansville, Indiana.

Beyond physical location, place can be metaphorical or even virtual. Cyberspace provides places for people to chat, worship, buy, sell, meet other people, as well as numerous other possibilities. A person can hang out in a chat community with peers whom they may have never met in person. Some people attend virtual church services on Sundays through an Internet connection. In addition to cyberspace, one can experience metaphorical places. Metaphorical places are located in the human imagination and allow us access to stories and symbols beyond the limitation of physical reality.

Next Steps to Ministry

Individuals and Place

Place engages our identity, our relationships, and our history (Sheldrake 2001, 9). Individual stories are located in places, and those places form and shape us. We are products of our environment. Kathleen Norris, in her book *Dakota: A Spiritual Geography*, explored the connection between place and spirituality. For her, Dakota was her spiritual geography, the place where she "wrestled her story out of the circumstances of landscape and inheritance" (Norris 1993, 2). A person who grew up on a family farm in Ohio may be shaped by small town values and the centrality of family. Family-farm stories are quickly disappearing as more and more generations are born, raised, and shaped by suburban and city landscapes. People from Montana are formed by the wide-open spaces and rolling landscapes. Those from New York City have a sense of community: being a New Yorker, representing a city with millions of people from hundreds of cultures. Place shapes our values, worldview, personalities, and religion. Growing up as a Southern Baptist in Georgia may form a person's understanding of the world that would stand in contrast to growing up as a Unitarian Universalist in Boston. Place matters when contextualizing the gospel.

Individual spiritual journeys go well beyond physical places and reach into the realm of metaphor. Landscape metaphors are one example of how place can be more than physical. Most people know what a spiritual desert is like. They can describe the experience in detail, including the variety of emotions associated with deserts. Spiritual deserts strip away the baggage of life and refocus attention on the basic needs and issues that require reflection. Who has not had a mountaintop experience at some point in life? Mountaintop experiences are inspiring, with their warmth and overwhelming feeling of assurance and energy. These experiences, while metaphorical, relate to the physical landscapes they describe. Mountaintop experiences can be awe-inspiring. The view from the top allows one to see the lay of the landscape and gain perspective. Deserts are often places of struggle and death, and yet they reveal a beauty and sacredness.

Kathleen Norris brought together metaphor and landscape in *Dakota*. The vast space of the Great Plains, the heartland of America, forms its people in a fruitful silence that breeds peacefulness. "The silence of the Plains, this great unpeopled landscape of earth and sky, is much like the silence one finds in a monastery, an unfathomable silence that has the power to re-form you" (Norris 1993, 15). Place forms people and impacts our contextualization of the gospel.

Community and Place

Each region of the country, each area of a state, has an impact on the stories and symbols of it inhabitants. Southern culture has distinctive characteristics, which are very different from New England culture. Ministry in innercity Chicago is not the same as pastoring in Cairo, Illinois, a small town in the southern part of the state. Each context requires its own type of ministry. Some regions of the country have dominant religious institutions and structures that hold significant places in the society: Southern Baptists in Texas, United Methodists in Nashville, Roman Catholics in Boston, or the Church of God in Anderson, Indiana. Ministry in these places is shaped by location for better or worse. The context both empowers and limits ministry.

In contrast, the Pacific Northwest has never had a dominant religious organization. Because religious institutions are relatively weak in the Pacific Northwest, religion had never been a strong mechanism of social control or influence (Killen 2004, 11). A number of Southern or Midwestern clergy have come to the Pacific Northwest with great plans to start churches only to be greatly disappointed with the general lack of interest. Ministry in the "None Zone," so called because a high number of people who select "none" as their religion on census surveys, often requires ecumenical collaboration and interfaith conversations.

Congregations and Place

Congregational location is a determining factor in contextualizing the gospel. The physical location of a congregation is central to its ministry. A downtown church in Los Angeles presents a different context for ministry than a rural congregation in Iowa or a suburban church in Dallas, Texas. Each place has its own culture, needs, possibilities, and liabilities.

Congregations have another sense of place beyond their physical locations. Metaphorically, where is the congregation located? A church can be in one of the four seasons of its life. Is the church in the fall of its life? Is the congregation 150 years old, struggling to keep the doors open and hold on to its identity? Is the congregation in the spring of its life? Is it a new church plant with a lot of freshness and energy? Perhaps the congregation has reached a plateau and is struggling to discover the next step in its evolution. Much like individual spiritual journeys, congregations can experience periods of spiritual deserts, mountaintops, or valleys. These are metaphorical places, but very real places nonetheless. Each context requires a different approach to doing ministry.

Conclusion

Contextualizing the gospel requires an awareness and intentionality. Story, symbol, and place simply provide one avenue to approach ministry in postmodernity. Learn the stories of those around you and those you hope to reach. Learn the stories of the communities and congregations with whom you work and serve. Pay close attention to the symbols that people use to express their journey, spiritual and otherwise. Learn the stories behind the community and congregational symbols that represent important aspect of their identity. Be mindful of your location, the place that you do ministry—the small towns and the big cities, the rural congregations and the suburban megachurches.

The story, symbol, and place rubrics allow Christians to face the challenges of postmodernity. The body of Christ needs to introduce Jesus, not religion, to hyperspiritual generations who have little use for or knowledge of the church. We need to invite seekers to discover themselves in the biblical stories as they tell their stories and not simply require people to conform to standard interpretations. We need to breathe new life into historical symbols so new generations can claim and value them for themselves while creating new symbols born in the spiritual imaginations of pilgrims on their journey of seeking God. We need to provide safe spaces for people to struggle and doubt and own their faith, which may look different from the religiosity we had structured in denominations and nondenominations. The Spirit of God is moving in, through, and around us, infecting the world with a spiritual curiosity that cannot be satisfied by mere religiosity. We have a great opportunity to invite seekers to interact with the stories and the person of Jesus.

Endnotes

[1] The term *church* is used to denote the larger body of Christ, both mainline and evangelical denominations and movements. While styles and structures may differ, the church is entrenched in modernity from theology to its need to maintain controlling structures.

[2] Cited in Killen and De Beer (2004, x); originally from Shea (1978, 41–49).

[3] See House (2005).

[4] There are a number of books that outline the tendencies of postmodernity. For an evangelical perspective, see Grenz (1996) and Erickson (1998). Grenz provides a great overview of postmodernism for beginners. Erickson explores the views of six evangelical writers; three writers consider postmodernism incompatible with Christianity while three other writers embrace many of the values of postmodernity.

[5] See www.npr.org for essays submitted for the "This I Believe" segment of *Morning Edition*.

[6] Visit www.emergentvillage.com.

[7] Alta Mira Press has published a very helpful series of texts on religion by region, co-published with the Leonard Greenberg Center for the Study of Religion in Public Life at Trinity College. The Religion and Public Life series divides the country into eight regions. These are a must read for anyone who hopes to contextualize the gospel in their community.

Reference List

Adler, Jerry. 2005. In Search of the Spiritual. *Newsweek*, September 5.

Erickson, Millard J. 1998. *Postmodernizing the Faith: Evangelical Responses to the Challenge of Postmodernism*. Grand Rapids, MI: Baker Books.

Grenz, Stanley J. 1996. *A Primer on Postmodernism*. Grand Rapids, MI: William B. Eerdmans.

House, Rutba, ed. 2005. *School(s) for Conversion: 12 Marks of a New Monasticism*. Eugene, OR: Cascade Books.

Killen, Patricia O'Connell, and John De Beer. 2004. *The Art of Theological Reflection*. New York: Crossroad Publishing.

Killen, Patricia O'Connell, and Mark Silk, eds. 2004. *Religion and Public Life in the Pacific Northwest: The None Zone.* Religion by Region Series. Walnut Creek, CA: AltaMira Press.

McFague, Sallie. 2002. *Speaking in Parables: A Study in Metaphor and Theology.* Canterbury, England: SCM Press.

Moll, Rob. 2005. The New Monasticism: A Fresh Crop of Christian Communities Is Blossoming among the Urban Poor. *Christianity Today,* September.

Norris, Kathleen. 1993. *Dakota: A Spiritual Geography.* Boston: Houghton Mifflin.

Roof, Wade Clark. 1999. *Spiritual Marketplace: Baby Boomers and the Remaking of American Religion.* Princeton, NJ: Princeton University Press.

Shea, John. 1978. *Stories of God: An Unauthorized Biography.* Chicago: Thomas More Press.

Sheldrake, Philip. 1998. *Spirituality and Theology: Christian Living and the Doctrine of God.* Maryknoll, NY: Orbis Books.

———. 2001. *Spaces for the Sacred: Place, Memory, and Identity.* Baltimore, MD: John Hopkins University Press.

Taylor, Daniel. 1996. *The Healing Power of Stories: Creating Yourself through the Stories of Your Life.* New York: Doubleday.

Webber, F. R. 1927. *Church Symbolism.* Cleveland, OH: J. H. Jansen.

Chapter Thirteen:
Douglas L. Talley: *The Art of Influence: Learning to Be a Leader*

There are hundreds of definitions of leadership. A common denominator in most, perhaps all, of them is the concept of influence. Leadership is influence. It involves influencing the thinking and behavior of others.

Robert Clinton defines leadership as "a dynamic process in which a man or woman with God-given ability influences a specific group of God's people toward his purposes for the group" (1988, 14). I like the focus and scope of his definition. As pastors and staff members in local churches, one of our most important responsibilities and biggest challenges is to influence people so that God's purposes are accomplished.

Being and Doing

Leadership involves both being and doing. Today's culture keeps trying to separate the function of leadership from the character of the leader, but that is a false dichotomy. They cannot be separated because the character of the person forms the foundation upon which the task of leadership is carried out. Therefore, to be an effective leader you must focus on developing godly character *and* leadership skills, the former being the most important.

Corporate and political scandals remind us that merely having leadership skills is not enough. Character and integrity must also be present. People misuse leadership abilities when character is compromised. Instead of serving others and serving God, they become self-serving. Greed, personal gain, and ego gratification become the driving forces and will eventually cause the destruction of the leader and the enterprise.

NEXT STEPS TO MINISTRY

In ministry the task of leading grows out of the leader's relationship with God. If the relationship is not vibrant, healthy and growing, then the leader will lack the necessary foundation for influencing people to accomplish God's purposes. He or she can still influence people to some degree, but that influence will be tainted and the leadership task will be compromised.

Before God uses a leader to make a significant impact, God does a work in that leader's heart. While the Bible has many examples, let us look at Moses.

Moses was the perfect candidate to lead the Hebrews out of slavery to the Promised Land, or so he thought. He was groomed to be the successor to the pharaoh of Egypt. He received the best education available as he was schooled in a wide variety of subjects, including law, governance, leadership practices, public speaking, and military strategy. His natural leadership abilities were nurtured and honed for greatness. He was well-suited to be a world-class leader.

Long before the Exodus event, Moses seemed to know in his heart that God had called him to set the Hebrews free from Egyptian domination. Though raised an Egyptian, Moses knew his biological and spiritual heritage. His true identity was found in the God of the Hebrews, not the gods of Egypt. He had watched the Egyptians mistreat the Hebrews for forty years and had decided in his heart to champion the Hebrews' cause before he impulsively struck and killed the Egyptian who was beating the Hebrew slave.

Moses was dumbfounded that the Hebrews did not realize he was the answer to their prayers for deliverance. His education and training made him the perfect candidate for the job. He had a killer resume. If he was ready to lead Egypt, then surely he was ready to liberate the Hebrews.

What Moses did not realize was that leadership is about more than training, skills, and technical competency. It is also about one's heart. He could not be the leader God needed until God did an extreme makeover of his heart. While in the desert for forty years hiding from Pharaoh, God reshaped Moses' heart. Then Moses was ready to be the leader God needed.

What God calls leaders to do is greater than what we can do on our own. While we need to develop skills and competencies as a leader, what is most important is the heart of the leader. We can only lead God's people in the pursuit of God's purposes if we have a close personal walk with him and are allowing God to produce the character of Jesus in us.

Integrity

Integrity is the mortar of godly character. It holds the life of the leader together. It is the byproduct of letting God shape and reshape a leader's heart. Integrity emerges when you settle character issues related to honesty, morality, motives, commitment, and ego. It is choosing to live a life above reproach (1 Tim 3:2) and worthy of our calling (Col 1:10) by allowing your heart to be vulnerable to the transformational work of the Holy Spirit. While integrity is important for leaders and non-leaders, it is absolutely essential for the Christian leader.

A lack of character will eventually cause an integrity implosion in a leader. It will undermine credibility. It will leave people feeling betrayed and used. It will also cause some to feel like God is no longer trustworthy, thus causing a spiritual crisis. However, integrity fosters confidence and increases influence.

The Christian leader must value integrity more than image. The political and corporate worlds are prone to focus on image and outward appearance, but a Christian leader cannot make that mistake. When integrity is cultivated, image manipulation is not necessary, and Christ is more visible in the leader.

Trust

Integrity fosters trust, and trust increases influence. When people trust you, they will give you permission to lead. People do not follow persons just because they are in leadership positions. They follow people who have earned their trust. If there is a lack of trust, people will not follow you no matter how skilled you are or how inspiring your vision. If people trust you, they will give you a chance to lead them.

I have been fortunate that my first pastorate has lasted over two decades. What I have discovered is that it takes time for people to trust their pastor so that he or she can influence them in significant ways. After I had been senior pastor for about six or seven years, the people had learned to deeply trust me. From what I have heard and read, that time frame is typical. Unfortunately, many pastors get frustrated because the people are not willing to follow them, so they change churches every three to five years. They leave before they have earned the right to influence the people. After I had invested the time necessary for trust to develop, I did not want to leave and start that process all over again. And my influence increased!

Some people have significant issues with trust. Due to traumatic experiences in the past, they have difficulty trusting persons even when trustworthiness has been demonstrated. You are likely to encounter people like this in your ministry. They will challenge your leadership in ways that make you feel like you are a defective and incompetent leader. Do not assume they are right. If they have trust issues, realize they are unlikely to follow anyone.

One of the benefits of a long pastorate is that once the people in your church trust you, they help new people trust you. By knowing you and your heart, they are able to vouch for your integrity and expand your influence. As a result, you do not have to wait for new persons to attend for five to seven years before they will follow you.

Servant's Heart

Jesus taught and modeled an important component of leadership that was widely overlooked prior to his ministry—servanthood leadership. The Egyptian and Roman style of leadership employed force to coerce people to serve those in leadership. Contrast that approach with Jesus' willingness to lay down his life for those he served.

Even the disciples were influenced by the power paradigm. They argued among themselves about who was the greatest and fought for positions of power in Jesus' kingdom (Matt 20 and Mark 9). This power struggle took place while Jesus was traveling to Jerusalem to make the ultimate sacrifice. After hearing their argument, he must have wondered if they would ever understand what leadership was really about.

He said to them,

> You know that the rulers of the Gentiles lord it over them, and their high officials exercise authority over them. Not so with you. Instead, whoever wants to become great among you must be your servant, and whoever wants to be first must be your slave—just as the Son of Man did not come to be served, but to serve, and to give his life a ransom for many. (Matt 20:24–28 NIV)

Leadership is not about being important and having power over people. The focus must not be on the ego needs of the leader or what makes the leader happy. It is not about using force to make people comply. Servant leadership is about serving others, self-sacrifice, and building people up so that God's agenda can be accomplished.

Jesus did not have a problem with authority. He knew what it meant to live under God's authority and to exercise authority. When Jesus was in the desert at the beginning of his ministry, he fought the ego battle that determined the kind of leader he would be. He refused to misuse his authority for personal benefit. Instead, he chose to serve regardless of the cost.

Leaders can never underestimate the lure of power and the temptation to misuse authority. This is not a battle we simply fight once. It challenges us again and again. That is just one reason why leaders need persons to hold them accountable. Early in your ministry identify several people (pastoral colleagues or lay persons) whom you trust and respect. Give them permission to ask you the hard questions. Their input can protect you from letting your ego undermine your ministry.

The most important ingredient in a servant's heart is love. Paul gives us a poetic and moving description of love in 1 Corinthians 13. Of the three things that last forever—faith, hope, and love—he says that love is the greatest. He tells us to make it our primary aim in life. Servant leaders are driven by love—love for God and love for others.

When I began my first pastorate, I had just graduated from seminary where I was at home in the world of academia. I had also just finished

Next Steps to Ministry

serving a one-year assignment at the church as an associate pastor, so the people knew me pretty well. As I was invited to move into the role of senior pastor, one man in the church told me that if I would learn to love the people, I would make an excellent pastor. I was a bit irritated by his remark. After several years at the church, I began to understand what he meant. He was not telling me not to lead or avoid difficult conversations with people. Nor was he telling me to spend all my time holding people's hands or trying to please them. He was trying to help me understand that if I did not make loving others my greatest aim, then I could never influence them to accomplish God's purposes.

I have taken his advice to heart. Through various assessments I have gotten to know myself pretty well. I tend to be task-driven rather than people-oriented. I can be strong minded and a bit too focused at times. I am more of a thinker than a feeler. But I think I am learning to make love my greatest aim. And as I do, my influence increases. People are willing to follow someone they are convinced loves them.

Shortly after the disciples were arguing about who was the greatest and fighting for position, Jesus washed their feet. What a contrast! With tension from that argument still in the air, Jesus took the towel and the basin and gave them an unforgettable visual about leading with a servant's heart. It was so contrary to the leadership culture they had grown up with that Jesus' action bothered them. In their minds that was not what leaders did. After Peter's protest, Jesus taught them about the essence of leadership.

A leader is not above others. A leader is not positioned to be served and pampered by others. Rather, he or she is to take the lead in serving. It is through having a servant's heart and through genuinely loving God and others that we are positioned to lead.

Spiritual Gift of Leadership

In Romans 12:8, Paul establishes that there is a spiritual gift of leadership. This is a special, supernatural ability to envision what God wants to do and influence others to partner with God in doing it. Every Christian has at least one spiritual gift (1 Cor 12:7), but all Christians do not have the same spiritual gifts (Rom 12:4–6). It appears to me that the Holy Spirit frequently gives spiritual gifts in combination and to differing degrees. That contributes to the uniqueness of each Christian and is a tribute to the creativity of God.

The spiritual gift of leadership is often a natural ability to lead that God supernaturally transforms into a spiritual gift. This gift is given in a rudimentary form and needs to be cultivated and developed in order to accomplish God's purposes. The gift of leadership does not compensate for a person's failure to develop a heart for God. There is still a need for God to do a work in the heart of the person so that God can be served and honored.

Made or Born?

There is an age-old debate as to whether leaders are made or born. While convincing arguments can be made for either side, my answer is, yes. Some people are born with natural leadership abilities, and some learn the art of influencing others. From my perspective the difference between the persons who are born leaders and those who learn to be leaders is potential. Those who are learned leaders may not make as great of an impact as those who are born leaders—especially born leaders who intentionally develop and hone their leadership skills.

Regardless of your perceived level of leadership potential, learn all you can about leadership. Even if you do not believe you have any leadership tendencies, learning about leadership will make you a better follower. In the process you might discover you have more leadership potential than you realize. Even if you do not have any leadership tendencies, you will learn how to support and complement those who do.

Sometimes people who have leadership ability convince themselves they are not a leader because of past failed attempts at leading. After Moses' false start setting the Hebrews free (Ex 2), he gave up on being a leader. When God appeared to him in the desert forty years later, Moses was so reluctant to lead that he gave God multiple excuses why he was not the man for the job. He was thoroughly convinced God had picked the wrong person. God trumped each excuse, and Moses became one of the greatest leaders of history.

God is looking for leaders who have a heart for him and a heart for others. As we surrender our hearts to him, he does an extreme makeover in us. He grows us from the core of our being into someone who is increasingly reflecting the likeness of his Son. As he transforms our hearts, we become more qualified to lead and people are more likely to give us permission to influence them. Then we are able to pursue what God wants to accomplish through us.

Leadership Dynamics

The heart of the leader is the foundation. With that in place, let us take a look at some important leadership dynamics.

Vision

Leaders lead. They spend time talking with and listening to God and others in order to discern the preferable future that God wants to bring to pass. Various authors define vision somewhat differently. Some say that vision involves the big picture, and some say it is very specific and focused. I think it can have elements of both because people need to see the big picture, and they need to understand how what they are doing fits into it.

The Bible never tries to define vision. Only the King James Version uses the actual word in Proverbs 29:18—"Where there is no vision, the people perish." The passage is actually talking about God's laws. The idea is that if God does not give guidance to people in how they should live, chaos reigns.

While I am not so sure the biblical writer was referring to vision as we tend to think of it, I do not think vision as a desirable or preferable future is totally missing from that verse. Think about it: without a revealed word from God—which is God's guidance—our lives are chaotic and directionless. Vision is a revealed word from God. It is God-given direction for our lives and ministries.

God has not designed you to be Brian McLaren, Dan Kimball, Rick Warren, Daniel S. Warner, your favorite professor, or your favorite author.

Neither has he assigned their unique vision to you. He does not want you to evaluate your worth by comparing yourself to any of them or anyone else. God has uniquely designed you for the vision he has for your life. Too many of us in ministry lose sight of the vision God has given us because we are investing too much energy comparing ourselves to other leaders.

People who do not live for Christ are free to dream up their own vision. However, those of us who have given our lives to Christ have given up that right. Our desire is to know his vision for our lives and ministry. He gives the vision, and we embrace it.

Which comes first, the vision or the call to ministry?

- God gave Moses a vision of setting the Hebrews free when he was a child or a young man. When he was eighty, God said it was time to pursue the vision.
- Isaiah had an incredible encounter with God and immediately volunteered for service. After his response to God's call, God gave him a vision of his ministry.
- God called Paul to the ministry through an event which involved the loss of his physical sight. Then later God gave him the vision of reaching the Gentiles for Christ.

Which comes first? It does not really matter. The important thing is listening for God's call and embracing his vision for your life. The call and the vision are God's responsibility. Ours is to obey.

Vision has both personal and corporate components. The personal component concerns itself with the individual leader's unique design and what God is calling her or him to do. The corporate component has to do with God's vision for a local church. When the pastor's personal vision and the church's corporate visions intersect, godly energy is released and God is able to do incredible things. However, when the pastor's personal vision and the church's corporate vision do not align, chaos and conflict usually follow.

Vision Must Be Missional

Churches have a tendency to become survival and comfort oriented. When either of these perspectives molds the vision, church members tend to think the church exists for them and to take care of them. The job of the leader is redefined as taking the lead in providing the care. Shepherding is reduced to caring for the sheep. Maintenance is substituted for mission, and the church disengages from its God-given vision.

The church in the twenty-first century desperately needs leaders who are mission focused, not maintenance or refuge focused. It needs leaders who embrace Jesus' mission of seeking and saving those who are lost (Luke 19:10), rather than reducing vision to caring for the found. God is looking for leaders who share the missional passion of Jesus.

George Hunter III observed over a decade ago that the church in North America no longer has the home field advantage (1996; 1992). We live in a culture that is spiritually sensitive but does not understand what Christianity is all about. And most are not interested enough to ask. They assume that Christianity is irrelevant to their spiritual needs, and many churches and Christians are not doing much to disprove them.

Being missional includes Christians becoming more adept at talking to pre-Christians about Christ in their everyday lives. It involves trying to understand the culture so that we can build bridges between pre-Christians and Christ. Missional leaders look for ways to take God's love, forgiveness, and acceptance to those outside the church so that they can become part of God's kingdom (Matt 28:18–20; Acts 1:8).

Winning people to a life-changing relationship with Jesus Christ is at the heart of being missional. This involves more than a moment of decision. The emphasis is on continual life change and helping people take the next step in that process. Even leaders have a next step. None of us fully becomes the person God wants us to be on this side of eternity, leaders included.

Jesus had a compelling sense of God's vision for his life: "The Son of Man came to look for and to save people who are lost" (Luke 19:10 CEV).

Though Jesus performed miracles, healed and comforted people, and challenged people's misconceptions about God, the vision that drove his life was to look for and save lost people, i.e., to win people to a life-changing relationship with Jesus Christ. He understood the missional nature of his vision so well that he was able to disregard the popular expectations people had for the Messiah and go all the way to the cross, thus making salvation and life change possible.

Self-Awareness

Leaders need to understand themselves. Personality and behavioral tendencies, family of origin, life experiences (both positive and negative), strengths, weaknesses, spiritual gifts, and natural abilities influence who you are and how you lead. They impact your relationships with people and can foster or undermine trust in you as a leader. If you are not aware of how they influence you, they are far more likely to sabotage your ministry.

There are many assessment tools available which can be used to help you better understand yourself. The additional insights provided by an assessment counselor can also be extremely helpful. Tapping into these resources early in your ministry can help increase your influence and make you more effective, as well as help you avoid some major leadership blunders. But do not limit your quest for self-awareness to the early years of your ministry; make this a lifetime pursuit. The older you get, the better you should understand yourself.

Since leadership is highly people intensive, leaders also need self-awareness of their relational skills. The ability to relate to people in healthy ways and develop healthy relationships is critical to influencing people in a positive manner. A lack of people skills has derailed many an aspiring leader. Many a potential leader has unknowingly undermined his or her effectiveness by being abrasive, inconsiderate, demeaning, controlling, intimidating, unapproachable, or self-centered. If leadership were merely a task, people skills would not be so important. But it is more than a task. Fortunately, people skills can be learned; but before you can learn them, you must be aware that you lack them or that your skills are not as developed as they need to be.

As an emerging leader, how do you know what kind of continuing education and self-development you should pursue? Self-awareness helps answer that question. In *A Work of Heart,* Reggie McNeal writes, "Self-understanding forms the fundamental building blocks for the leader's personal development" (2000, 77). As you avail yourself of assessment resources and grow in your self-understanding, you will be able to develop a strategy for personal growth that will take you to the next level as a leader.

As you become aware of your strengths and weaknesses, focus more on developing your strengths than trying to improve your weaknesses. It has typically been assumed that to maximize your leadership abilities, you need to grow in the areas of your greatest weakness. But research by the Gallup Organization indicates that you should build on your strengths and not be too concerned about your weaknesses unless they are keeping you from maximizing your strengths (Buckingham and Clifton 2001).

For example, a Clydesdale is built for strength, not speed. To force the Clydesdale into speed training in order to run in the Kentucky Derby would involve trying to overcome a weakness. That training strategy would require that strengths be ignored and would destine the horse to failure.

Too often in ministry strengths are ignored while weaknesses receive primary attention. The result is that ministry effectiveness is compromised. Build on your strengths. Play to them. Team up with others in the body who bring complementary gifts and strengths. If a weakness is causing problems in your ministry, address it. Find ways to compensate for it, but focus on maximizing your strengths.

Criticism

If you lead, you will be criticized. There are not many sure things in life, but that is one. Developing a vision, even God's vision, and seeking to influence people to pursue it is like drawing a bull's-eye on your forehead. People will take shots at you.

Criticism, even if well intended and deserved, can be so disheartening for an emerging leader. Even veteran leaders who have learned to deal with criticism still find it at least a little disheartening. But to lead effectively, persons must find a healthy balance between learning from the criticism and having a thick skin.

Someone has likened criticism to a caricature. In a caricature, certain physical features are overexaggerated or grotesquely distorted. Criticism can be similar in that a fault is overemphasized and blown out of proportion. But that is not always the case with criticism. Sometimes a criticism is someone's attempt (though not always a loving attempt) to help us see our faults more clearly—faults we may be overlooking and which may be hampering our leadership. The challenge is to interpret valid criticism so that it grows us rather than defeats us.

When you are a leader, it often feels like people are using a microscope or an overactive imagination to find things about you to criticize. All leaders probably feel that way at times. I certainly have.

A person that I highly respect once told me that the very thing some people criticize about me is what makes me extremely effective in certain areas of ministry. Then he gave me an example. His insight helped me realize that to pay too much attention to the criticism would actually minimize one of my strengths. He also helped me understand that though a criticism may be somewhat valid, I have to be careful not to apply it too extensively.

Many tend to react negatively to any criticism because they have had it used as a weapon to attack them. Not everyone intends criticism to build us up and grow us. Some use it to inflict pain, hoping to hurt or distract us. The art of handling criticism involves learning to determine if there is any truth to the criticism. If there is not, ignore it and move on. If there is, apply it in a way that you become a better person and leader.

People in today's world love to take cheap shots at leaders. Such criticism seems to be an American pastime. Leaders seek to bring about change, and there are always people who will criticize anyone who tries to change anything. Unfortunately, this hypercritical atmosphere in which we live has caused many pastors and church leaders to resign from ministry.

While leaders can never be above criticism, we must not let our critics define us. Leaders like Moses, David, Nehemiah, Jesus, and Paul were often criticized, but they never lost sight of their vision. They understood that criticism could be wise counsel (Prov 12:15) or toxic (Prov 12:18), but they never let it become more important than God's assignment.

There are two kinds of criticism that every leader should refuse. The first is anonymous criticism. Some persons like to deliver criticism through an anonymous letter or a third party (who refuses to reveal who the criticism is from). Not only do you not have an obligation to receive this kind of criticism, but it is recommended that you always refuse it.

The second kind of criticism to always refuse is abusive criticism. If a person is willing to respectfully share a criticism with you, listen attentively. But if the person turns abusive or demeaning, explain that the conversation has become inappropriate and that either the conversation needs to become more respectful or should be discontinued.

Never respond to a criticism through e-mail. Doing so is much less stressful than talking to the person but far less effective. E-mails can be easily misunderstood, especially when they involve personal relationships and emotional subjects. Protect yourself by talking directly to the person.

Conflict

Criticism and conflict are closely related. Criticism often escalates into a conflict between the criticizer and the person being criticized. Those kinds of situations frequently become very messy.

Most people hate conflict. There are a few who seem to thrive on it, but most people will go to great lengths to avoid it. It makes us uncomfortable, agitated, and edgy. Yet, leaders must deal with conflict.

Reggie McNeal has an interesting perspective on conflict. He writes, "God uses conflict to shape a leader's heart" (McNeal 2000, 155). That is how I am choosing to view conflict. It is an occasion for God to search my heart and bring to my awareness an area in which I need to grow (Ps 139:23–24). That does not mean I find it easy to deal with conflict situations. They are still stressful. I just do not want to waste them. If God can use a conflict to shape my heart, then I do not want to miss the opportunity to grow.

There are some very insightful tools, such as the Thomas-Kilman Conflict Mode instrument, that enable us to understand how we tend to handle or mishandle conflict situations. It is not unusual for a person's conflict resolution style to cause a conflict situation to escalate. The better we understand our responses and tendencies, the more likely we are to respond to conflict in a constructive manner and bring satisfactory resolution.

Dr. Newton Maloney offers a different way of looking at conflict. He says that disagreement is what happens between two or more people. Conflict happens inside an individual and occurs when someone involved in a disagreement feels so emotionally and psychologically threatened that his or her personal survival is in jeopardy. Protecting one's feelings of worth and value then becomes more important than the relationship(s) and resolving the disagreement.[1]

Have you noticed that in some disagreements, the issue that seems to have prompted the discussion is never really talked about? Instead, the dialogue deteriorates into attacks and defensive posturing on the part of one or all parties involved in the disagreement. The issue never gets resolved because one or more parties are fighting for their existence as a person of worth and value. The disagreement cannot be resolved until all parties are out of intrapersonal conflict.

Conflict resolution skills are a special kind of people skills that leaders need to develop. Leaders are in the change business. Change creates tension between people and makes people feel threatened which gives birth to conflict. Disagreement is inevitable. Intrapersonal conflict is not. A leader must be prepared to deal with either or both.

Influencing Attitudes

In times of crisis or opportunity, leaders set the tone that will either build confidence and momentum or create doubt and anxiety. Emerging leaders do not always understand this. They find themselves in a difficult or challenging situation and become rattled by it. Others sense that and become anxious. The congregation becomes unsettled and the crisis gets worse or the opportunity is missed. Leaders must rise to the occasion and take the initiative in influencing others to be faith-filled and confident that God is in control and will accomplish his purposes.

This is not to suggest that leaders manipulate circumstances or people. Such leadership is irresponsible and will fail sooner or later. Responsible leadership sets the tone so that God is able to work and build people's faith.

The church I pastor was preparing to conduct its eighth consecutive three-year capital fund campaign. Ten months earlier we had moved into a newly constructed $2,000,000 multipurpose worship center, and now it was time to convert the construction loan into a mortgage. The minimum financial commitment we needed was about $600,000. Since we had been in a perpetual campaign for the past twenty-one years, I was a little anxious. I feared that people were campaign weary. I wondered if we could do it.

Before a campaign team was formed and the emphasis was launched, I knew I had to settle that issue internally. While I realized that God was the key to the success of the campaign, I also knew that as the point leader of the congregation, my attitude would set the tone. If I did not believe we could do it, it was not likely that anyone else would either. And they would know if I was faking it. I had to genuinely believe that we were going to at least reach our minimal goal or my attitude would negatively influence others.

God and I had some lengthy conversations before he fully convinced me that we could do it. I had several restless nights as we talked it over. Finally, I believed we would not only meet our minimal need but surpass it. I was fully confident.

Shortly before the campaign launched, the husband and wife team who were the lay directors of the campaign asked me, "Do you really think we can do this?" Without hesitation I responded, "Absolutely!" And I believed we could. I was able to lead the campaign from a position of confidence, and we exceeded our goal.

The attitude of the leader influences others. Through God's Spirit cultivating confidence in us, we can convince people that an opportunity can become reality or that a crisis is manageable.

When Moses and God talked at the burning bush about the assignment to set the Hebrews free, Moses had no confidence at all that it could happen. Sending him back to lead the Hebrews at that point would have been disastrous. After they talked it through and God was able to convince Moses that he would make it happen, Moses had a convincing attitude. Even when they encountered resistance from Pharaoh and the Red Sea, Moses believed God would take care of things. And God did. Moses's faith in God was contagious and influenced the other people.

Attitudes are contagious. And leaders influence attitudes.

Levels of Leadership

In *Developing the Leader Within You*, leadership guru John Maxwell identifies five levels of leadership:

- Level 1: Position—People follow you only because of the position you hold.
- Level 2: Permission—People give you permission to lead because they believe you care about them.
- Level 3: Production—People follow you because of what you have accomplished for the organization.
- Level 4: People Development—People follow you because you have empowered them.
- Level 5: Personhood—A lifetime of effective leadership causes people to follow you.

Maxwell says that each leadership level builds on the previous level. Each time you reach a higher leadership level, your impact increases (1993, 5–16).

When I first began pastoring, I naively assumed that people would follow me just because my name was on the door of the pastor's office. I quickly discovered that positional leadership has narrow limits. Either through accident or God's guiding hand (I choose to believe it was the latter) and as my tenure extended, I began moving to the next level of leadership. As I did, people demonstrated more willingness to follow me. After several more years, I felt a tremendous responsibility to lead wisely because the people looked to me to lead and had become very loyal and committed not only to where we were going but also to me.

People are influenced by people they trust. And trust takes time and leadership success to develop. As people allow you to move from one leadership level to the other, leading becomes more rewarding and fulfilling—and more humbling.

Developing Others

Leaders develop other leaders. This is one of the most important responsibilities of being a leader, probably the most important. As leaders multiply themselves, so much more can be accomplished. We tend to think that the job of leading is to get things done and that we must therefore be about the task. However, as we multiply ourselves through developing other leaders, considerably more can be accomplished and the level of fulfillment rises.

Leaders are in the people development business. That includes helping people understand leadership, but it also includes helping them identify what they do well and encouraging them to do it. Look for leadership potential in others. As you identify emerging leaders, spend time with them so you can cultivate their potential. Talk about leadership, and give them opportunities to lead.

Developing leaders is more than simply giving someone an assignment and turning him or her loose. That can actually do more harm than good for an emerging leader. While on-the-job training is often the best training, leaders need feedback, input, and instruction. They also need lots of encouragement.

Encouragement is more than simply being a cheerleader. It means to give another person courage. Leadership experts James Kouzes and Barry Posner have found that encouraging the heart is one of the most important leadership functions. It empowers people to become their best and to do their best. They explain that encouragement is "about toughness and tenderness. Guts and grace. Firmness and fairness. Fortitude and gratitude. Passion and compassion. Leaders must have courage themselves and they must impart it to others" (1999, xiv).

Surround yourself with the best and most capable people you can find. Being the leader does not mean that you should be the best at everything. Do not be afraid of people who are more gifted and more skilled than you are. Instead of seeing them as a threat, realize that they will make you a more effective leader and will be a blessing to your common ministry. Too often leaders only want people on their team whom they feel comfortable leading. This sacrifices the effectiveness of the team. Recruit the highest level of leaders that you can, and pour yourself into them. They will make you and the team better.

Lifelong Learner

Most people in school are eager to graduate and move on in life. After reading scores of books, writing research papers, and pulling all-nighters before exams, there is a feeling of relief when the final class is completed. We tell ourselves, "I'm finally through with my education." I hope not!

Always be a learner. Never complete your education. Our world is constantly changing, so we need to be continually growing in order to influence it for Christ. Every one of us has unlimited room for growth as a person, a disciple of Christ, and as a leader.

Commit to being a lifelong learner. Be an avid reader. Attend seminars and conferences. Learn from others. Pursue an additional degree. Be teachable. Develop new skills. Expose yourself to a variety of learning opportunities so you can be a good steward of the gifts and abilities God has entrusted to you. Never stop learning.

Being a lifelong learner is more important today and in the future than ever before. Cultural shifts that used to occur over five or six decades now take place in just a few years. A new world is constantly emerging. Only lifelong learners will be prepared and positioned to lead.

Endnotes

[1] From a course by Newton Maloney on conflict management.

Reference List

Buckingham, Marcus, and Donald O. Clifton. 2001. *Now, Discover Your Strengths.* New York: The Free Press.

Clinton, Robert. 1988. *The Making of a Leader.* Colorado Springs, CO: NavPress.

Hunter, George G., III. 1992. *How to Reach Secular People.* Nashville, TN: Abingdon Press.

―――. 1996. *Church for the Unchurched.* Nashville, TN: Abingdon Press.

Kouzes, James M., and Barry Z. Posner. 1999. *Encouraging the Heart.* San Francisco: Jossey-Bass.

Maxwell, John C. 1993. *Developing the Leader Within You.* Nashville, TN: Thomas Nelson.

McNeal, Reggie. 2000. *A Work of Heart.* San Francisco: Jossey-Bass.

Chapter Fourteen:
Ronald V. Duncan: *Effective Meetings and Anointed Budgets*

Meetings and budgets have been around since the early church began. They were not called meetings and budgets in those days. They were gatherings where issues and needs were discussed and resolved. The process of conducting meetings and developing budgets has changed dramatically since Acts 4 and 6. In our modern era, many have seen meetings and budgets as instruments of disgust, frustration, and hopelessness. I tend to disagree. From my point of view, meetings and budgets are spiritual activities that assist the church in having effective ministries. If we can view these activities as using legitimate spiritual gifts (e.g., administration, mercy, helps), then we have established the proper foundation on which to build effective structures.

So where are we going? We must understand our times, our culture, and our heritage. The following excerpt from the FRONTline column that I wrote for the February–March 2005 issue of *ONEvoice!* magazine helps to set the stage:

> There are no prepackaged models of polity within the New Testament, though the New Testament does provide some guiding principles. Today, when difficulty occurs in the life of the church because of personalities or roles, many scramble for the bylaws, standard operating procedures, and other resources to resolve the dilemma. Most systems of church governance will work with some level of effectiveness if the personalities involved have the right spirit. But a congregation that is seeking to be faith-

ful to Kingdom purposes in the twenty-first century must have a polity that allows for even greater effectiveness.

Two issues continually emerge in all congregations: control and/or power and the development of ministries. Those who have the power or control in a local congregation will determine to a great extent the types and quality of ministries. I am aware of observations by some who say that the structure we use will determine our effectiveness and growth as a church.

We know certain facts: God created the church; power and control issues exist; and the personalities of individuals influence how a system is used. The goal is to discover the most effective polity for the fulfillment of Kingdom directives.

In Acts 6, three principles stand out to me as starting points. The first is recognition and acknowledgement of a problem. The Greek widows and the orphans were being overlooked in the daily distribution of food. Today, we often have difficulty admitting that we have a problem. In order to protect our polity, we may deny that a problem actually exists.

The second principle, after recognition and acknowledgement of the problem, is communication and dialogue. It was clear that the spiritual leadership of the early church understood the problem and knew they could not solve it alone. Therefore, they began a dialogue with those who were concerned.

The third principle demonstrated in this text is that the solution must have results. Verse 7 says, "So the word of God spread. The number of disciples in Jerusalem increased rapidly, and a large number of priests became obedient to the truth." Remember, the disciples dealt with a human need (food for widows and orphans), but a spiritual result occurred.

Acts 6 is just one text that provides principles on how to organize the work and ministry of the church. Romans 12, 1 Corinthians 12, and Ephesians 4 are also very instructive. The key question to ask ourselves is, does our polity and governance help us fulfill Kingdom directives?

As you look at the church world, some churches have provided through their national structure the precise methodology to use in both of these areas of meetings and budgets. The Nazarenes, for example, provide a manual every four years that includes their history, constitution, government, and ritual. The Methodists provide their Book of Discipline.

Some churches have been reticent to offer national structure and precise methodology. The Church of God of Anderson, Indiana, has been one of those groups. In 1927, Russell R. Byrum of the Church of God wrote *Problems with the Local Church*. This book provided the organizational framework that has been used voluntarily by many congregations. Then in 1951, Earl Martin wrote *Work and Organization of the Local Church*, and in 1957, Harold Linamen wrote *Business Handbook for Churches*. These Church of God efforts were intended to offer suggestions on procedure to local churches.

How the church's ministries are administered today has been greatly impacted by legal requirements, the business world, and the development of Christian management. Legal requirements began to emerge with the 501(c)(3) designation for not-for-profits issued by the Internal Revenue Service. The original reason for the 501(c)(3) was to relieve the church from tax liability on donations and to provide for the donor a tax deduction.

The church in America looked to the business world in the late 1960s and early 1970s to make it more efficient and effective. Christian leaders attempted to glean from successful businesses proven strategies and methods to improve their stewardship effectiveness. As with any process, sometimes more was brought to the church than was intended. Church boards began to struggle with the role of faith in their decision making: should they base their decisions on faith or on trend lines that predicted rather accurately the giving of their constituents? When difficulties arose, the choice seemed to be driven by management principles that called for reductions in program and staff. This issue continues to surface throughout the church.

Because secular business practices did not always take into account the ethos of the church, a new endeavor began to gain momentum. This might be called the development of Christian management. Seminaries began to teach church administration as full-semester classes. Larger congregations began to have church business administrators. Seminars, conventions, and organizations focusing on administration and management appeared throughout the country in the '60s and '70s. Now numerous multimillion-dollar companies and corporations provide consulting, fund-raising, and management skills to the church community. Whereas in the early '60s, the church was looking at the business world for proven concepts and practices, now the business world is looking at the church community for its models. This change has been fueled by the success of Robert Schuller, John Maxwell, Stan Toler, Bill Hybels, and others.

With this background, let us address the two main issues: the development of effective spiritual meetings and anointed efficient budgets.

Effective Spiritual Meetings

A plethora of books tell us how to run effective meetings. The "how" is certainly an important aspect, and we will address it later. However, I think that the reason most meetings fail to reach their stated objective (if they have one) is that the participants ignore the context of the meeting.

Just as in biblical exegesis, the context is essential to getting the best result. Context is often overlooked because it is assumed that everyone knows it. I believe this to be a fallacy. Allow me to illustrate:

The pastor has called for the official church board to meet at 7:00 PM. The agenda has been published or will be distributed when members arrive. The first person to arrive is the chairperson. She is an assistant junior-high principal with one thousand students in her school. She has already met today with the administrative staff of the school and the assistant principals of the district. After school, she met with the PTA executive committee to plan fund-raising for the next year. She then hurried home to develop dinner plans with husband and children. Imagine her state of mind as she arrives for this meeting.

The next person to arrive is the vice-chair, who is a real estate broker. He has just dropped off two prospective buyers and delivered a bid proposal to a seller. He is watching his cell phone for a response. Imagine his state of mind as he arrives for this meeting.

The next person to arrive has been home all day alone. She is in desperate need of some adult conversation about anything. Imagine her state of mind as she arrives for this meeting.

The pastor, who called the meeting, has been very active today in ministerial duties: office work in the morning, hospital visitation across town in rush-hour traffic, and two calls about his car that is in the shop for repair. Imagine his state of mind as he arrives for this meeting!

I think you get my point. The context of the day's events must be understood. In actuality, multiple contexts are in play: issues borne by participants from their day, the relationships among the board members, board members and the pastor, and the effectiveness of this board.

Effective spiritual meetings must start with a common understanding of the context(s). When this is absent, numerous problems can emerge along the way.

Understanding the Context

In our scenario, the pastor is just one of the participants. The board has a chair. We can assume the board has met together before. Here are some critical questions for these leaders to consider as they strive to develop a spiritually effective meeting:

Next Steps to Ministry

1. Have they developed rapport with one another? Do they see one another as spiritual leaders? Do the leaders pray for one another regularly? Do they care for the other board members between meetings?
2. Have the leaders discussed agenda items and prepared for the meeting? Do the board members have the background information needed in order to make a decision? Has follow-up occurred since the last meeting so answers can be given to previously asked questions?
3. Have they coordinated with other groups within the church that will be impacted by the board's decisions? Has input been sought from all stakeholders? Have the pros and cons of the issues been given fair hearing?
4. Have the leaders painted a vivid picture of how the issues affect the mission of the church? Have the board members prayed for wisdom and guidance?

Spiritually effective meetings are possible when the contexts are thought about. To understand the contexts, we must consider relationships, agenda, coordination, and mission/vision fit. Now let us consider a few things about the how.

Managing Meetings for Great Results

Here are questions to ponder as you begin to think about managing the meeting: Does every participant know they are valued? That they are important to the process? That they are a representative of God? And do all understand the process to be used in this meeting?

Establishing the context helps bring each of the participants from their varied daily activities to focus on the purpose of this meeting. To restate the purpose may seem like you are wasting time, but it paints the picture for the participants. Beginning from the same place will assist greatly in your trek to a decision. A possible introductory statement by one of the leadership team might sound something like this:

"Tonight, as disciples of Christ, we have gathered to do some Kingdom business. Each one of us has been placed on this board because our colleagues believed in us and have given us the responsibility to care for this ministry. We will be discussing four issues. No decisions are anticipated tonight. As is our custom, we desire input from each of you. We have also gathered input from other stakeholders, and that information will be shared. Our plan is to conclude by 8:00 PM. The Lord has laid on my heart this scripture to share with you tonight before we pray: Ephesians 4:16. As we pray, do you have special needs you would like to share?"

This statement has covered many issues of context for us. The tone of the context is critical for future success: the tone of cooperativeness with others, the tone of the meeting's purpose, the tone of care and concern, and the tone of expectations.

So it is evident that the how starts with context and tone. From the context and tone, we move to process. Process is a tool to effect discussion and perhaps arrive at a decision. To illustrate, let me use a simple example: Let us suppose you need to move a mound of dirt. What process would you use? Would you present the facts about the need? Go look at the mound of dirt? From my perspective, I want to know how much dirt needs to be moved. Where is it going? When does it need to be moved? And what resources are available? If we only have one cubic yard to move within the next month, this would determine timing and resource required. If we have a thousand cubic yards of dirt to move by the end of the week, then our solution would be different. So one of the early stages of the decision-making process is determining the parameters of the issue.

How many meetings have you attended where a twenty-dollar decision consumed one-quarter of the meeting time? Process includes asking, What decisions should this committee make? We can streamline many committee meetings by bringing only the essential questions to the board. Using my illustration above, the essential question for the board would be, Does the dirt need to be moved? If it needs to be moved, then make the decision and allow the managers of the project to work out the details.

Process may also detail the methodology. Back to my dirt story. A local congregation was building a new complex in a new location. Mounds of dirt had accumulated from various construction activities. The church, wanting to save money, took on the task of cleaning up the construction site. Families came with wheelbarrows and shovels on a Saturday morning to clean the site. Resources were present, but no plan had been shared as to where to move the dirt. Wheelbarrows were filled with dirt before the workers realized they had no location for dumping. Effective board process works toward a complete plan. How many work days have you attended at your local church and found that no plan had been prepared to take into account the priority of jobs, skill level of workers, or resources needed to complete the projects?

Effective board process also includes closing the loop. This means adequate and complete follow-up has occurred on the decisions made by the board. A board may make a great decision but forget to assign responsibility for carrying out the decision or even recording it in the official minutes. Delays in projects and ministries often occur for the lack of follow-up or follow-through. The leadership team must establish a process to check on the decisions of the board (i.e., accountability). Sometimes this occurs at the next meeting; however, some decisions need to be monitored between meetings.

Effective process also includes evaluation: How did our decision work? Was it effective? Did we reach our goal? Were the expectations reached? Another story to share with you: A congregation wanted to offer an alternative to trick or treat on Halloween. The committee assigned to the task developed a rather elaborate Saturday afternoon of activities for children on the church grounds. Publicity was generated for not only the church family but also for community families and children. The day arrived for the alternate Halloween activity: the weather was great, the crowds came, the children had great fun, and the planners were delighted. Upon evaluation, expectations for next year were generated as well as new collaborative efforts established. If no evaluation had occurred, the process would have stopped with the success of the event. Because there was an evaluation process, new and expanded ideas emerged for the next year. This is just one of the reasons to include evaluation in your process.

Running spiritually effective meetings starts with context. The process includes parameters, methodology, closing the loop, and evaluation.

Using Budgets to Stay on Mission

Foundational Thoughts

A church budget is a collection of ministry ideas attached to dollars that empower the mission of the church. Budgets generally have three categories: have-to-be paid items, essential-for-ministry-to-occur items, and hoped-for items. Every congregation makes a determination on what to include in each category.

The way the congregation looks at its budget will reveal a great deal about what is valued by the congregation. A budget can be systemized in numerous ways. Some congregations organize around an accounting chart of accounts (see Chart 1). Some organize around departments or boards: trustees, Christian education, church council, etc. (see Chart 2). Churches that have one board or a group of elders may organize around ministries or major subjects: property, personnel, missions, education (see Chart 3).

How the budget is organized will help determine the presentation of the budget to the congregation. In some churches, congregants want to see a very detailed budget. In others, detail is left to the boards and only the bottom-line numbers are shown to the entire church.

The amount of money allotted to each major area will also vary from church to church, based on size of congregation and ministry components. Personnel costs (pastoral staff, secretary, custodian, bookkeeper, etc.) will make up the majority of a small church's budget[1]. Depending on the situation, property costs will be the next major budget item, followed by ministry-related items and missions giving.

As a church grows, the budget percentages will change. Personnel and property will be the largest two budget items for most churches, regardless of size. In larger churches, however, there will be a bit more flexibility in ministry options, both in quantity and quality. This means the congregation is able to do more with a little flair.

Next Steps to Ministry

Developing a Budget

Unless the congregation is new, most congregations have had some experience in developing a budget. In many instances, this has been a painful and, at times, unhealthy process. Like board meetings, the development of the budget should be a spiritual experience that develops the participants as disciples of Christ and teaches stewardship principles to the congregation.

The manner in which the process of budget building is approached is a responsibility of the leadership team. The leadership team is defined differently by each congregation, but it most likely includes such key personnel as the pastor, significant stakeholders, financial experts, and chairs of departments or ministries. The leadership team's setting of the tone for budget planning is just as important as their ability to crunch the numbers.

Setting the tone means preparing those involved in the process, both spiritually and practically. Spiritually, the participants need a basic foundation established of what the Bible teaches concerning stewardship. This can take the form of readings, sermons, dialogue discussions, or retreats. Part of the spiritual preparation is the need to think with godly vision about the future. The leadership team can pose questions like, What would God have us be about in this community? What would we believe God is leading us to do if we believed we had no financial restraints? What would we do if we could start with a blank sheet of paper? What does the Bible teach about stewardship? To deal responsibly with questions such as these, those developing the church budget need to be spiritually mature in their faith.

The leadership team's setting of the spiritual tone is crucial to building, presenting, and sustaining a budget in the life of the congregation, yet this task is often overlooked or deemphasized. A rule of thumb is to spend as much time in spiritual preparation as you do in the practical aspects of budget preparation. Stewardship education is a year-round, every-year activity. You may have special stewardship emphasis times, but consistent teaching in church school classes, newcomers classes, and preaching is crucial to building a sound foundation.

The practical aspects of preparing the budget include: detailing the steps, providing the necessary data, deciding on the format, creating the presentation to the congregation, implementing procedures, and follow-up on the decisions. In the practical phase, you must have one or more detail-oriented people who can monitor the process. Sooner or later, all the ideas and suggestions have to be placed in some well-ordered form for discussion and decision.

A framework decision will have to be made by the leadership team in order to give direction to the budget workers. Do they begin with a blank sheet of paper? Do they look at last year's budget and evaluate the ministries and decide what to continue or discontinue? Do they keep the same and add a small percentage increase? Do they do all of these things? Are they given a predetermined amount of money within which they must plan their budget? The leadership team needs to have these issues clearly decided and the rationale explained to the participants before they begin their work. This is the practical framework or parameter of the budget process.

Thus far in the development of the budget, we have addressed spiritual preparation, initial decisions to be made by the leadership team, and establishing the framework. Now let us move to the actual process. I am choosing to use the broad-category approach. Personnel, property, education, ministries, and missions will be the categories used for this discussion.

Within the personnel category, you need to solicit input from stakeholders (people who care deeply or are involved) and the people responsible. The personnel committee, church council, or trustees often deal with questions of personnel compensation. This can be a very volatile area unless it is managed well. Managing the personnel arena means establishing clear guidelines for evaluation, seeking input from the parties involved, explaining your decisions to the personnel before the congregation receives your recommendations, and putting in place appropriate feedback mechanisms.

A congregation's approach to compensation for pastoral staff usually occurs in one of two ways: (1) The responsible group establishes a lump-sum figure and tells the pastoral staff member to divide it up anyway he or she wishes. (2) The group establishes a reasonable salary, then adds appropriate benefits and expenses. The latter is the best way. A congregation is responsible for the welfare of all its staff, within the means they have available. To make a staff member choose between having an adequate pension or having adequate health-care coverage is an abdication of responsibility on the part of the church.

How staff are evaluated is also a crucial component of this process. Staff evaluations are a must. Evaluations serve as opportunities to develop a team to the next level of spiritual leadership. Obviously, this is not done in one hour or in a vacuum. Within the Christian management world, numerous models have been developed to help churches with staff evaluation. With proper evaluations, the group responsible makes recommendations to the budget leadership team.

Questions about what is appropriate staff compensation surface regularly within church communities. Some have taken the approach that the staff compensation should be tied to the average of the community in which you serve and work. This means the average salary of the community would be the average salary of the church staff. Others have decided to use other measurements more closely tied to the type of work done. Teachers' salaries are one norm used in this comparison. Still others refer to church compensation surveys conducted nationally; these surveys usually include all sorts of variation in church communion, congregation size, staff education, and longevity. The lesson is that congregational leadership needs to be informed and must put together a consistent approach toward staff compensation.

The issue of multiple-staff compensation also deserves consideration. The trend in today's churches is to hire additional staff to cover specific ministry areas. In such situations, how does a congregation structure an equitable staff compensation plan? Having a plan in place that provides some flexibility will support staff morale. Too often there is no plan, and each year poses a problem to the budget workers and to the staff. Allow me to present a model for consideration.

The plan for church staff compensation has two parts: (1) salary and housing allowance, and (2) basic fringe benefits. If the congregation can agree that all church staff will receive the same basic fringe benefits, then you have covered a multitude of issues. Basic fringe benefits include health insurance and retirement (both Social Security and pension). The salary and housing amount is now determined using the other criteria that the congregational leadership team has established. Some congregations consider salary and housing to be one amount. Each eligible pastoral staff person then determines what portion of that amount will be designated as housing allowance, based upon Internal Revenue Service guidelines. (Note that I am not including other ministry expenses such as car and entertainment in this discussion. These expense items should be kept separate from staff compensation issues. When they are placed together, you present a false picture of what the staff member actually receives.)

So how should the senior pastor's salary relate to those of other staff members? This question involves several variables. Among the variables are each staff member's time in ministry, education, and tenure at the local church. A senior pastor with forty years of experience, a master of divinity degree, and fifteen years at this church should have a substantially higher salary than the recent college graduate who has no experience. If the leadership team has established a chart or grid plotting out these variables, then initial salary issues are more easily resolved.

Merit raises, bonus raises, and cost-of-living increases are issues for the leadership group to review annually. Each year the congregation should do their best to take care of the compensation of the staff. All of us recognize that congregations have up and down years financially. Yet it seems to me that a congregation that gives adequate consideration to staff compensation does better in the long haul. Regardless of the process used, the team that is dealing with staff compensation should arrange for a discussion with the staff concerning the process used and the rationale followed. They should give the staff time to ask any questions. It does not feel like a team when you simply get a letter reporting what has been done or the decision is not mentioned at all.

Property considerations in the budget can be categorized into two subsets: (1) maintaining and (2) expanding. Maintaining means paying your mortgage (if you have one), insurance, utilities, and maintenance. Sadly, property maintenance is often forgotten in the budget process. It is forgotten because we become accustomed to our surroundings and fail to recognize that they are becoming run down. These questions should persistently be on the minds of the property keepers: How does a first-time visitor view our facilities? How would the city or county building inspector view our facilities? A good rule of thumb is to apply 2 or 3 percent of your annual budget to property maintenance each year.

Education, nurture, or discipling expenditures depend on the array of classes or opportunities for growth established by the congregation. These amounts include curriculum, books, resources, seminars, conventions, retreats, and revivals. These expenditures may be made by numerous groups within the life of the church (e.g., Christian education, worship, youth, women, men, children). It is important to provide the resources necessary for carrying out these ministries. A fire department would be greatly hampered in their mission if they could not have fire trucks and water hoses. As a church, we sometimes call people to serve and fail to provide the essential tools and resources for them to accomplish the task we have given them.

Missions stands at the heart of the congregational life from my point of view. I have a very wide definition of missions: any activity that seeks to proclaim Jesus Christ in an outward thrust from the congregation. This definition can include community, state, national, and international work. A congregation must find a healthy balance in its missional activity. It has been proven over and over that a congregation with a clear and vibrant missional thrust will grow and thrive. Why is this so?

Beginning with Luke 4:18, Jesus focused his ministry on those in need---spiritually, mentally, and physically. Any local church that stops with the spiritual aspect of human need has short-circuited the gospel pattern. Every generation of believers must reach a healthy understanding of New Testament mission. This is a very difficult task for the local congregation, and it requires intentional efforts. Too often congregations have formed a missions committee and the remainder of the church has basically forgotten about missions. Missions, like witnessing, is essential to being a disciple of the Lord Jesus.

The leadership team developing the budget should lead the congregation in finding a balanced missions thrust. A starting point is the tithe (one-tenth). It is my belief that each congregation should tithe their income to missions.

This tithe can be used to support numerous missional thrusts. Beyond the tithe, special offerings may be taken to alleviate particular concerns.

Budget development reflects the life and ministry of the church. It is a spiritual activity that deserves the highest level of leadership within the congregation. Budgets can be rallying points and benchmarks for the life of the congregation.

Conclusion

I have heard many pastors remark, "I am not gifted in administration, so I let the trustees do all that work." My thesis is that church meetings and budgets are all spiritual activities. You may not have the gift of administration, but you are still the spiritual leader of your congregation. By the same token, you may not be musically inclined, but you are still the spiritual leader of the church's musicians. The amount of spiritual leadership needed for congregations to function according to New Testament principles is enormous. My hope and prayer is that you will not abdicate your important role in leading spiritually in these essential and everyday activities of church life.

Chart 1: Chart of Accounts

    10—Staff
        11-Staff Compensation
        12-Staff Fringe Benefits
        13-Staff Expenses
    20—Christian Education
        21-Adult
        22-Young Adults
        23-Youth
        24-Children
        25-Babies
    30—Trustees
        31-Property
        32-Utilities
        33-Maintenance

40—Mission
    41-National or International
    42-State or Region
    43-Local

Chart 2: Departments or Boards

Trustees
    Property
        Payments
        Utilities
        Insurance
        Maintenance

Christian Education
    Church School
    Small Groups
    Youth
    Adults
    Children

Church Council
    Staff Compensation
    All Church Events
    Missions

Chart 3: Elder Board

One Board
    Personnel
    Property
    Christian Nurture
    Missions

Endnotes

[1] I am defining a small church as one with under one hundred people in regular attendance.

Reference List

Anderson, Leith. 1999. *Leadership that Works*. Minneapolis, MN: Bethany Press.

Barna, George. 1997. *Leaders on Leadership*. Ventura, CA: Regal Books.

———. 2001. *The Power of Team Leadership: Finding Strength in Shared Responsibility*. Colorado Springs, CO: Waterbrook Press.

Bennis, Warren, and Bart Nanus. 1997. *Leaders: Strategies for Taking Charge*. New York: Harper & Row.

Blackaby, Henry, and Richard Blackaby. 2001. *Spiritual Leadership: Moving People on to God's Agenda*. Nashville, TN: Broadman and Holman.

Bossidy, Larry, and Ram Charan. 2002. *Execution: The Discipline of Getting Things Done*. New York: Crown Business.

Crocker, H. W., III. 2000. *Robert E. Lee on Leadership*. Roseville, CA. Prima Publishing.

De Pree, Max. 1997. *Leading without Power: Finding Hope in Serving Community*. San Francisco: Jossey-Bass.

Ellis, Lee. 2003. *Leading Talents, Leading Teams*. Chicago: Northfield Publishing.

Gangel, Kenneth. 1994. *Feeding and Leading*. Wheaton, IL: Victor Books.

Goleman, Daniel. 2002. *Primal Leadership*. Boston: Harvard Business School Publishing.

Huszczo, Gregory E. 1996. *Tools for Team Excellence*. Palo Alto, CA: Davies-Black Publishing.

Hybels, Bill. 2003. *Courageous Leadership*. Grand Rapids, MI: Zondervan.

Kinnaman, Gary, and Alfred H. Ells. 2003. *Leaders that Last: How Covenant Friendships Can Help Pastors Thrive*. Grand Rapids, MI: Baker Book House.

MacMillan, Pat. 2001. *The Performance Factor: Unlocking the Secrets of Teamwork*. Nashville, TN: Broadman and Holman.

Malphurs, Aubrey. 1997. *Values-Driven Leadership.* Grand Rapids, MI: Baker Books.

———. 1999. *Advanced Strategic Planning.* Grand Rapids, MI: Baker Books.

Miller, Calvin. 1995. *The Empowered Leader.* Nashville, TN. Broadman & Holman Publishers.

Nutt, Paul C. 2002. *Why Decisions Fail.* San Francisco, CA: Berrett-Koehler Publishers.

Patterson, Kerry, et al. 2002. *Crucial Conversations:Tools for Talking When Stakes Are High.* New York: McGraw-Hill.

Wall, Bob. 1999. *Working Relationships.* Palo Alto, CA: Davies-Black Publishing.

Wirasinghe, Errol. 2003. *The Art of Making Decisions.* Houston: Shanmar Publishing.

Other Resources

Christian Management Report. Published by Christian Management Association, San Clemente, CA. http://cmaonline.org.

AFTERWORD
The First Five Years

When I took my first ministry assignment, fresh from college graduation, I had little idea what I was getting into. I affirmed that God had called me. I enjoyed the opportunity to speak God's Word and to care for God's people in internship experiences. I completed an undergraduate degree that prepared me for further study more than it prepared me for life in the church. A couple of friends helped me move the five-hundred plus miles to my new home. For the time being, I would bunk in the unheated upstairs attic at the parsonage where the senior pastor and his family lived.

I learned of this ministry opportunity from two classmates who were serving nearby congregations. Their presence aided my courage in taking this initial step. Indeed, their presence and that of the three pastors with whom we served became a source of life to me.

Forrest Plants lived and served in the key of doxology. His spirit breathed affirmation on those he touched. I will never forget Forrest or his warm counsel in my life. I thank God that, though he was a very busy man at the height of his powers, he did not think my occasional "hanging out" at his office a bother. When he died, a decade on, I prayed, "Lord, give me a portion of my brother's spirit!"

Don Smith was spiritually alive and relationally vital. He and Forrest tutored us in the ways of effective small group life as it applied to youth camping and as it applied to learning and growing as people. They took us with them as they sought to spread God's kingdom across our state.

John Bobak, Jr., the son of Slovak immigrants, was not always well understood by those he served, but John had a heart of gold for God and for God's people. He loved me like a son—still does. He allowed my gifts for ministry to bud and to blossom as we served together.

My peers, David Noel[1] and Jeff Frymire[2] have gone on to fruitful lives in Christian service. Three decades ago, we were just beginning. We had so much to learn. Forrest, Don, and John saw that we would have much to give.

Travels in the "First Church" van to ministers meetings, regional gatherings, scouting a site for the next youth camp, or just to have lunch together became mentoring sessions. Truth be told, we did not know the term *mentor* in those days. Each in their own way, our pastors invested themselves in us. Providentially, God supplied a network that we now know is most essential to survival in the early years of a life in Christian ministry (and to thriving at any point along the way)—a supportive and accountability-bearing colleague group.

Preparing for the Future

As one who has given considerable time and energy to preparing the next generation for a life in Christian ministry, I have sometimes taken comfort in Jesus's words to his disciples in John 16:12: "I still have many things to say to you, but you cannot bear them now." I think that there is truth in that for the person on the road toward their first assignment in Christian ministry. This is true both in regard to the pitfalls that await and in the opportunity to be an instrument for God's glory.

For example, William Willimon writes helpfully about the nature of temptation as it relates to this vocation. It may come to us as a hidden desire for power. That may find expression in the guise of money or power or sex. These temptations are real, and they will come to you. Willimon asserts that such temptations have no end in this life:

> Maybe this lack of ending is meant to throw the thing back into our laps, to remind us that the story on temptation and ministry is never quite finished for any of us. No

pastor sleeps secure, even if you sleep alone. You and I are still busy finishing this story and the head upon which the heavenly dove alights is also the head to be turned by beasts. (2004, 101)

Often in those first years, and somewhere in the early months or weeks, I pray that in the midst the fog of your uncertainty, the inexorable crush of weekly deadlines, and the sometimes molasses-like slowness of the people of God to move forward, a glimpse of the glory of what we are about in this life will break through and you will know that it is worth it after all. Richard Lischer (2001, 113) narrates an experience with a middle-aged couple in a small-town Illinois hospital emergency room. Their names were Ed and Doral. Doral's gall bladder had burst and new pastor Lischer had been called in the middle of the night to come to their side. They were elated to see him, but he suddenly realized he had no idea what to say:

> Suddenly I realized that I hadn't brought a little book or any other tools for ministry. I wasn't sure what was expected of me. But I did take a good look at Doral, her hair undone, expressive eyes moving from my face to Ed's and back, her face and arms pasty with sweat. She was the most frightened person I had ever seen.
> They looked at me expectantly, but I didn't know what to say. I didn't know the Francos. I must have known people like them in my boyhood congregation. Surely, we had a great deal in common, but at the moment what we had was silence. It was very quiet in the alcove.
> What came, finally, was the fragment of a shared script. I said, *The Lord be with you*
> To which Ed and Doral replied in unison, *And with thy spirit.*
> I said, *Lift up your hearts.*
> They said, *We lift them up to the Lord.*
> And suddenly the Lord himself became as palpable as Ed's love for Doral. What was disheveled and panicky recomposed itself. The Lord assumed his rightful place as Lord of the Alcove, and the three of us wordlessly acknowledged the presence. It was as if Ed and Doral and

I had begun humming the same melody from separate childhoods.

While we cannot prepare you for every temptation or pitfall or anticipate the particular circumstances where the glory will break through for you and those you serve, there are some things we do know. What I learned experientially with David and Jeff and our pastors we now know with a greater base of research data. Dash, Dukes, and Smith review the literature pertaining to recent American Theological School graduates in a 2005 article in *Theological Education*. In the section focused upon the first five years of service, each of the studies cited (from the United Church of Christ, the Evangelical Lutheran Church in America, and the Roman Catholic Church) highlighted "the need for mentoring relationships that include genuine accountability and peer support groups—each geared or focused on these first five years" (Dash, Dukes, and Smith 2005, 68). In addition, capacities to "know a congregation" and to "learn from the experience of ministry" (70) were essential to thriving in one's initial assignment.

At the moment, surrounded by friends, perhaps several of whom are quite close to you, it may be a stretch to imagine the solitary journey that a life in Christian ministry may become. Gary D. Kinnaman and Alfred H. Ells, veterans in the formation of Pastors in Covenant groups that enable ministry leaders both to survive and to thrive, point to the problem and its cure in their work:

> We won't survive—and our churches won't survive—if we don't invest in long-term, transformational relationships with one another.
>
> Leaders don't seem to be lasting...we are convinced that the primary problem is this: Most people in full-time ministry do not have close personal friendships and consequently are alarmingly lonely and dangerously vulnerable. (2003, 10)

Their book, *Leaders That Last: How Covenant Friendships Can Help Pastors Thrive*, offers practical guidance in establishing a group that is safe, guided by a covenant agreement, and that fosters peer relationships that are life-giving.

THE FIRST FIVE YEARS

Our prayer is not only that you will survive the first five years of a life in Christian ministry but that you will thrive in it! This is not easy, but it can be done. But rest assured, it cannot be done alone. This book is written to make this an achievable reality in your life. We write so that you may be empowered to start well. Others write and speak so that all of us may finish well:

> A network...of relationships is *not an option* for a believer who desires to grow, minister effectively and continuously, and finish well. *It is imperative!* In our studies of leaders, we can clearly conclude with few exceptions that those who experienced anointed ministry and finished well had a significant network of meaningful relationships that inspired, challenged, listened, pursued, developed, and held one another accountable. Those that failed to reach full maturity and finish well did not have it, or cut all or part of it off at some point. *We have personally determined that we will develop and maintain an active relational network for ourselves and pay whatever cost is necessary to do it.* (Stanley and Clinton 1992, 159)

There is no way that I may predict the specific circumstances of your first ministry placement, but I do want to share one word of advice with you, based upon my own experience and what the literature shows us today: Take the initiative to place yourself in a support and covenant group with your peers in ministry. Seek for the group to be intergenerational. Establish guides that build confidential safety and trust. In that climate, give one another permission to ask the tough questions. Keep faith in relationship and participation with your friends across a span of time. Build a climate of faithful listening and responding to one another. Call forth the best from each other. Travel in the company of the servants of the kingdom of God!

Blessings as you go forth!

David E. Markle
Park Place Church of God
Anderson, Indiana

Endnotes

[1] See David's musical compositions at www.praisegathering.com and www.everynationindy.com.

[2] Jeff recently published his first book: *Preaching the Story: How to Communicate God's Word through Narrative Sermons* (Anderson, IN: Warner Press, 2006).

Reference List

Dash, Michael I. N., Jimmy Dukes, and Gordon T. Smith. 2005. Learning from the First Years: Noteworthy Conclusions from the Parish Experience of Recent Graduates of ATS Schools. *Theological Education* 40 (2): 65–77.

Lischer, Richard. 2001. Open Secrets: No One Could Have Prepared Me for My First Week as Pastor in New Cana. *Leadership,* Fall: 108–113.

Kinnaman, Gary D., and Alfred H. Ells. 2003. *Leaders That Last: How Covenant Friendships Can Help Pastors Thrive.* Grand Rapids: Baker Books.

Stanley, Paul D., and J. Robert Clinton. 1992. *Connecting: The Mentoring Relationships You Need to Succeed in Life.* Colorado Springs, CO: NavPress.

Willimon, William H. 2004. Theological Table Talk: Vocational Temptation. *Theology Today* 52 (1): 98–101.

Other Resources

Sustaining Health and Pastoral Excellence (SHAPE): This program provides pastors with the opportunity to join other pastors on their journey as they each invest in knowledge, leadership, vision, spiritual formation, and connectedness. Healthy leaders enable healthy churches to transform the world for the kingdom of God. Through the Life and Ministry Plan (LAMP), pastors develop skills for life and ministry assessment, reflection, mapping, and goal setting. SHAPE allows pastors to experience strong, supportive, caring relationships in safe space. That kind of connectedness creates an opportunity for our ministry culture to move from autonomy to interdependency, from pastoral isolation to connectedness, from fragmentation in the movement to common direction, from crisis-oriented to purpose-driven. To learn about SHAPE opportunities in your region, e-mail shape@chog.org or call 800-848-2464, ext. 2184, or 765-648-2184.

Biographies

Christina T. Accornero is an adjunct professor of Christian leadership and mission at Asbury Theological Seminary in Wilmore, Kentucky, teaching for the E. Stanley Jones School of World Mission in the area of cross-cultural leadership, organizational leadership, and urban missiology. She is also registrar at the seminary, managing student retention and leading a staff team of academic advisors and enrollment specialists. Previously, she taught at Mid-America Christian University, Indiana Wesleyan University, and Anderson University School of Theology. An ordained minister of the Church of God, Dr. Accornero holds a PhD in intercultural studies from Fuller Theological Seminary.

Ronald V. Duncan is currently the general director of Church of God Ministries, Inc., in Anderson, Indiana. He received his call to ministry at the age of sixteen and recalls that many mentors have aided his ministerial career over the course of his ministry. He has served the church in many capacities of leadership, including pastorates in Indiana, Ohio, and Texas. In April 2006, he concluded twenty-five years as an army reserve chaplain. Dr. Duncan graduated from Anderson College (now University), going on to earn an MDiv from Ashland Theological Seminary, and an MRE and DMin from Christian Theological Seminary.

Edward L. Foggs, a native of Kansas City, Kansas, has been in ministry since his teenage years, including more than a decade as pastor, thirty years in national church staff positions, and numerous interfaith assignments. After eleven and a half years of service, he retired from the office of General Secretary of the Leadership Council of the Church of God (Anderson, Indiana). In that capacity, he led the Church of God in a major restructure of its national ministries—now known as Church of God Ministries, Inc. He remains very active in retirement with speaking engagements, writing assignments, and consultation with pastors and congregations.

Martin D. Grubbs is a third-generation leader in the Church of God (Anderson, Indiana). His father, David Grubbs, served as pastor of First Church of God in Kingsport, Tennessee, and Salem Church of God in Dayton, Ohio. Marty graduated from Anderson College with degrees in sacred music and religious studies. In May 1981, he joined the staff of Crossings Community Church (then known as Westridge Hills Church of God) in Oklahoma City, Oklahoma, as minister of youth and music. When he became senior pastor in 1985, average attendance was 143. The church has since grown significantly, with more than four thousand people now attending.

Cynthia Rembert James is pastor of two congregations in Oakland, California (Landmark Ministries and Twenty-Third Avenue Church of God); chairperson of the Interstate Association of the Church of God; prominent speaker, trainer, and conference leader; and a Christian psychologist. She has earned two doctorate degrees, a PhD in psychology from Rutgers University and a DMin from United Theological Seminary. She offers a scholarly yet fervent approach to sharing the good news of the gospel.

Steven Lewis is associate professor of historical theology and director of spirituality and church relations at the Northwest House of Theological Studies in Salem, Oregon. He earned his PhD at St. Louis University. Steve's research focuses on theology and spirituality in American culture. He is the author of *Landscape as Sacred Place: Metaphors for the Spiritual Journey*. He is an ordained elder in the Missouri Annual Conference of the United Methodist Church and serves as theologian in residence at Vancouver (Washington) First United Methodist Church. Previously, he served at Warner Pacific College as chair of the Department of Religion, associate professor of historical theology, and dean of the chapel.

David E. Markle serves as senior pastor at Park Place Church of God in Anderson, Indiana. He conceived *First Steps to Ministry* (Warner Press, 2001) and this current volume while serving as associate professor of religion and Christian ministries at Warner Pacific College in Portland, Oregon. A graduate of Asbury Theological Seminary (DMin in preaching), Anderson School of Theology (MDiv), and Anderson College (BA), David has logged more than twenty-five years of pastoral ministry with Church of God congregations in North Carolina, Michigan, Oregon, and his native Indiana.

Rand and Phyllis Michael are active in counseling and family and marriage therapy. Rand is associate professor and clinical director of marriage and family therapy at George Fox University, Portland, Oregon. He is a licensed marriage and family therapist and holds graduate degrees in both theology and counseling. Phyllis is associate professor of human development and family studies at Warner Pacific College. She holds graduate degrees in communication and counseling. Currently, the Michaels are training marriage and family therapists in East Asia and sending teams of mental health clinicians to other underserved areas of the world. Through their counseling, speaking, training, teaching, and consulting, they have ministered across the globe.

Arlo F. Newell is a prominent leader of the Church of God (Anderson, Indiana). After pastorates in Indiana, North Carolina, Missouri, and Ohio, he served as editor in chief of Warner Press, the Church of God publishing house, from 1977 to 1993. He has written several books of theology, including *Receive the Holy Spirit*, as well as magazine articles and adult curriculum material. He continues to be in constant demand as a speaker, pastor, and conference leader.

Steven L. Rennick joined the Church at the Crossing, in Indianapolis, Indiana, as senior pastor in 2003. From 1995 to 2002, the Rennicks served as Church of God (Anderson, Indiana) missionaries in Kenya, East Africa, where Steve was the founding principal of Kima International School of Theology (KIST). He graduated from Gulf-Coast Bible College (now Mid-America Christian University), in Houston, Texas, and then studied at Anderson University School of Theology before earning a PhD from George Mason University in the field of character education. He has also served on the National Youth Ministry Team of the Church of God.

Fredrick H. Shively has been teaching Bible and ministry classes at Anderson University since 1974, having previously taught at Fuller Seminary, Arlington College, Azusa Pacific University, and Warner Pacific College. He has also taught classes at Mediterranean Bible College in Lebanon and at C.E.M.D.I.D. in Costa Rica. His pastoral experience includes pastorates in three states and more than twenty interim assignments in churches in six states. He graduated from Anderson College and then earned an MDiv and a DMin from Fuller Theological Seminary.

Gilbert W. Stafford is professor of Christian theology at Anderson University School of Theology, where he also serves as associate dean, dean of the chapel, and director of the doctor of ministry studies program. From 1986 to 1996, Dr. Stafford was the speaker for the Christian Brotherhood Hour (now Christians Broadcasting Hope). He is the author of many books, including *Theology for Disciples*. Before joining the AU faculty, he pastored churches in Massachusetts and Michigan. After graduating from Anderson College, he went on to complete an MDiv at Andover Newton Theological School and a ThD in systematic theology at Boston University School of Theology.

Andy L. Stephenson is the leader of youth and family ministries for Church of God Ministries in Anderson, Indiana. Having served for almost a decade as a youth pastor, Andy is passionate about teenagers and about seeing God use them to change the world. He has coauthored a four-level discipleship series titled the Ultimate Adventure that helps equip teenagers to use their God-given gifts for the kingdom. Andy graduated from Mid-America Bible College (now Mid-America Christian University) and holds an MS from Oklahoma State University and a PhD from the University of Texas at Arlington.

Douglas L. Talley serves on the staff of Florida Church of God Ministries as state church health coach. His responsibilities include serving as a church consultant, coaching pastors and church leaders, directing the SHAPE/Maximum Impact Ministry for pastors, and serving as a consultant for capital campaigns. Previously, he served as senior pastor of Westlake Community Church in Indianapolis, Indiana. During his twenty-five-year tenure, the church significantly changed its philosophy of ministry, relocated, completed three building phases, and conducted eight consecutive capital campaigns. Doug graduated from Anderson College (BA) and Anderson School of Theology (MDiv). He received his DMin from Fuller Theological Seminary.

Gregory A. Wiens serves as state pastor for Florida Church of God Ministries, Inc. Previously, he founded Hope Community Church in Oviedo, Florida, where he served as pastor for fourteen years. He has also taught at the University of Central Florida and at Warner Southern College. Greg received a BS in industrial and operations engineering from the University of Michigan and then worked on an MBA in corporate finance. He received his MDiv from Anderson University School of Theology. In 1995, he was awarded an EdD from the University of Central Florida in research, testing, and assessment.